Corporate Culture

Geoff Sheffrin
Dinah Bailey

ISBN 978-0-9949698-0-4

Table of Contents

Acknowledgement

Many thanks to our brilliant editor (I will re-emphasize the brilliant and add very knowledgeable and very supportive), Marjorie Lamb, who guided us through numerous revisions, and made crucial suggestions and amendments to the manuscript.

Marjorie is the author of several books, including the best-selling *Two Minutes a Day for a Greener Planet* (HarperCollins, 1990), published in Canada (English and French), U.S.A., and Australia, and co-author of *Dying for a Hamburger: Modern Meat Processing and the Epidemic of Alzheimer's Disease* (McClelland & Stewart Ltd., 2004), published in Canada, U.S.A., U.K., Japan, and China.

Marjorie's career has included radio, television, speaking engagements, and guest appearances all across Canada and in the U.S. Her published work runs the gamut from books, magazine columns, and newspaper articles to corporate reports and poetry.

As an editor, she has enhanced the work of numerous authors, ourselves included. See her web site: http://tinyurl.com/writerinres.

Foreword

This book is divided into four parts:

Part 1: Puts contemporary management into context with a brief review of some of the history of management evolution and goes straight into the meat of the book by defining the elements of Corporate Culture and its diagnostic process.

Part 2: Looks at management styles of individuals and groups and puts these things into context regarding decision making and how some styles are more holistic than others in helping create a strong Corporate Culture.

Part 3: Provides an extensive review of change tools and change processes – after all, you cannot walk around in a dream with a vision of wanting excellence. You need to make it happen with a "boots on the ground" strategy, tactic, technique, or tool. Many of these tools are ever present in contemporary organizations but even in today's "over-connected age" several of these tools are still very valuable in shaping and locking in a Corporate Culture.

Part 4: Puts strategies and tactics and the implications of these activities into context in organizations and adds further perspective on what to do and how to shape the Corporate Culture. The last chapter closes with the author's opinion on several organizations that have had (and may still have) a strong Corporate Culture, and sheds some light on what makes them strong.

Introduction to Corporate Culture

How to go from Average to Excellent

Do you work for a truly excellent company? Odds are that you do not. Could you turn your place of work into a truly excellent company? With awareness of and attention to the Corporate Culture of your company, the answer is yes.

This book will show you how to define the Corporate Culture of your company and how you can influence and even change it for the better—the key to making an average company a truly excellent one.

While everyone can learn and benefit from the knowledge of how Corporate Culture functions—the more senior people have proportionately more influence on the outcome and its sustainability. The head honcho usually has the most direct impact.

I have always marvelled at the apparent simplicity of modern day business management. What's the big deal? After all it's just a question of being organized, staying focused and getting on with the business of business. Throw in a bit of accounting—to keep score of the process—and you are literally "in business". Oh, and don't forget the cash flow—the accountants and the banks seem to get a little upset if there is some shortage of that.

What's wrong with this picture? A hermit working alone in a garret might manage just fine with that kind of business model. But get two people together, and complications start to set in. That's when you start to get the dynamics of human interaction. Make it three people and the dynamic becomes significantly more difficult. Make it an organization full of people and the complexity increases exponentially.

So if the people element of the business makes for all that complexity, how do truly great organizations become truly great?

Indeed, it raises the broader question: are they truly great or are they just lucky to be at that point in their existence?

Quite often, and much more commonly than you may expect, the excellence characteristic resides in one or two key people. These people may not influence the entire organization, but influence sufficient sectors by their span of control or their breadth and depth of interaction so that you see one or more microcosms (and even some macrocosms) of the cultural impact that their style and approach brings.

A brilliant chess master

Brian D. (names are changed to protect the innocent as well as the guilty) was not very senior in a hierarchical sense, and had a modest job title that disguised his considerable value to the company. In fact, he was one of the most influential movers and shakers in one of the world's largest consumer goods companies. I remember vividly working for Brian, who was not my boss—but to whom I reported.

The Chairman, who saw this man's talent as far more than just the technical role he filled, had deliberately placed Brian in his unusual role. Brian's mandate was to be the international chess player and identify the best pieces to go into all the right places. In other words, his daily job was deciding where to place people internationally in a way that disproportionately affected the entire organization very positively. He of course had the ear of the decision-makers who would authorize the moves. Seldom in his office, he spent most of his time travelling the world, connecting, networking, reviewing talent at the place of work, and discussing the prospects of talent with his network of people, a somewhat exclusive inner circle that Brian used solely to further the needs of the Corporation—in a rather secretive fashion, as we will see. He always made it clear up front what was his role, what he expected of you, and the level of discretion that he expected of you.

At this time I was not aware that I had been identified in any special way, though I was very aware that my move (a promotion) came early and not necessarily to my current boss's satisfaction (he wanted to keep me). I had been identified as one of those who were on his list of prospects, and Brian had arranged my move from a technical management position to a more senior position at the corporate centre. He had decided I should join the corporate group in a role that would raise my profile in the company and, due to the nature of the work, would have me travelling quite extensively, thereby broadening my exposure to others in the company and to the world at large. Eager to take on new challenges, I figuratively packed my bags and moved. Actually it was only the office—but what used to be a pleasant 30-minute country road commute now became a chore. For those who know London, England, you may appreciate that living two hours and fifteen minutes by train north of the City made for too much snooze (or catch up) time and too little time with my young family.

After my move, I was called to my first meeting with Brian in his corporate office at the international headquarters of this company. The office was relatively ordinary but Brian's demeanor was not. Even though he was more senior than me, he chose to meet with me not across his desk, but face-to-face in a relaxed manner sitting at the side of a small meeting table in his office. At that time, several decades ago, offices had a fairly traditional layout with the desk forming a barrier between the office occupant and the visitor. The furniture in the "big executive's" office had a couple of informal love seat type couches for décor and not for meetings. Brian's office was not like that. First, he was not one of the "big executives", and second, he had removed the barrier of the desk by setting up a small conference table and chairs so that he and his visitors could sit at right angles to each other.

Brian greeted me warmly, asked about my move, and then got right to business. He was very clear and candid about his role, my role, and his purpose. He explained to me in simple terms that in addition to his job as might be expected from his job title, he also had this talent coordination role in the company. He was very unassuming about it and very modest. He was also very straightforward and low-key about the confidentiality of the discussion that we were having. He positioned the discussion in such a way that I had no inclination to share the confidentiality with anyone else. Indeed, as I continued with the company over the following years, I got to know many of the people who were similarly placed by Brian, and we never shared any discussion about our role and how we supported Brian.

The mandate he gave each of us was very simple in its intent (and over time was equally simple in its honesty). "Identify talent wherever you think you see it and the next time we meet tell me about it. Don't discuss it with others—keep it just between the two of us. I will call you when I am next in town and we will have a follow-up meeting."

Meanwhile, I reported to Mac who was in charge worldwide of the corporate engineering group. I would be one of the international group of engineers who serviced the operating units with whatever corporate support they needed beyond that which they already had in house. My job obviously got me in front of all parts of the organization and at all levels throughout a large part of the world. Whenever I spotted talent, whether in Turkey or Toronto it would go on my mental list for discussion with Brian on his next visit.

Brian's organization was vast. He had a few dozen people like me all over the world. You can imagine the collective power of the network that this created and the power it ostensibly gave Brian. Yet if you were not part of the group, you would never know that this network existed. To those not on "the inside" there was always some speculation about Brian's "other responsibilities" and the fact that his department was so small compared to others (Brian had two engineers on his staff, yet they served the corporate world of over three hundred operating units). The

important thing was that the power was never obvious, never used, never discussed, and to most people it was transparent.

The role that any of us filled in helping Brian was both training for each of us and a continuous test of our ability to fill this and future roles. To be a part of the identified group you had to have certain qualities that were essential to the future senior manager. You had to have the maturity and wisdom to be able to handle important things in a discreet manner. The networking and feedback role that Brian gave you was important and inconspicuous. In filling Brian's needs, you were on a continuous training curve, one that required you to assess people's attributes and maintain discretionary judgment about them for a later benefit. As an identified contributor to this network you were also under constant self-imposed scrutiny. As the contributor you also failed if you did not maintain the confidentiality. By failing, you demonstrated that you were not worthy to be on the list and were then quietly dropped from the network. In an extremely simple process, being an ongoing part of the network you continued to demonstrate your credentials and ability. If you failed, you were quietly sidelined. No tests, no big drama, and no extensively documented process—just a simple succeed or fail by your own hand. The most elegant things are often the simplest.

It is a role I never saw again in any company anywhere, including those in which I worked and those for whom I consulted. When Brian died prematurely (one night in a hotel room on the far side of the globe) this role vanished and was not replaced, largely I think because the individual made the role due to his unique mix of skills and personality. He was one of the few truly irreplaceable people that I ever came across—a mentor that I will never forget.

In this book, you will explore the most fundamental requirements of the organization, the people, and how they interact. You will learn that the most elusive and the most challenging aspect that distinguishes the excellent organization from the rest is how the people interrelate, cooperate, and respond. You will discover what makes the group dynamic click and how the excellent become and stay excellent versus the rest that remain average or even second-rate. You will see that Corporate Culture is the essential element that differentiates one from the other.

But before all the high-flying consultants and big bucks executives tell me "It's this process", or "that focus", let me hasten to add a caution. All the tools and management techniques in the entire business world (and I have used and installed a lot of them for a lot of different clients in a lot of different industries) succeed or fail based upon the strength of the people. That in turn leads you right back to the Corporate Culture.

Through this book you will appreciate how much of a Corporate Culture can be created by design, how much can be managed into existence by thoughtful and skilful management and, I regret to say, how much of it is pure luck. Many people will be very upset when they find out that a big part of the "excellence"[1] in their company is pure luck. But by the time you finish, you will also see how luck can be managed. (I'm not the first to steal/plagiarize the line that luck is what happens when opportunity meets preparation.)

So, what is Corporate Culture anyway? Well I can tell you what it is not—it has nothing to do with the corporate donation to the local opera company (as a company President that I once worked for assumed) or encouraging your employees to participate in a multicultural event. As you move through the book you will see how Corporate Culture is actually made up of several different elements, each of which is distinct and unique and each of which has its own reason for being. You will explore and examine how four primary critical elements, Values, Expectations, Attitudes,

---

[1]In many cases the word excellence and excellent are used as the noun and adjective they are supposed to be. In many other cases the term "excellence" is used (in quotation marks). This is in part in reference to the Peters and Waterman book *In Search of Excellence* (1982), a book that always intrigued me since some of those notable companies that were excellent stayed that way, while others did not.

6

and Beliefs, actually shape the Corporate Culture, sometimes by design but too often by accident—or luck.

You will see how two of these elements can be moulded and steered to give desired results. You will discover how two of them are very significantly locked in by virtue of the influential members of the enterprise. You will explore the importance of the lesser elements such as the myths and mystique that through time make up part of the fabric of the organization. You will also see where the larger than life figures, the heroes and the anti-heroes, fit in and what impact they have on shaping the Corporate Culture.

You will learn how two critical attributes of the leadership of the organization can make a dramatic—no, more than dramatic, the absolute, undoubted, quintessential—difference to the excellence of the company. These two attributes are, in fact, the only thing that matters when you try to differentiate the excellent from the ordinary. Innumerable surveys done at every level of the organization and done in every different type of organization always, and without fail, flag the same two excellence characteristics.

Through this book you will also appreciate even more the absolutely vital nature of the leadership factor. It will become very clear why excellent companies are excellent and why that exact same company, at a different point in time can be as mediocre as any of the thousands of other organizations that daily compete to provide us with their products and services.

You may already work for a truly excellent company. If so, you may be surprised to learn that the excellence that you enjoy in your day-to-day work environment frequently comes from circumstance and not necessarily by design. When it comes by design, it's a pleasure to see it in action.

I have had the good fortune to work in one or two companies that have had the exact correct cultural requirements to make them organizations that I would define as excellent. Curiously, the companies did not know what the key attribute of this success was or why they had it or even how to keep it.

For me, it was always sad to see that elusive key characteristic slowly wither away and progressively die in each of these organizations.

A great culture in action

Several years ago I had joined a large international company at a senior level. There were several reasons for the decision to join them since my incentive to do so was not that strong.

At that stage I was running my own very successful business and had no pressing need to change any of the many things that were going well for me. However, one of my key reasons for the move was that this was a large company that had many elements of the "excellence" that I had by now come to identify and recognize as a defining success factor in any business. For me it was an opportunity to see my expectations of how an effective Corporate Culture operated and how it delivered its business results.

I had already done a number of strategic development exercises for a number of clients over a wide spectrum of industry and had clearly formulated my thinking on Corporate Culture and how the "excellence" factor is created, delivered, and maintained. In this instance the senior management team was very cohesive. The focus was on the business and the delivery of its products and services. There was a straightforwardness and openness to the actions and interactions. The people down through the company had a clear and obvious level of respect for the Principals. The Principals in turn had a simple, charismatic, and almost visionary style of leadership and communication. They were open, approachable, honest, and straightforward. The vision and mission for the business were two simple long-lasting objective statements about growth and their position in the world market. You could ask most people anywhere in the company and they could articulate the substance of the message.

As I watched the company grow, I saw these elements slowly being diverted. Other agendas were creeping in. Some new added senior managers had their own interpretations of the Mission and the Vision. I had a closed-door meeting with the Principals and described to them what they had achieved and what was slowly happening around them that was diluting this achievement.

What was happening was that as the company grew further, the need to expand the senior group made the dynamics and the chemistry harder to maintain. Employees, while still loyal to the founding principles (and Principals), had started to form other allegiances—driven largely by the new "camps" that one or two of the newer senior managers were bringing to the table. These "camps" or allegiances had progressively different agendas—not dramatically different but these were now focused on different senior people, which in turn started to create the "camps" or divisions within the various functional areas. With different focus areas emerging people would respond to their local senior leadership in a way that was not fully in step with the overall corporate approach.

The sad part about this case was that the death of the cultural success factor was both predictable and avoidable. Yet even pre-emptive discussions failed to bury the risk, and the inevitable happened. Their excellence started to fray at the edges and slowly but certainly it began to fade away, even though several of the key characteristics stayed alive and vibrant with the principals involved. They outgrew their capability to exert the key influence parameters over the whole organization and the result was inevitable.

So, you may ask, where do I fit in and how do I know if I am in an "excellence" organization?

Where you fit in will become clear as you explore this book and understand the subtle elements of corporate culture and how these key attributes apply to you. You will be able to assess your place in the cultural mix and you will be able to understand why it is that you like (or dislike) this company and the people. You will understand why the culture at your company is the way it is and why the excellence exists or fails to exist.

You may already have a good instinctive knowledge of whether yours is an excellent company or not. It is often as simple as the old "Monday morning" symptom. If you go to bed on Sunday night and have that sinking feeling that the weekend was the best part of your life and you are not looking forward to Monday, then guess what? You are not where you need to be—either you must look elsewhere for a fulfilling work situation, or you must work towards creating excellence in your workplace. If on the other hand you actually look forward to Monday as much as you look forward to the weekend, then part of that may relate to several of the Corporate Culture "excellence" standards being in place—knowingly or by chance.

As you explore this book, you will learn how you can clearly define the Corporate Culture for yourself, diagnose the Corporate Culture at your place of work, and decide if indeed you are prepared to invest the effort necessary to bring your company to excellence. This book will help you figure out exactly what is needed to go from average to excellent. You will be provided with the tools to make your own decisions regarding "excellence" and how to judge your place, your role, and your opportunity in your current or future work environment.

I have tried to model this book on a format that I much appreciate. Give me what I need to know fast, concise, and easy to find. Give me the explanations in a way that compliments the fast track read. Give me some examples of real life so that I can put the point into a context that I can understand. Sort of three books in one.

The bulk of the book is in the regular typeface that you are now reading.

The story line is in this font style. The story line provides real life examples of the Corporate Culture at work. It is the bread around the sandwich. It provides the response to your comment, "explain this to me please", and answers the question, "how does this work?"

For the speed-read fanatics and those who want to get to the meat fast, you've guessed right—it's in this bold font so you can find it quickly and refer to it easily later.

When you see how the corporate culture is diagnosed, assessed, and understood, you can manage it with knowledge and purpose. When you manage with knowledge and purpose, you are on your way to excellence. Let's get started—the journey is exciting, stimulating, and very achievable—but not easy. (Hey, if it were easy, everyone would be there.)

The Crackpot

No – management is not always crazy. It just seems that way sometimes.

PART I: THE EVOLUTION OF MANAGEMENT

This section of the book puts contemporary management into context with a brief review of some of the history of management evolution and goes straight into the essence of the book by defining the elements of Corporate Culture and its diagnostic process.

Chapter 1.   The Keys to the Kingdom: the Purpose of Enterprise

What exactly is the purpose of enterprise?   A simple answer suggests that in most societies the purpose of enterprise is to create wealth and well-being. The more socialistically inclined would argue that the well-being part of the equation is clearly the most important. Business purists would argue, equally vehemently, that without the wealth component there is no enterprise.

I would love to argue in favor of the social component being the more critical, but I have to agree that the wealth component is fundamental and essential. In our international society the only universally agreed-upon measure of progress and success that we have is the wealth component. Without some form of sustaining financial "fluid" to course through the veins of the organization, there will soon be no organization. This is true for a business or a charity or any other form of organization whose purpose is sustainability beyond a purely social existence. (One of these days we may actually get smart enough as a species to recognize that sustainability is far and away the most critical element of an enterprise.)

It is unfortunate, however, that most business spends a disproportionate amount of energy on the financial achievements, although it's probably not surprising, since the financial aspect is the only consistently measurable part of the daily activity. The human part is far more difficult to measure on a consistent and objective basis.

Many organizations speak in volumes about the importance of their people in all sorts of eloquent ways. I don't know how many times I have heard the phrases "our people are our most valuable asset", "without our people we would not be here today", or "our people make the difference". All these statements are no doubt well-meaning and are delivered with much sincerity. Mostly the statements are even well-deserved and accurate. The problem usually is that, having made the statement, the person delivering the message then spends the next 90% of the allotted time talking about the financial results and the related implications.

Few organizations actually deliver a true partnership of employees, customers, and stakeholders. Those that do are often the types of "excellence" company that I refer to here. The companies that handle this delicate balance well often have learned the critical aspects of these three very different audiences.

The **employees** have to feel and have tangible, frequent, and ongoing reinforcement that they matter, they make the difference, and they are respected and highly regarded. Once a year when the President stands and delivers the year-end state of the nation address is not sufficient reinforcement of this crucial message.

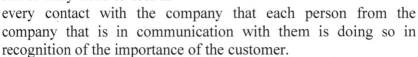

The **customers** must be able to get a tangible sense that they are the kingpins that the business is trying to serve. They need to feel in every contact with the company that each person from the company that is in communication with them is doing so in recognition of the importance of the customer.

The third component of the partnership, the **stakeholders** or shareholders, have a very different motivation and are often only focused on the financial benefit side of the equation. This is the group that drives the senior management to the financial goals that must be achieved if the business is to thrive and prosper. Note, we said the financial goals — again the money side of the equation takes precedence. Why? Because it is the only aspect that can be consistently measured and dissected and then analyzed every which way to judge the outcomes and the successes (or shortcomings) of the organization. This is a process that cannot be applied to the people side of the equation. The human aspects are always too indefinable, too indirect to lend themselves to analytical measurement. The human side of the enterprise, as critical as it may be to the success of the organization, is always the intuitive and intangible part of the equation.

Those companies that have found the balance among the needs of the employees, customers, and stakeholders, and can maintain the focus to serve each of these needs well are often the "excellence" companies that others envy.

In such organizations, it continues to be a key responsibility of management to increase the effectiveness and the delivery capability of the organization. To accomplish this, the company has to focus on the Culture. The Culture of the organization is the critical factor that motivates the employees to strive constantly to deliver their best in all that they do. Employees who are fulfilled are motivated to perform, and are the ones who actually wake up on Monday morning and look forward to the prospect of going to work. Why? These are the people who have their basic needs met and exceeded. They have recognition, they have fulfilment, they have autonomy and the opportunity to contribute, and they feel that their contribution is recognized and important. In addition they also have their "hygiene" factors met. (We'll discuss this concept in more depth in Chapter 4). In other words, they feel that they are well compensated, they have a sense of security, they have appropriate benefits, and all the indirect motivators are not an issue since they feel themselves to be fairly treated.

Given the competing interests of the disparate groups (employees, customers, and stakeholders), the employee group is the first key. If that group is in focus and committed, then the needs of the other groups can be met. If the employees are fulfilled, it shows in how they act and communicate. This in turn shows itself very directly in the quality of what they do and how they do it. This directly impacts the customers, since the customers benefit from all the best outputs created by a motivated employee group. This can be in the quality of the end product or service right through to how customer service is managed and even to how the accounts payable group interacts with the suppliers. What employees say and do exudes quality everywhere.

Furthermore, motivated employees can provide satisfied repeat customers. From there it's not rocket science to figure out that the outcomes have a very strong probability of satisfying the stakeholders.

Thus it is important that the organization develops and maintains an environment that nurtures the employee group to constantly exceed their previous best. I use the term nurtures in a very deliberate, directed, and to some extent, forceful way. Yet I mean it in a way that is supportive and encouraging so that success builds upon success.

What is also interesting in the process of business is the cyclical nature of the economic forces that so significantly impact the short and medium term outcomes. During one of the recession cycles in the early 1980s my father wrote me a letter about the state of his manufacturing business (he was the head of the largest European fashion manufacturing house – i.e. ladies dresses by the hundreds of thousands) at that time. He wrote:

> *"Trimming an operation is inevitable in the recessive conditions we have today. It is not a matter of conscience to go lean, it is a matter of good husbandry and efficiency and no service to <u>anybody</u> is done by perpetuating the preposterous anomaly of excessive numbers or inadequately skilled staff that arrogant unions and weak*

16

management foisted on us. [While I apologize to our union colleagues for the slight, I do not apologize for the weak management comment.] *Now is the crunch of the times, and only the strong mindedness of capable men, who have been placed in responsible front line positions, will give the lie to the addled thinking of the last fifty years.*

It is time for clinical study and action and nowhere is the need for clear thinking greater than in industrial management. Not to rise to the occasion now is to commit professional and economic suicide – there are no alternatives."

The interesting thing about his observations from a previous era of economic and management circumstances is the sameness of the message. It could just as easily have been two years ago instead of twenty. What it does show is that a successful business must keep its eye on many priorities at any one time. Those with well-balanced plans and a consistent Corporate Culture can ride out these variables far more readily than their less attentive competitors.

The trouble with business in our environment is that it is all too easy to lose the focus of the key items noted above.

Business needs two key components to flourish:
- **A simple, focused business plan and**
- **A Corporate Culture that works.**

In contrast, many senior managers think that it is all about the Income Statement, the Balance Sheet, and the Cash Flow, coupled with sales and marketing. Clearly, those are crucial. However, if you stop to think what has the disproportional long-term positive impact it's easy to see that the people component—the Corporate Culture—and a clearly articulated business plan make the most difference.

In the context of the business plan, a good friend of mine, Bernard T. Smith, a whiz at manufacturing systems software and everything connected thereto, has a wonderfully simple business model analogy in his book *Power Planning for Business.*[1]

He writes:
"The basics of planning can be simply stated:

- Know where you want to go
- Know where you are
- Fill in the middle."

My supporting endorsement would add:

- Do it in a Corporate Culture that works.

Chapter 2. The Elements of Corporate Culture

This chapter starts our journey to defining and understanding the Corporate Culture. We have seen that any organization is a sum of all of its parts. The style of all of the individuals of that organization collectively forms the Corporate Culture.

All organizations, from the excellent to the mediocre have two things in common when it comes to Corporate Culture:

- **Every organization has a Corporate Culture that is as unique to them as your fingerprint is to you.**

- **Every organization has a mixture of people whose individual styles directly impact that Corporate Culture.**

The current Corporate Culture of any organization is made up of hundreds of thousands of small, subtle, and not so subtle elements. We will group all of the influential elements under six headings, four of which lend themselves to definition and two of which form part of the heritage and evolution.

The six influential elements of Corporate Culture are:

- Values
- Attitudes
- Expectations
- Beliefs
- Myths, History and Legends
- Heroes and Anti-heroes

Corporate Culture Definitions

Culture can be defined in two primary ways:

- **The total of attainment and learned behavior of a people for a specified period.**
- **The refining and learning of the individual.**

Organization: The collective will and experience of a group formed to fill some defined common purpose.

Corporate Culture: The attainment and learned behavior of a group of people who elect to use their collective will and experience in the pursuit of a defined common purpose over a specified time.

That is a pretty heavyweight definition and can be re-stated as follows by using the four more definable elements of Corporate Culture.

> **A Corporate Culture is the collective values, attitudes, expectations, and beliefs of those who create, shape, and work in the organization.**

Values: The standards of something desirable, a moral precept. In the context of individuals in an organization, values are largely conditioned by an individual's age, their origin, their education, and formative experiences.

Attitudes: A state of mind, conduct, or behavior indicating opinion or purpose. In the context of Corporate Culture, attitudes are created by an environment and by expectations largely shaped by peer interactions. While attitudes are largely individual, the leadership also significantly influences them. They can be shaped and influenced by a number of mechanisms.

Expectations: A state of mind looking forward to probability and anticipation. In the context of Corporate Culture, expectations are purpose, direction, wants, and desires both in an individual and group context. These too can be shaped and influenced by a number of mechanisms. The leadership can also significantly influence these.

Beliefs: Trust and confidence in something held true—a doctrine. In the context of Corporate Culture, beliefs are substantially an inbred part of the heritage of the organization and the individuals that do (and did) shape it into what it is today. This is an aspect that can be amended. Modification is not easy and often happens most notably when the organization goes through some major trauma.

What we have looked at so far are the four current essential elements of a Corporate Culture: values, attitudes, expectations, and beliefs.

At any point in time these elements are what they are. This may sound like a patently obvious comment, but it is the simple reality of any organization. Any and every organization has a current Corporate Culture. In almost every case it just exists. People are aware of it, they accept it, and they even acknowledge it. But it continues to just exist. For most people it is there from the moment they walk in to work until the moment they leave. It is all consuming of everybody all of the time. This is not a negative—it is just a reality.

In a few cases the leadership is more than aware that it exists and actively tries to influence its evolution. Because of the awareness and the attempt at influence some success is often attained. Much of any success that accrues is due to the intuitive skills of those managing the influence process. This is most successfully done from mainly the senior levels of the organization and is rarely accomplished from lower levels.

In very rare cases I hear of an organization that is knowledgeably moving its Corporate Culture. (If someone asked me to name one—I am not sure that one comes to mind.) In Chapter 20, "Organizations", we will review some excellent companies both current and from the recent past. In that review we will appreciate how Corporate Culture is part of the process and why organizations that are excellent at one point in their history are not excellent at another.

All organizations are shaped by their evolution. At any point in time they are what they are by virtue of their evolution. This status can be summarized as **Myths, History, and Legends.** History is usually the subject of some formal record. For employees in general, the history is often summarized in the form of legends—a colloquial potted history of one or more significant events that shaped the company into what it is today. The myth portion derives over time from the potted history and the story becomes a little larger than life, occasionally shared around the coffee machine and usually told to new employees as part of their informal orientation. New employees may already know many of these items of informal history before they join. For larger organizations, particularly public companies such as General Electric, Hewlett-Packard, Bombardier, Apple, or Microsoft, these parts of the organizational background are often public knowledge through the business press and other communications media. This is particularly true where the senior management is somewhat charismatic and in turn, garners media coverage.

As part of their evolution and significant contributors to the myths, history, and legends we have the **Heroes and Anti-heroes** of the company. These are the usually larger than life characters and personalities that have shaped the past and influence the future. In this context and relating to the above companies we can cite Jack Welsh (GE), Paul Tellier (Bombardier), Steve Jobs (Apple), and Bill Gates (Microsoft).

These attributes are visible to the outside world for many companies, particularly the more high profile businesses. They also exist in every organization since the leadership and the defining incidents that make them what they are today are very real and ever present.

The Dependency Hierarchy

If accounting practices can define the organization in terms of conventional measurements, then the human capital and its health and well-being can be defined through its Corporate Culture. Of the six elements of Corporate Culture noted above, two just "are" and at any point in time, they just exist. Two are very much the product of the current organization and its leadership and two are more capable of manipulation.

We can rank each of these elements as prospective change agents. We will undertake a more detailed review of this ranking and explain the logic in Chapter 3, "Corporate Culture Diagnostics". This ranking we call the **Dependency Hierarchy:**

- The quickest and easiest to change is **expectations.**
- The next is **attitudes.** This too can be changed reasonably quickly.
- To change **beliefs** takes time and is usually slow. The results accomplished are often superficial.
- **Values** are probably the most difficult to change and again yields slow and superficial results.
- **Myths, history, and legends** just exist. There is no point in changing them and trying to change them in a democratic system is often counterproductive.
- **Heroes and Anti-heroes** also just exist. Trying to change them is irrelevant.

Why do Presidents and CEOs have such relatively short lifecycle in most American and Canadian organizations? The answer lies in Corporate Culture needs and the perceived need for change in the organizations' operating success. As we've already seen, the leadership of the organization is the most significant current influence on the Corporate Culture. In my experience, the majority of North American companies do not understand Corporate Culture, its influence and value. I have witnessed and been involved with many North American companies who turf out the CEO, the GM, or whoever is the most senior person responsible for the business unit affected in a very short space of time. If the latest Head does not provide the magic bullet within a period of a year or two, then he or she is GONE. Sometimes they don't even get a year or two—they can be gone in less than a year. Witness Hewlett-Packard President and CEO Léo Apotheker, who lasted a mere 357 days (September 30, 2010 to September 22, 2011). Why is this? In my opinion far too many of the average North American Company does not know how to create a coherent strategy, how to deliver a consistent set of performance goals and how to focus on the key attributes of their business to deliver consistent shareholder expectations.

During the past several years I have been working with a large North American manufacturer of consumer products. In one of the units the senior person was ousted and replaced four times in a period of two years*. As each new Head came in, they barely had the time to assess the lack of results from the previous regime before they too were out the door. The corporate management had high expectations for an efficient, productive, and quality-oriented delivery from their operating units. Each Head of the operating unit was faced with the same problem—too much cost, not enough trained and well qualified labor, poorly experienced middle management and a price structure that was so lean that the unit could only make a profit under ideally efficient circumstances.

As each Head came in the inevitable musical chairs would take place and some of the middle management would change. Then came the task of assessing what needed to change to make the unit profitable. The action plan was formulated, a serious and well-meaning attempt was made to upgrade the operator skills, reduce the cost, and increase efficiency. But in their location premium skills were in short supply as was capital to upgrade and automate. (If you cannot get premium help then you must automate to remove the labor skill.) As the well-intentioned plan lumbered on, corporate decided that this was too slow and needed something more effective and dramatic, *i.e.* the magic bullet. Before the plan had any chance to deliver— the Head was changed again. Once more the music played and all the players danced to see who could sit on which chair when the music stopped.

*See below the suggested time line for effective Culture change to deliver.

Expectations and attitudes can be and are influenced daily in many different ways in every organization. Beliefs and values are very much driven by the influential players in the organization.

24

So, if you want to change the beliefs and values, fire the CEO and watch the new CEO change some other key players, and you have created a shift in the Corporate Culture. In that process everyone has new expectations and attitudes also shift noticeably. What then happens, depending on how it is done, we have successfully added another chapter to the annals of "myths, history, legends, heroes, and anti-heroes".

Optimisation of Culture and the Maximization of Purpose of the organization can be shown as a continuous loop that constantly feeds on improvement. In the context of Corporate Culture it is obvious that strong and constructive leadership is an essential to deliver such a process. With this combination it is easy to see how the use of the available value standards can be maximized and the corporate purpose and capability advanced (*i.e.* stronger values and

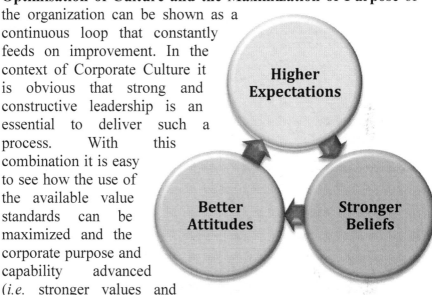

strong beliefs foster better attitudes which in turn creates higher expectations which requires the stronger values and beliefs to foster even better attitudes leading to even higher expectations which in turn—the cycle goes on).

It is also worthy of note that the closer the "mesh" (the strength of the relationships) amongst the senior managers (the leadership group), the quicker the improvements can be achieved. It is for this reason that when a CEO is changed that you often see several other key positions change. The closer the mesh of the influential managers to the leader, the greater the opportunity to capitalize on the strengths needed to achieve the goals. In the final chapter of this book, I will tell you about just such a close-meshed group, of which I was lucky enough to be a part.

Corporate Culture in action—My first exposure
As we begin to understand Corporate Culture and the significance of each of its simply defined elements it's worth recognizing the value of a strong Corporate Culture.

We have previously defined Corporate Culture as the values, attitudes, expectations, and beliefs of those who create, work in, and who are the organizations. A strong Corporate Culture that is compatible with and builds upon the strength of its leaders and participants will create a strong organization. Employees as individuals and as groups who can identify with the Corporate Culture will thrive and make more effective contributions in almost all that they do than will those in a disjointed culture.

"Hygiene Factors" at Texas Instruments
One of the earliest examples of a strong Corporate Culture that I personally experienced was at Texas Instruments in the U.K. Interestingly enough their Corporate Culture was based on the Herzberg philosophy of management (see Chapter 4). At that time I was a fresh graduate engineer looking for my first full-time job in the many available fields of engineering. When I went in for the interview I remember very clearly the all-encompassing message that was delivered by the Human Resource department by whom I was interviewed and also from the engineering management. The message was very clear and was totally focused on the delivery of the "Hygiene Factors" (*e.g.* company policies, supervision, working conditions, inter-personal relationships, money, status, and security) as described by Herzberg. The whole company spoke with almost one voice. The organization had many prominent communication notices about the operating philosophy.

As I toured and went through the interview steps I remember the consistency of the mantra. At that time I was not experienced enough to recognize that this was one of my first exposures to a very deliberate attempt at operating a business based on a very clear and defined Corporate Culture. Texas Instruments was at that time considered a leader and far ahead of its contemporaries. I have to admit I don't remember if they rejected me or if I declined. My feeling is that they rejected me—likely because I may not have been a good fit into the Corporate Culture. It was not that I couldn't identify with the Culture—it's most likely that my personality characteristics were not considered to be as good a fit as they needed to ensure the ongoing harmony of the Culture.

Without recognizing it at the time—my interview with Texas Instruments was my first memorable exposure to Corporate Culture in action.

In today's environment there are far fewer examples of enduring and all-encompassing Corporate Cultures such as that at Texas Instruments. This is, I speculate, for at least two reasons. One is that all-encompassing styles likely don't carry the same favor with corporate executives as they once did. Secondly, particularly in the North American business environment, the tenure of the CEO is usually too short for that approach to be effective. For the all-encompassing Corporate Culture to work the company usually has to be privately owned so that the longevity of the process can provide the continuity of style necessary to ensure consistency of Corporate Culture. An example that comes to mind is Husky Injection Molding Systems. This company was privately held for many years and had a very clearly defined set of values and beliefs that clearly shaped the attitudes and expectations of all the employees.

Why is the identification and recognition of Corporate Culture so important? If you don't know what the Corporate Culture of your company is, then it is likely that the people are not working in unison. As a result the programs that are expected to create constructive change and progress in the organization do not flourish. Corporate Culture does not have to be stated and "in your face" to the extent it was in my observations at Texas Instruments. It can be (and most often is) much more subtle and much less obviously defined. What's important is that it exists with sufficient clarity that it is identifiable to the vast majority of the people that work within the Culture. What's important is that the senior management and specifically the CEO are operating in a consistent and complementary style. It is this consistency that provides the basis for progress and allows people to identify with the expectations of the company. The greater the degree with which people can identify with the Corporate Culture, the greater the chance of the various programs and initiatives being successful.

The Corporate Culture shapes the work behavior of individuals, groups, teams, organizational units, and divisions within the company. Ultimately, an effective and coherent Corporate Culture has a positive impact on the whole company.

The much-quoted New York Yankees catcher and manager, Yogi Berra, once famously said, "If you don't know where you're going, you'll wind up somewhere else". An incoherent Corporate Culture is exactly that—an opportunity to end up somewhere else.

Rampant incoherence

A North American pharmaceutical manufacturing company consisting of several hundred people, all working very hard and with a lot of applied skill and intelligence, were getting nowhere very quickly. Major cross-functional projects involving a number of different operating departments would take a very long time to deliver and would need significant re-planning several times through the life of the project. The people involved were all highly educated, skilled, and experienced. The project was easily defined into clear deliverables. The objective was easily articulated. The resources were (in the most part) readily available when they were needed. Yet the program consistently failed to deliver on time and on budget. The program should have taken about a year to deliver at a specified cost. In the final analysis, the program took over two years to deliver and cost significantly more than twice the budget.

The factors that hindered the success were many-fold. Most significantly:
- There was no clear single owner of the expected end result.

- The one department that had the largest stake in the outcome did not have any jurisdiction on the related elements of the project.
- Five separate organizational heads were involved in the successful delivery of the project.
- Each of the organizations supporting the project had separate priorities that were not linked to the success of the project. Only one department had the project as a key deliverable, while others had related aspects as a lower order of priority.
- Many people within each of the organizations had dual reporting relationships in the form of a matrix management structure.
- In looking for the most senior executive responsible at the location involved, you could point to at least three people and possibly a fourth senior manager as being accountable.
- In looking for the classical "the buck stops here" figurehead you actually needed to go to the international president of the parent company who did not even work in the country let alone at the location.

To me, what was even more alarming is that all the senior management were fully aware of the dysfunctional nature of their process yet were powerless to change it. The most they could do was to persuade and constructively cajole the staff into maintaining progress. The bottom line is that they ended up with a late project delivery (many months), significant cost overruns (about 60% if I remember correctly), and an inability to validate to the required global standards.

What makes up a Corporate Culture?

Clearly, the key elements of a Corporate Culture are predominantly driven by the style of the CEO or the leader of the business unit in question. This is mostly exemplified through the leadership values and beliefs. The Culture is further reinforced by the attitudes and cemented by the expectations of these same leaders. As many of these elements are undeclared and not even articulated, it raises the question of how the Culture is perpetuated. After all, in anything other than a very small organization, the leadership cannot be hands-on and interacting with everyone at all times.

In western society and business culture we tend to interact with our peers, colleagues, bosses, and subordinates in a relatively open way. But even in this fairly free environment, we tend to assume a mantle that is our interpretation of who we are within the Culture in which we find ourselves. When you arrive at work to start your day, you become the you that is part of that organization. In a number of subtle and sometimes not so subtle ways you fall in line with a series of value and belief parameters that are the essence of that particular organization. As you progress from day to day and become a more fully integrated and participative member, you will have adopted specific attitudes and be attempting to fulfil various expectations. These will largely fit into a broad framework that makes up the organization. The list of elements in this framework is extensive, and the larger and more diverse the organization the more extensive the framework.

Some of the more obvious elements of the framework of an organization include:
- Communication patterns
- Job descriptions
- Recruiting practices
- Organization structure
- Training
- Space and the environment
- Authority
- Freedom
- Rewards
- Motivational elements
- Peer support and pressure
- Bonds and barriers between people and departments
- Identification with the mission and the goals
- Sense of purpose.

It's easy to see how each of these elements is a topic in its own right. Each can generate a sub-list of its own. As these lists expand, so more of the Corporate Culture is clarified.

As interesting as it could be to explore the list further, the list is only the effect of the Corporate Culture in action. To understand the Corporate Culture it is critical to examine the causes that create the style and tone that emerge from the above elements.

This leads us nicely into the next chapter. But before we get there—it would be worth exploring a "potpourri" of cultural values from several different sources and viewpoints.

An organization's values will be reflected in behavior and attitudes. Values represent basic convictions about what is important and what is right, good, and desirable. These, as we have already explored, are the essence of what the senior people bring to the organization. Values are relatively stable and enduring. When managing a strong and diverse organization, values are essential to achieving business goals, and where diverse viewpoints are needed for creativity and progress, skilled and strong leadership is required.

Organizations can mould a workplace by hiring people with values that align with the organizations. This results in better retention of employees who have a clear understanding of their job roles and responsibilities and organizations values. They adjust more quickly to their new roles faster and more efficiently. Shared values lead to positive work attitudes and greater productivity.

National Cultural Values
When managing an organization with a large diversity of ethnic origins and backgrounds, it becomes increasingly important for all individuals at management levels to be aware of national cultural values and become adaptive and capable of working with people from different cultural backgrounds.

National cultural values are not new to corporations of any size. Over 30 years ago, social scientist Geert Hofstede surveyed 116,000 IBM employees in 64 different countries

about their work-related values. He discovered there are five value dimensions of National Culture.[2] Adapted for our purposes, these are:

> Power Distance: the extent to which society accepts power in an organization and is accepting of the fact that it is distributed unequally.

> Individualisms *vs.* Collectivism: the extent to which people will act independently or in groups/teams.

> Quantity of Life *vs.* Quality of Life: quantity is considered to be the degree to which values such as assertiveness, material goods and compensation are more important to people. Quality is considered to be what people value such as relationships and showing sensitivity and concern for the welfare of others.

> Uncertainty Avoidance: the extent to which people prefer structured over unstructured situations. The more uncertain people are of things, the higher their levels of stress and anxiety.

> Long Term *vs.* Short Term Orientation: long term is equal to looking into future and value persistence. Short term is equal to values of the past and present and more emphasis is put on respect for tradition and social obligations.

Although the original survey was conducted over 30 years ago, some cultural values remain the same within some countries. For example, Asian countries tend to be more collectivist than individualistic. The US ranked highest on individualism in the original survey. Their values and focus have shifted from quantity of life to quality of life due to the influence of women and younger entrants into the workforce. Furthermore, all parts of the western world are far more multi-cultural than ever before, and company management needs to be aware of that.

Following are a few examples of the above five value dimensions. Remember that these are constantly changing in all parts of the Western world.

Canada:
- High Individualism
- High Quality of Life
- Low Long-Term Orientation
- Moderate Power Distance
- Moderate Uncertainty Avoidance.

United States:
- High Individualism
- Quality of Life
- Low Long-Term Orientation
- Low Power Distance
- Low Uncertainty Avoidance.

China: has high Power Distance and Long-Term Orientation but low Individualism. They have moderate Quality of Life and Uncertainty Avoidance.

Hong Kong: has high Power Distance and Quality of Life but low Individualism and Uncertainly Avoidance.

Japan: has high Quality of Life and moderate values in the other four categories.

Mexico: has high Power Distance and Quality of Life but low Individualism.

Russia: has high Power Distance and Uncertainty Avoidance but low Quality of Life and low Long-Term Orientation.

West Africa: has high Power Distance and low Individualism and Long-Term Orientation. They also have moderate Quality of Life and Uncertainty Avoidance.

From Hofstede's study, the following are a few highlights of major countries that Canada finds itself closely related to in the corporate world.

Mexico: The managerial style in Mexico tends to be more autocratic and paternalistic. Mexican workers are less likely than Canadians to tolerate abrasiveness and insensitivity by their managers. Mexican managers are greater risk takers than those of us in North America. They feel free to take risks because of their higher Power Distance and autocratic style. Mexican workers are more accepting of teamwork and less likely to stand out as individuals. Overall, workers expect more from their managers.

United States: Workers are more competitive and self-focused than workers in other countries. Children are taught from an early age about the values of individuality and uniqueness. American students focus on learning, analyzing, and asking questions.

Japan: In Japan, children are taught to be "team players" and work within groups. They are taught to conform, make decisions, and be able to produce results in a short period of time. The Japanese prefer to work in a team environment and perform better working with standardized tasks as part of a team, with group-based decisions and goals.

East and South East Asia: Asians value being able to connect between two independent individuals. Relationships are based on reciprocation and are longer term and enduring. They rely on less institutional law and more on personal power and authority. These values are more important than location, price, strategy, or product quality. For Westerners to be successful business partners with Asians, we need to build lasting relationships.

When organizations are looking to expand overseas, or even across national borders, a better understanding of the culture of other countries is important, especially if employees and/or management are transferred to foreign locations on assignments and promotions.

There are differing opinions of cross-cultural training. Most organizations don't offer cross-cultural training for employees. Those employees who find themselves going overseas on assignment often face unnecessary challenges. Studies show that only 30% of managers who receive cross-cultural training prior to working in a foreign country will last from one to five years in their assigned role, which is an indication that a large proportion fail to retain the sensitivity required to manage in that culture, or tend to ignore the culture values in which they are immersed. This lack of cultural sensitivity is a detriment to an organization striving to progress in an off shore environment.

Cross-cultural training is both good and needed for those companies that do it. The problem is that there is usually no follow up and reinforcement support to make it effective and enduring. And many don't do it at all.

Organizations that do not offer cross-cultural training make a grave mistake. Training leads to higher performance, and can improve relationships and help a person adapt more quickly to their new surroundings and values of the country. So why don't more organizations offer cross-cultural training? Upper management believe that "managing is managing" no matter where you are or what country you are in. The skills a manager has are transferable and not something you can learn in a training program over the course of a few weeks to a month. Others just don't feel it is effective and don't want to invest the time or money. They ignore the cultural differences and make decisions based on a person's past performance—the reason that they got the promotion in the first place.

Cross-cultural training may consist of documentary training, which is the review of written material on the country such as economics, history, the people, geography, etc. Another option is to study cultural institutions, or to hire a consulting company that specializes in the field of cross-cultural training. In this training program, individuals are involved in role playing exercises that give them exposure to various social settings and situations in which they may find themselves. This allows them to "feel" their new culture before arriving at their intended destination.

A final option for organizations that are looking to promote someone to travel overseas on their behalf would be to hire someone to work for you who is of the same nationality of the country the person would be working in. For example, if you are sending someone on assignment to work in China, it may be beneficial to hire someone who is Chinese, and send that person to China.

Cultural Values of different Generations
In the context of Corporate Culture the synergy or differences between generations makes for some interesting dynamics. Each generation is born and raised in a specific set of circumstances that dictate how they will grow up and perceive things. Some will have been born in times of prosperity and well being, others will have been born in times of economic difficulty and some social turmoil. In the chart below, the "seminal event", as it is referred to, sets the stage at a high level for the difference between generations. It is not difficult to fill in some related items of less significance from the background experience each of us has. These events and the surrounding social circumstances happened mostly in the formative years of each of us and therefore became a significant part of our individual values and beliefs.

The values of Canadians have changed a lot over the past 10 years, and continue to change. There are 4 distinct age groups of adult Canadians—Elders, Boomers, Generation X, and Millennials (or Generation Y). Each age group has at least 12 distinct "values". (This analysis substantially applies to U.S., U.K., and Australian generations as well.)

Elders are classified as adults born between 1922 and 1945; Baby Boomers were born between 1946 and 1964; Generation X includes those born between 1965 and 1980; and the Millennials or Generation Y were born between 1981 and 2000. These year ranges are not cast in stone but are generally accepted as the descriptive norms to define a group of people.

The following table, adapted from Lawrence Smith's definitions, lays out the characteristics of each generation.

Characteristics of Generational Groups (based on US population numbers)[3]

Characteristic	Elders	Baby Boomers	Generation X	Millennials (Generation Y)
Birth years	1922 - 1945	1946 - 1964	1965 - 1980	1981 - 2000
Seminal event	WWII	Vietnam	A weak USA	9/11
Population	55 million	78 million	47 million	80 million
Style	Traditional	Personal satisfaction	Self-reliant	Modern traditional
Ethic	Respect, loyalty	Ambitious, political	Progressive, cynical	Loyal, conservative
Gender roles	Classic	Mixing roles	Unclear	Gone
Work	Respect the system, work for security	Respect experience, like to work	Respect expertise, work to live	Work to live
Heroes	Strong heroes	Some heroes	No heroes	Anti-heroes
Upbringing	Traditional family	Traditional family	Absentee parents	Protective parents
Rewards	Job well done	Money, title, recognition	Freedom & time	Work

Elders like to play by the rules. Their core values are order, authority, discipline, and the golden rule (do unto others....). They are loyal to a single employer and they expect the same loyalty displayed towards them. They show up on time for work, take orders appropriately from their employers, and show respect to their elders and those of authority. Elders do not see the need to be in debt, and therefore are considered to be frugal.[4] Famous Elders: Warren Buffett (Chairman and CEO Berkshire Hathaway), Michael Eisner (former CEO Walt Disney).

Boomers fall into four categories: Rebels, Communitarians, Enthusiasts, and Disengaged. Boomers are fragmented in their views, reject authority, possess scepticism of business motives and government, are concerned for the environment, and have a strong desire for equality. Some are angry, intimidated by change, and anxious about their professional life and finances. They understand the principle of working hard for a living and are of the mentality that you work until you die. Famous Boomers: Tim Cook (CEO, Apple), Bill Gates (former CEO, Microsoft), Melinda Gates (Co-Chair, operator, Bill & Melinda Gates Foundation).

Generation Xers share common values of experience. They are considered to be seeking and adaptable to change, and feel their personal image is the key to their individual success. This group falls into five categories: Thrill seekers (desire money and material items), Dependant (seek security and stability), Social (committed to own pleasure), Aquarians (ecologically minded), and Post-materialists (self-fulfilment and concerned about human rights). They come from homes where both parents typically worked and witnessed their parents go through setbacks such as downsizing and being miserable in their jobs. This generation is keen on flexible work hours and four-day work weeks, and expect sabbaticals for education and paid parental leaves. The main focus is to have fun working, earn a good income, but have a balance between work and family life. Famous Gen Xers: Larry Page (CEO, Google), Marissa Mayer (President and CEO, Yahoo), Sheryl Sandberg (COO, Facebook), Galen Weston (President, Loblaw).

The name Generation Y implies the generation following Gen X, and may also derive from those who are always asking "why?". This group is now usually known as **Millennials**. This is a generation of creative individuals who work where they are allowed to express their creativeness and ideas. They have a flexible approach and control over their working hours and in the workplace have been known to show little loyalty because they know they will have more than ten careers in their life time. Most don't stay with an employer for more than two years at a time.

38

Generation Y is known for its ability to instruct and guide the Elders and some Baby Boomers with today's technological changes and advancements. They are loyal to friends and have a casual relationship with authority. They are one generation that has openly accepted diversity in their lives and workplace. Famous Millennial: Mark Zuckerberg (Chairman & CEO, Facebook).

These days, many individuals in senior management positions are held by Elders but are gradually being replaced by Boomers. The concern here is that Boomers are known to dislike rules that were part of their parents lives and are considered to be workaholics and may expect those they surround themselves with to be the same. The risk is that organizations become dissonant from a lack of rules. If Boomers create an unstructured organization, other generations may feel dissatisfied in the corporate culture. A smart Boomer leading an organization will recognize the need for structure, but will also be sensitive to how his or her generational peers will appreciate a more fluid environment.

Generation Xer's are comfortable with adapting to change and will work well with the Boomers, but are seeking better and more experiences in their positions. However, Gen Xer's are not in awe of authority and not interested in being workaholics. To manage this group, managers must be flexible, observant, and willing to adjust to the individual needs of the different groups.

Values and Fairness
Different departments within the same company can have different cultures. For example, the Human Resource department values interpersonal skills while the Accounting department appreciates policies and rules. Specific values in each department help emphasize behavioral expectations of the employees.

But organizations must have consistency in relation to employee treatment and performance. If employees perceive that someone is being unfairly treated, motivation and performance will suffer and decline. Employees may perform negatively, which ultimately affects the organization and undermines or contradicts the culture of the company. Managers must ensure they treat employees fairly and consistently and enforce values highlighted by the departments to maintain a competitive advantage.

The Walt Disney Company, for example, makes a point of stating their values publicly:

> So what does it mean to be part of the Disney team?
>
> Values Make Our Brands Stand Out
> * Innovation
>   o We follow a strong tradition of innovation.
>
> * Quality
>   o We strive to follow a high standard of excellence.
>   o We maintain high-quality standards across all product categories.
>
> * Community
>   o We create positive and inclusive ideas about families.
>   o We provide entertainment experiences for all generations to share.
>
> * Storytelling
>   o Every product tells a story.
>   o Timeless and engaging stories delight and inspire.
>
> * Optimism
>   o At The Walt Disney Company, entertainment is about hope, aspiration and positive resolutions.
>
> * Decency
>   o We honor and respect the trust people place in us.
>   o Our fun is about laughing at our experiences and ourselves.[5]

See Appendix A for an exercise in determining what you value.

Attitude Measures and Indices

Attitudes are feelings concerning objects, people, and events, and these feelings affect job behavior.

Job related attitudes consist of job satisfaction, job involvement, and organizational commitment. Job satisfaction is the general attitude an employee has toward his or her job. The higher the level of job satisfaction, the more positive attitude the employee will have (versus a negative attitude).

Job involvement measures the degree to which an employee identifies with their job and performance level. The higher level of job involvement that an employee has, the more the employee cares about the position and its role in the organization.

Organizational commitment is the employee's buy-in to the organization, its values, and mission. The higher level of organizational commitment the employee has, the more the employee identifies with the organization. The lower the organizational commitment, the greater absenteeism and turnover.

There are various methods of assessing the attitudes of employees. One approach is to conduct an attitude survey which can provide insight into how and why employees approach their work the way they do as well as inform management what they may want to consider changing about the organization. Many firms have used this method to identify respect and diversity issues within the workplace.

Ideally, the survey statements are customized to obtain the information management desires within a particular organization. The overall score is achieved by adding up all values from the ratings and summarized by groups, departments, divisions, or the organization as a whole. From there, it is up to management to decide how to execute a plan to improve employee attitudes and develop the areas that are weak. See Appendix B for a sample Attitude Survey.

Attitudes and their Modification

Attitudes can be defined as evaluations of statements or judgments concerning objects, people, or events. For example, if I were to say, "I like my job and what I do", I am expressing my attitude towards my role or responsibilities. Now do I really mean it? Do I truly like what I do? Most individuals will allow their attitude towards a company to appear rational. Another example: suppose I were a Gen X individual going to interview with a company that has a great reputation and I know that if I got the job I could go places with my career, and the growth opportunity would be fantastic. But, what if I didn't get the job? My response might be "Well, they aren't that great anyway. Who needs them?" This seeming shift in outlook exhibits a classic sour grapes attitude adjustment.

An individual's behavior can predict his or her attitude towards a situation. This idea can be summarized in the theory of Cognitive Dissonance, first proposed by Leon Festinger in the late 1950s.[6] Cognitive dissonance is the incompatibility between two or more attitudes or between behavior and attitudes. Inconsistency is uncomfortable and people will attempt to reduce dissonance and discomfort whenever they can. In other words, the demands of their job may mean that a person may be required act in ways contrary to their attitudes or beliefs. In order to decrease their discomfort and to be consistent with what they say and/or do, they may modify their attitude.

Can you change a person's attitude? Yes, it is possible, but success depends on the person, their strength of attitude, the scale/size of change, and the technique that is used to change the attitude. People will respond more to someone they like and/or someone they feel is credible.

Attitudes can be altered when change is presented in a positive, believable manner. How to help with attitude changes:
- Use a tactful tone.
- Show supporting evidence whenever possible.
- Be an effective listener.
- Be empathetic to fears and frustrations.

Change in attitude *can* lead to a change in behavior, but the reverse is also true: change in behavior *can* lead to a change in attitude.

Changing Corporate Culture

What is the most opportune way to create the most effective change in a Corporate Culture?

Psychologists would describe the incident that becomes the catalyst for Corporate Culture change as "a most significant emotional experience" (one of those life-changing moments), the type of experience that would be considered as very high on the stress scale of life's experiences.

In the context of a corporation, in order to effect a change in Corporate Culture, the significant change would need to be:

- An impending bankruptcy
- The change of the most senior unit head (the president, location director, and key team members)
- A takeover
- A major merger or amalgamation of a major acquisition.

While the above are normally considered imposed events, they are not the only mechanism for effecting change in the Corporate Culture. It is quite common for a progressive senior management team to introduce a major change tool, such as 6-Sigma for Motorola or zero-based budgeting for the new owners of Tim Hortons. Chapters 10 through 14 discuss these and many other types of available tools, but one of the biggest challenges is that they are often implemented as "quick fixes" to render substantial improvements over a short time frame. As such they often fail to meet their expectations because they were not given enough time and resources to deliver the required outcome.

Chapter 3. Corporate Culture Diagnostics

Remember the **four key variables of Corporate Culture— values, attitudes, expectations, and beliefs**. We are now getting into the core of the matter as we diagnose Corporate Culture through an evaluation of these key elements. We will look at the elements in the form of an Assessment Matrix and then assess the underlying background elements that are intrinsic to the process.

Finally, we will look at a culture analysis process that I have used many times to evaluate organizations. This is where **the complexity of something as all encompassing as a Corporate Culture can be distilled down to just a few words.** Not just any words—but words that are very specific and that capture the essence of the Corporate Culture under consideration. From these few words, we will see how two key words arise from this process. We will also see that the stronger the shared perception is that these two words are paramount within the organization—the stronger and more durable the Corporate Culture.

Key people in key organizations are always looking for that competitive edge. Those who are thinking people realize that that edge comes from their people. Once that first realization is in place, they are eager to participate in the diagnostic process of their Corporate Culture.

This diagnostic process starts with someone seeing a need or having the desire to analyze the current status of the existing Corporate Culture. It is usually best to have this undertaken by an experienced individual who is not intimately involved with the day-to-day operations of the culture being evaluated. The detached and more objective approach that is brought by a third party individual is very helpful since internal people often see things through filters that can be tainted by personal prejudices, politics, and an inability to step back and get a fully objective view of the current situation. Nevertheless, a few corporations are now following Google's lead in appointing a "Chief Culture Officer" to keep an eye on the renowned company atmosphere.

(The appointment of Stacy Sullivan to the position led to some criticism of implied conflict of interest, given her role as Google's Head of Human Resources.)

Through a series of questions—most of which are not very specific—you (the facilitator—the more senior the better, or else with very strong support from the top) can start to get a very clear picture of the organization and what the leadership intends. Also, while you as the facilitator are getting this clarity, you also accumulate a very clear perception of how each of the key characters interact, communicate, and lead. I am often delighted at how candid people will be if they are motivated by the belief that this process can raise their people and the company to another level.

Below we classify the questions under our four key elements to bring more clarity to the picture.

The Value Diagnostic

We have already said that values cannot readily be changed. They tend to be predominantly a reflection of the leadership and can be modified to a minor degree. But the more they are modified and the less they reflect the true values of the leadership, the more the Corporate Culture is dysfunctional.

The values of the organization are much more an extension of the leadership values than of anything else. The organization through its various declarations and mantras can attempt to articulate values (and often they do) but these are not the true values of the corporation. The true values are a combination of factors that can be diagnosed by interviewing top management as follows:

- In what decade was the leader born?
- What is the individual's place of birth?
- What is their background (formative years age 1 to 5, developmental years age 6 to 17, educational years 18 to 24, and career years 25 on)?
- What is their education?
- Were they an only child, a second child, or a middle child?

45

- What was the major occupation of the leader's parent who was the household provider?
- What were the individual's key attainments?
- What were the individual's key traumas or setbacks?

In many environments today some of the above questions cannot legally be asked directly, so the answers must be deduced from general conversation. For example, you might say, "Tell me a bit about your family". In fact, the accuracy of the answers is not critical. It is the directional implications (information in the right ballpark) of the combination of the questions that provide the needed insight.

The Attitude Diagnostic
Attitudes are one of the more malleable of the Corporate Culture elements. Here we are trying to assess how things work within the organization. The further down the organization you go asking, the less the value of the answers to these questions.

The sorts of questions we are asking of senior management are very different from those asked of middle management or lower levels, and they clearly are part of the evolution of the company. Senior team questions tend to be more strategic, middle management tend to be more tactical, and lower levels are more executional. Regarding culture, senior questions are the most important.

- What do the performance appraisal documents look like?
- What are the verbal communication patterns?
- What are the written communication patterns?
- What is the day-to-day focus of attention?
- What is the vision or the purpose?
- What are the Human Relations policies? (Both real and perceived need to be evaluated).
- What are the participation mechanisms? (Who gets in on the action and how?).
- Approachability of the individual?
- Objectives programs?

- Rituals?
- Space and environment?
- What levels of authority and freedom exist and at what price? (Consequences).
- Support and pressure up, down, and laterally?
- Bonding within peer groups?
- Bonding within higher and lower hierarchical groups?

While some of the questions in this group are relatively straightforward it is clear that many of them are to some degree subjective. In other words they will be assessed through the eyes and the filters of the observer. There is nothing wrong with that. Indeed, it is this aspect that makes the process unique and also allows for the individual who is making the assessment to judge his or her own compatibility.

The same list of questions could be asked of middle management, and the comparisons would provide some valuable insights.

The Expectation Diagnostic
Of all of the elements of Corporate Culture, expectations are the most readily steered—it's the one element over which the biggest impact of change can be exerted. A series of relatively open-ended questions to the upper management group give a good sense of how the organization has been trying to influence the shorter term thinking of its contributing employees. Some of these have clear and potentially documented answers. Others are far more judgmental.

- Appraisals (again) but this time not the structure but the content—how do these documents steer and prioritize what is important for the individuals at the receiving end?
- Promotion policy (both real and perceived)?
- Corporate goals and targets?
- Links to individual's objectives?
- Training? (Functionality—does the rubber hit the road or is it window dressing?)

- Record of Absenteeism? How does this jibe with the expectation of management?
- Record of Turnover? How does this jibe with the expectation of management?
- Succession planning?
- Importance of year-end results *vs.* the longer term?

The Beliefs Diagnostic

Like values the belief systems are much more locked in. They are more intrinsic to the leadership, though with effort and conviction they can be moved to create a shift in Corporate Culture.

- What is the mission?
- What is the philosophy of the organization (both real and perceived)?
- What is the organization structure? The span of control? The levels? The influence of key members?
- What are the recruiting practices (who does what and who decides)?
- What do the job descriptions look like? How realistic are they?
- Decision making approval mechanisms (financial and key ventures)?
- What is the internal perception of the organization and its place in the world?
- What is the external perception of the organization by its suppliers, clients, and the public? This may be determined superficially by internal review, and more thoroughly by external interviews.

In all the questions above, it is the intended result versus the actual results that is key to the process. What does all the structure say it is trying to accomplish? What is all the structure actually accomplishing? The more open and transparent the process and the more honest the intentions, the more coherent the Corporate Culture will be.

The more senior management is on the same page, the stronger and more enduring the Corporate Culture will be.

48

The Assessment Matrix

All of the above diagnostics can be summarized into an Assessment Matrix shown below.

The Assessment Matrix is a list of many specific attributes that exist in virtually all organizations. The attributes are normally very visible to all the employees and are often measurable. If the measurement capability is not direct and tangible then the item is likely still clearly enough documented that an informed judgement can be made about its appropriateness. For example, absenteeism and turnover can be directly measured and tracked whereas appraisals need to be judged in terms of their context, balance, and objectivity.

Each factor in the Assessment Matrix has a greater or lesser impact on the Corporate Culture. Values, as has been suggested above, is the most "locked in" of the Corporate Culture attributes and is the characteristic that most reflects the leadership. As noted previously, attitudes and expectations are the most easily manipulated in the organization. Beliefs can be steered and progressively changed with some specific focus and effort.

The Assessment Matrix is not a change management tool—it is an assessment list that ensures that all the elements, whether core to a change process or not, are considered and evaluated to ensure each is appropriate to the Corporate Culture required.

The following table shows the impact that a change in any particular corporate attribute brings to the key elements of Corporate Culture. A change in an attribute can bring either a significant change in a key element—shown with an "S", or a relatively minor change—shown with an "M".

As you work on any attribute, that attribute will either have a significant or minor effect on elements of Corporate Culture.

Looking at the table below, a **change** in any "Attribute" will bring about a change in any or all of values, attitudes, expectations, and beliefs to the extent shown in the table.

The Assessment Matrix: Change in corporate attributes and their impact on key elements of Corporate Culture

	Attributes subject to change	Impact on Values	Impact on Attitudes	Impact on Expectations	Impact on Beliefs
Corporate View	Corporate Goals	M	S	S	S
	Focus		S		S
	Vision/Purpose	M	S	S	S
	H.R. Policies		S	M	M
	Philosophy		M	S	S
Employee-driven	Communication		S	S	
	Participation Mechanisms		S		M
	Rituals		S		M
Employee-centred	Appraisals		S	S	
	Objectives (individual)		S	S	S
	Training		S	S	M
Outcomes	Absenteeism/Turn-over		M	S	
	Corporate Perception in/out				S
Cultural philosophy	Promotions		M	S	M
	Succession Plans		S	S	
	Year End Emphasis		S	S	
	Approachability		S		S
	Space/Environment	M	S		
	Authority/Freedom		S	M	
	Support/Bonding/Pressure		S		
	Organization Structure		S		S
	Recruiting Practices		M		S
	Job Definitions		S	S	S
	Approval Mechanisms		M		S
	Employee Induction		S	S	S

For example, the matrix shows that if corporate goals change, we can expect "significant" change in the areas of attitudes, expectations, and beliefs with only "minor" changes in values. The reason is that corporate values (as we keep confirming) are largely a given, as they are intrinsic to the key people, and are exhibited most strongly in the leadership. A major event or need that changes the corporate culture will have little impact on the values that the leadership brings to the corporation.

However, if a seminal event changes the corporate goals, then all of the more malleable of the culture attributes also change. The attitudes will change as dramatically as the expectations, since whatever forced the change in the culture will have a dramatic impact on these two attributes. I'm reminded of the era when the charismatic but temperamental Steve Jobs left Apple, during which time the company floundered. Jobs later returned to bring the company back to profitability. Both his departure and his return were indeed seminal events for Apple, with corresponding corporate culture changes.

The reason that beliefs also change is that beliefs are an attribute that resides in the organization in two parts; there is the part that is intrinsic to each of the employees, and there is the part that relates to what the employees project as "company beliefs"—"the way you get along around here." The only part of the beliefs that change is the part that relates to the organization changes. The beliefs that are intrinsic to the individuals do not change.

If we look at appraisals as another example, it is easy to see that a well-run, honest, forthright, well communicated, and objectively based appraisal system will have a direct impact on both the attitude and the expectations that the participants have of the process. Equally, each of the participants will not change their beliefs as a result of the appraisal process, nor will they change their values.

From the table, it is easy to see how various corporate attributes exert very little influence on the values, and much more influence on attitudes and expectations. The beliefs are less directly influenced by corporate attributes.

The attributes have been placed into loose groupings each of which have some related relevance. For example, the first group has the common element of "the corporate view" of things. These items tend to set the "tone" of the organization. They have a relatively broad impact across and down the organization since the leadership largely sets them. As an example, Google began with a well-publicized corporate motto "Don't be Evil"—which later came to plague them as various parties began to question their commitment to the ideal (especially when they started tracking users across all their services). Interestingly, they have dropped the motto, and now say in their Code of Conduct, "You can make money without doing evil," which is a far cry from the original imperative.

The next group, the employee-driven attributes, reveals how employees operate within the pre-determined "tone" of the organization. It is easy to see that these items have a disproportional effect on the attitudes of the employees.

That in turn is followed by the employee-centred attributes, a group that very tangibly affects the employees. These items have a direct impact at a personal level for each and every employee. How they are handled is critical to the consistency of the Corporate Culture. While very personal to each individual, the structure, the style, and consistency with which these attributes are handled has a large impact on the organization's culture. It's also easy to see how these items have the broadest impact on the expectations, attitudes and to a degree the beliefs. Within the context of the corporation since these items tend to be very specific to each employee they all follow a core "tone" of consistency.

The next group of corporate attributes are outcomes and are to a large degree measurable. The corporate perception item is the most difficult to measure.

The last group is all somewhat "philosophical" in nature. Yet each of these attributes puts its "stamp" on the company and on how the company's Corporate Culture is defined.

From this Assessment Matrix it is possible to determine the consistency of the Corporate Culture since items that are "out of step" with the majority of the "tone" of the remaining items tend to undermine the believability of the Corporate Culture. This is one reason why organizations with a very strong and consistent approach (remember the example of Texas Instruments as it was) tend to have an all-encompassing culture—a culture that almost envelops the employee in a cocoon from the time of arrival to the time of departure.

Equally, cultures where these items are not consistent and not coherently connected tend to have broader issues and challenges. This lack of consistency and connection is frequently a significant part of the reason why mergers and acquisitions often fail to deliver on their promised expectations. The same elements of an Assessment Matrix from two different organizations cannot be shuffled together like a deck of cards and be expected to produce a great result. Similarly, one cannot pick the apparent best from each contributing organization and expect that to yield a perfect outcome. For mergers and acquisitions to thrive the elements must be selected in the context of the new corporate values and then, adopted, modified, massaged, or created from scratch to deliver a package that sets the new "tone".

Values, Attitudes, Expectations, Beliefs—The Background
In this section we will see how the detail of the Assessment Matrix is evaluated and how this evaluation forms the foundation of the final diagnostic.

This diagnostic process provides a simple summary of the key elements that critically define the organization. The summary of these key elements then allows an objective assessment to be made regarding the two most critical aspects of the Corporate Culture, namely the level of **trust and candor**. This is the first time we have introduced these two key words.

> **These two aspects of the Corporate Culture, trust and candor, are the defining elements that distinguish an excellent culture from the rest.**

We will return to trust and candor a little further down.

Values Background

We have already established that values are the most difficult characteristic to change within an existing structure. To put it simply—if you want to change the values then change the leadership. Alternatively, if the values are largely in good order and reflect the potential of the desired end goals, yet they are not coherent across the organization, then some of the leadership will need to be changed.

A wrench in the works

I remember one organization that exemplified good leadership and a very effective Corporate Culture. The leadership over the years that they had been in operation had grown the company into a powerful and effective organization. The characteristics of the leadership style were very clear. The style and the approach of the leadership had consistently attracted the "right kind of people" into the company—particularly at the senior level.

The company continued to grow and prosper, and as it got larger and larger it started to lose the defining difference that separates an ordinary Culture from an excellent Culture. The *principals* of the leadership did not change, but the *principles* of one of the key lieutenants did over time. Although the fundamentals of the Corporate Culture as espoused by the principals remained the same, the influence of this key lieutenant grew, and as a result undermined the very essence of the success of the founding Culture. The individual in question progressively undermined the core principles of the Corporate Culture— trust and candor, both of which eroded. You may wonder why the founding leadership allowed that to continue—a good question for which there is no obvious or logical answer. Your next question rightly may be how did these core principles erode if the founding leadership was still in place and as committed as they had always been? The answer is simply that the organization grew to such a size that the hands-on day-to-day influence of the founders was progressively more diluted due to the need to delegate. Their choice in delegation was well considered and well executed. The problem was that they chose not to deal with the disruptive influence caused by the senior lieutenant and as the power and authority of that individual grew—the inevitable happened.

The company grew larger, and at the same time grew less efficient. The power-hungry lieutenant was building empires and was surrounding himself with underlings that would obey his direction without too much personal challenge. The result was reduced efficiency due to too many people who were not fully competent and most of them blindly obeying the edicts of this leadership. So instead of doing "more with less" the company continued to do "less with more". The cost structure became larger and the volumes (and revenue) did not increase proportionally. The result was (and is) a less cost effective company than it may have been. Followed by a catastrophic failure.

The sad part about this saga is that in the process of not addressing this emerging threat of dilution of the Corporate Culture, a number of other excellent senior lieutenants progressively left and further dilution of the Corporate Culture continued.

The most important starting point in a Corporate Culture Diagnostic is to establish the values of all the influential Principals involved. This is done through an interview process.

We have looked at the values diagnostic in general, but the more specific questions for senior management include the following:

- Approximate age (decade of birth)
- Origin (where raised and educated—0 to 5 years, 6 to 12 years and 13 to 21)
- Background (family during those years)
- Education keys (what were their major strengths and weaknesses)
- Only child (or second or third etc.)
- Family and parental occupations
- Key attainments
- Career traumas

- Self-image (as vocalized by the interviewee)
- Perceived image (as observed by you and vocalized by the interviewee)
- Body language & eye contact (observations by the interviewer throughout the process)
- Confidence (observations by the interviewer throughout the process)
- Incumbent's perception of their own management style
- Breadth of knowledge (are they a specialist or a generalist)
- What do they believe is their management style
- Approachability (body language, demeanor, office layout—inherited or chosen)
- Self-definition of their greatest strength
- Self-definition of their greatest weakness.

Finally, how do others perceive this individual? This is a separate question that will progressively come clear through the evolution of interviews throughout the organization.

The result of this interview process must be assembled into the structure of an organization chart. Even organizations that already have org charts rarely integrate these analyses into their charts. The reason the results are necessary to the org chart is that the influence of each of these senior individuals is paramount to the diagnostic process. It is critically important to be able to determine objectively whether the level of influence of each individual is commensurate with the title and the apparent position in the organization. Some people have inflated titles and some have more mundane titles. The influence that each exerts can be out of step with the title. Similarly, some people are placed specifically in very influential roles yet are out of the mainstream of the decision making process. There are often good reasons for this (sometimes not) so the influence by each senior person must be assessed to ensure the drivers of the Corporate Culture are recognized.

Attitudes Background

Attitudes are an attribute that is amenable to change. Such changes can usually be accomplished relatively quickly. Even in a large organization the attitude adjustment cycle (if thought through well and executed with consistency) can be radically shifted within a year.

The basis for the change process is in the information and documentation that people use to manage the day-to-day activities of the employees. Several key documents need to be assessed:

- Induction/Orientation programs
- Corporate focus/mission
- Human Resource policies
- Corporate or departmental objectives and incentive programs
- Job definitions/descriptions
- Training procedures and process
- Appraisals
- Authority and freedoms
- Organization structure
- Succession plans.

It's important to assess the degree of formality that exists in this area. How are these various attributes documented? What does the documentation convey—not in the pure and obvious words but in the intention behind the words and the method in which they are handled and communicated? How are they used and administered?

Many companies have well thought through documentation and processes that govern this area. Yet few have thought through the implications of coherence—the consistency between one document and the next. Do they each communicate a common theme regarding the corporate values? I have often seen examples of these documents assembled from other sources as being a "best practice" document. Being a "best practice" document is an excellent choice but only if modified to suit the corporate values or if they have been tailored to fit the desired Corporate Culture.

Think about this for a moment—if the values are largely intrinsic to the leadership and they are the people that determine how these documents integrate and function, it then follows that many key aspects of the corporate values are communicated through these documents. So, taking "best practice" documentation from various sources only works if they are tailored and thoughtfully modified to fit the intended purpose.

A series of less formal attributes also form an important part of the background of the above structure of all the preceding questions. These include:

- Style of written communication—what is the formality, frequency, impact of hierarchy?
- Style of verbal communication—how do people interact face-to-face and how frequently?
- Participation mechanisms—how are people invited into process steps?
- Approachability—are people open to *ad hoc* communications or is it very formally structured?
- Rituals—style of meetings, dress code, employee celebrations, corporate celebrations.
- Space and environment—offices, style, size, accessibility, open or closed door? (The work environment is significant in people's perception of top-level management. It also means more than just physical surroundings—employees must be able to trust senior management in order to create an environment free of discrimination and harassment.)
- Peer support, pressure, and bonding—how do people interact and support each other?
- Organization's vision and purpose.
- Orientation programs (also called "On-Boarding")—helps new employee feel part of the team from the beginning, giving a tour of the facilities, receiving literature such as a policy manual, company history and benefits. It's an orientation to the team, or department—who does what, reports to who? Allows a review of the job description

and how it fits into the organization. Without an orientation, some employees leave within three or four months.

On-Boarding consists of: establishing a plan to get the employee through the first three months, transition employee into happy, productive, well-integrated member of the culture, specify statement of purpose—so that the employee has a clear understanding of company vision and goals.

These items, while less formal than the preceding list of questions, are all individually a series of indicators that define the attitude element of the Corporate Culture.

Matrix mismanagement

Some years ago I handled an extensive project for a large international personal care product client who prided themselves on their matrix management structure and how it had successfully broken down the "silo mentality" that had previously been predominant. On the face of it the matrix appeared to work—until one went below the surface and attempted to handle a longer-term cross-functional project. From year to year various departmental goals and objectives would change. This in turn would change individual goals and objectives within departments. So far so good—nothing wrong or unusual about this. Individual bonus payments would be based on the combination of individual and departmental objectives. Still fair to say—nothing wrong so far.

The challenge came when the cross-functional aspect of the project was being organized. Each of the departments responsible for their aspect of the program delivery had their own corporate objectives and these were not aligned with each other. While the delivery of the primary goals of the project was the responsibility of the department that had primary ownership of the end result, the other functional areas had been given other key goals that placed this project on a different priority in each department. The problem was made worse by the fact that in the matrix structure, each department reported internationally and the international objectives were different from department to department. The end result was a project that needed support from each of the functions to be successful (on time and on budget) yet only one department had that as their primary objective—for the others it was priority number three or four. This lack of consistency was made worse by the fact that internationally this project was relatively low on the inter-company priority list. Guess what? It came in late and was considerably over budget.

Expectations Background

Employees' expectations are the most malleable of the attributes within the Corporate Culture. They can be successfully changed to a significant degree in a relatively short period of time.

The formal and stated elements can be "adjusted" or redirected to convey a new or substantially different set of requirements very quickly.

The formal attributes that affect expectations include:

- Corporate Goals
- Vision / Mission Statement
- Employee induction
- Training programs
- Job definitions/descriptions
- Individual objectives
- Appraisals
- Promotions
- Succession Planning

To bring about a change in expectations, it's easy to see how quickly the above elements can be adjusted to promote a radically new direction and sense of purpose within the organization.

The Corporate Goals, the Vision, and the Mission are all documented (usually) statements that, with forethought, can be changed very quickly by senior management and appropriately communicated. These would be some of the first things that would be addressed in a Corporate Culture change process.

With these instruments in place and becoming the "living and breathing" guide to the path forward, the formality of the next level of documentation can be adjusted to aid the change process. Induction programs, training programs, and job descriptions are the next obvious step. As mentioned above in the attitude section, it's important to modify these documents with care and thought since the style, tone, and content communicate very clearly to employees what the company thinks is important. As employees work with and understand these documents the expectations will become widely understood and adopted by all involved.

Individual objectives and the appraisal process are the next clear communicators of what the company thinks is important. These two documents set the stage for what an employee is to do (the expectations) and how the performance is judged.

Finally, promotions and succession plans round out the components of the expectations program.

Several of the above attributes are noted as being formal. That is they are documents, or a process that is documented, or shared through a written media. Several of them are also interpreted verbally. How this aspect is handled is equally important since there must be consistency in the execution and communication of the steps involved. For example, if the employee's job description is not in alignment with their objectives, there is the beginning of some confusion. If the departmental objectives are not in line with the key prioritized objectives of the employee, further confusion results. This is compounded if the appraisal process then places performance measures and rewards in a different priority sequence from either the individual's performance objectives or the departmental performance objectives. Clearly, coherence in all of these elements is a key to success.

Crisis management as the norm

Here's an example of how incoherent programs can contribute to failure in meeting expectations. A short while ago I did some strategic development and implementation work with a manufacturing client. The organization was desperately seeking to improve the use of its installed manufacturing capacity. There was ample capacity to meet the near term foreseeable needs yet the organization constantly failed to meet its own output targets. Senior management was constantly extolling the needs to organize for achieving the highest levels of output. They created good programs for organizing the production planning and control systems. They put in place an excellent measurement and analysis system. They had in place very good continuous improvement programs. Yet they failed over several years to meet their own expanded production goals.

Why? In spite of all the good programs and intentions, they measured success by how flexibly they could react to the constant change that they were prepared to inflict on their schedule. In other words, if I needed to impose another change on the schedule and bring this product forward for earlier completion, how quickly could I do that and how could I minimize the disruption? In addition, to compound the felony, they chose to delegate the key improvement programs to people who had no ownership or vested interest (except the individual's professional pride in accomplishment) in the end result. More importantly, the people that had the most to gain from the improvements being so diligently worked on by others were rarely at any of the meetings designed to move the improvement programs forward.

Finally, as you may have guessed, the performance rewards in the appraisal and bonus programs focused on flexibility in achieving the short-term production goals. Senior management was always and conspicuously visible in the production re-scheduling process and almost never at the meetings that were the foundation of the much-needed improvements where discussion was taking place. The outcome was obvious. Short-term changes and the crisis management were the norm. Everyone revelled in it and everyone complained about it and everyone was stressed out by the workload it created.

The solution to this challenge was very simple—fix and lock in the short-term schedule (do not change what is planned to be done for the next three to four days). Measure and report the success of on time delivery. Eliminate Work in Progress (WIP) as much as possible. (WIP is a safety blanket—as well as a financial drain. If you have no WIP then you must make what you do have the productive and on time outcome.)

Here is what should have happened. First, senior management should have focused on and measured success by "right first time and on time" for all the production needs, rather than by the flexibility of the production line. Then the departmental measurements of success would be consistent with the required outcome. Next, the production group—those who own the outcome and have the most to gain from the improved process—should have driven the improvement program. Finally, senior management should have ensured that they were high profile and visible whenever they could be to emphasize the importance if this initiative. "If the bosses are participating, then it must be important."

Beliefs Background

Some change can be created in the area of beliefs, but the change is not the most significant in the short term. The change tends to be superficial and slow in coming (unless values are changed by changing some key players). However directional adjustments can be made over time. The best method of accomplishing change in this area is to ensure that the "new beliefs" are consistently reinforced through the attitudes and expectations side of the equation.

In assessing the beliefs, some of the same attributes as expectations are reviewed—yet with a different objective. The items for review are:

- Mission statement
- Philosophy of the organization
- Organization structure
- Job descriptions
- Approval mechanisms—financial: how is spending approved and controlled?
- Approval mechanisms—how are key new ventures or initiatives approved and controlled?
- Corporate Goals.

In assessing these attributes we are seeking not to understand the characteristic of the attribute but rather the philosophy behind the attribute. What were the creators thinking when they crafted these attributes? What was the intent? Why is it this way and not some other way? Why does Google's mission statement read: "To organize the world's information and make it universally accessible and useful," while Avon's mission statement consist of six very long sentences? What was behind Nike's decision to use this short and simple mission statement: "To Bring Inspiration and innovation to every athlete in the world"?

You can see from this line of questioning that we are trying to dig into the thought processes that created several of the attributes that now form the organization and its characteristics. You can also see why beliefs are less readily changed than expectations and attitudes.

The wording of the Mission statement and the way in which job descriptions are crafted say a lot about the philosophy of the organization.

The organization structure also says many things about the philosophy. Is the structure flat or vertical? Is it arranged in "silos"? That is to say, are there parts of the structure that are isolated from the main or parts that are very different from the rest? If so, why?

Approval mechanisms say a lot about a company in terms of freedom and trust. Who can approve what, how, when, and how quickly (with and without reference back up the hierarchy) gives a clear indication of the beliefs part of the culture. It is an important indicator of the trust factor and the degree of freedom that people have within the organization.

Finally, the Corporate Goals also provide a foundation for the beliefs. These tend to reflect the vision and the mission (assuming these to have been coherently thought through at the time of their creation.

Any one of these attributes does not in itself create the opportunity for the beliefs to be diagnosed. But each of them contributes to a picture of what drove (or is driving) the current thought process and the organization to be the way it now is.

There are also some informal mechanisms that assist in assessing the beliefs. These mechanisms fall into two areas:

- Recruiting practices
- The internal and external perception that the people inside the organization have of the company.

Regarding the recruitment practices—we are again looking at the freedom and the decision-making authority that people within the organization have. There is no right or wrong in this area. There only "is". What "is" is what "is". The "how" of it indicates clearly the beliefs that exist and the degree of trust that exists within the structure.

Another interesting exercise that helps to get a clear understanding of the beliefs is a "self perception" exercise. A number of key people are asked to explain how they perceive the organization first from the inside. "What does this organization look like to you? How would you describe it?" Then again—the same question to the same people but this time they are trying to answer what they think an outsider would say about the organization.

As implied above, beliefs are not readily changed. But when the fundamentals behind the beliefs are understood, then in the context of changing (or adjusting) expectations and attitudes, the beliefs can also be adjusted.

Culture Analysis

Having explored the above aspects (values, attitudes, expectations, and beliefs) thoroughly, we can then perform a Culture analysis. The culture analysis is a very intuitive mechanism—that is to say it is not a clinical and measurable type of activity.

The culture analysis is assessed under a series of headings. Within those headings the detail will emerge from a mechanism that is much like a word survey. Appendix C provides the basic words for each of the headings under the analysis process. During the interview process the senior managers of the organization choose from the lists the words that best describe their company.

From the word survey process, some words will fit the heading better than others for that particular company. For example, during this interview process senior managers will have a relatively clear view of what words best describe their vision of the term "Expectations". The words "foresight" and "anticipate" create a very different picture than "probability" and "take for granted". Under the heading "Authority /Responsibility, the words "autocracy" and "supremacy" convey a very different impression than the words "administration" and "bureaucracy".

The headings for the Culture analysis are as follows:

- Values
- Attitudes
- Expectations
- Beliefs
- Communication
- Accountability

- Authority / Responsibility

A number of questions also need to be asked to help shape the detail and the understanding of the answers. These are:

- What is the culture now (not what you'd like it to be)?
- What elements are key to success?
- Where is the power concentrated both formally and informally?
- What is the distinctive competence and critical strength?
- Where does the top management spend its time?
- Do the functional objectives and strategic implications parallel the culture?
- What elements are weak?
- What explicit and implicit assumptions underlie the current goals and objectives?
- Are these consistent with the cultural ability? (Companies often have visions and expectations and they do not have a culture that can effectively capitalize on what is needed to accomplish the goals.)

Through a word survey process, based on having performed the previously mentioned analysis tasks, key words emerge that succinctly describe the organization and its culture.

Armed with this information (a word picture derived from the key words), and based on the understanding of the culture that currently exists, a discussion can commence to determine what the preferred culture should look like. In this context, the process now moves backwards through the same steps (in reverse order) to that which got us to this present point.

From the word survey, the preferred words are chosen (by senior management collectively or in small groups or individually) that more accurately and effectively reflect what the culture *should be*. Based on this, the mechanisms that shape the beliefs can be modified to better suit the need. The attitudes and expectations can then be adjusted accordingly. The final test, at this culture assessment and change planning stage, is to determine if the values of the incumbents can shift sufficiently to accommodate the new culture. What you are trying to assess is whether the key people have moved and are now aligned with the intended culture.

The ultimate goal is to have a culture that exhibits strong and consistent candor, which in turn will cultivate an environment of trust. If the shift in thinking and in the values of the individuals in power is too great—then the culture change required will not happen. The main reason for this is that people cannot *act* a part on a constant basis. The values have to be believed intrinsically by the people responsible for adopting them and disseminating them. If this is not the case—the whole process is just window dressing.

Trust and Candor
Trust and candor are the ultimate success factors of a coherent Corporate Culture and of a cohesive senior management team.

Trust occurs when organizational values are consistent and exhibited and followed by senior management. Values provide a benchmark for employees and lead to a sense of consistency, dependability, and reliability regardless of economic, environmental, or organization changes.

In every case where we have been involved in a Culture Diagnostic process, an assessment, a change process, or an integration status review and update—the bottom line always and without fail came out to be the same conclusion. If the values, expectations, attitudes, and beliefs are/were all in place and consistent across the spectrum of the senior management group—the higher this consistency the higher the trust. The higher the trust—the higher we found the candor to be. There has never been an exception and I do not expect to find one.

The elements that lead to this are self-apparent—if all the elements of the management structure function as they should in an open, honest, and cohesive way—the employees feel and see consistency of purpose and actions. The greater this coherence—

the higher the level of trust. The higher the level of trust—the higher the employees report the honesty to be. The perception of honesty comes directly from the level of candor that the employees see in the organization.

These three elements, trust, candor, and honesty are like a set of triplets—they thrive together and they thrive on each other. The higher one is, the higher the other two are. When one falters, it usually drags down the others.

The whole purpose of a coherent Corporate Culture is to consistently bring the key elements together in such a way as to ensure the highest level of integrity. The highest level of integrity comes from the highest levels of trust and candor.

I am sure you have heard the expression "honesty is the best policy". In the context of Corporate Culture—it is the only thing that matters.

Ultimately, if you are desperate for a single word approach to what I am trying to say then I would choose the word:

Transparency.

PART II: MANAGEMENT: STYLE, GUILE, AND WILES

This section of the book is a brief historical review of the evolution of management. It allows us to looks at management styles of individuals and groups in the context of decision making and illustrates how some styles are more holistic than others in helping create a strong Corporate Culture. Many portions of the evolution of contemporary management really set a solid foundation for today's managers and the need for a strong and coherent Corporate Culture.

Chapter 4. Hierarchy to Hygiene: Management Styles, their Evolution and Impact

It was the early part of the twentieth century before there was any tangible and articulated basis for starting to differentiate management styles. Prior to that time, most styles (if you could call them that) consisted of either a feudalistic master/servant relationship or an autocratic business owner with a group of distinctly subordinate employees. In each case the power of "the boss" was absolute. It was exactly this aspect of the work environment and the extremely dominant/submissive yet adversarial relationship that formed the basis of the organized labor movement. Trade unions were formed by the downtrodden workers who eventually found vocal and (in the early days) physical ways of expressing their frustration and anger.

All of this eventually led to a continuing evolution of analysis and mechanisms that various experts employed to characterize and quantify management styles.

Today there are almost as many management styles and approaches as there are people who have the title of manager, but most of these styles can be sorted into three to five collective groups. These groupings are nothing new; in fact the research that sustains the classifications today can be traced back to the very early days of "scientific management". After the steam age and the Industrial Revolutions that characterized the evolution of the work place in the 19th century there was some "structure" appearing in the work place environment. The best known of these is from popular history and can be traced back to Henry Ford and the Model T (you can have your car in any color so long as it's black). Charlie Chaplin helped characterize the plight of the hapless worker in his famous movie skit "Modern Times" in 1936. Then came the Second World War when mass production techniques were developed at a tremendous pace with little thought to the workers and management styles. (After all everyone was working for the war effort and patriotism is a strong motivator under those circumstances.) It was not until the post World War II era that management began to emerge as a science.

Maslow's Hierarchy of Needs
One of the earlier evolutions of management's awakening, which set the foundation for much of what followed, can be traced back to Abraham Maslow's "Hierarchy of Needs", proposed in his 1943 paper "A Theory of Human Motivation".[7]

The key elements of Maslow's theory can be depicted in a simple and historic diagram.

Maslow's Hierarchy of Needs

Self fulfillment
Realizing potential,
Self-development, Morality,
Creativitiy, Spontanaeity,
Problem-solving,
Lack of prejudice,
Acceptance of facts

Esteem, Autonomy, and Ego Needs
Reputation, Status, Recognition,
Respect, Appreciation, Self- Esteem,
Self Confidence, Autonomy,
Competence, Knowledge,
Achievement

Social Needs
Belonging, Giving, Receiving, Acceptance,
Love, Friendship, Family, Intimacy

Safety Needs
Security of body, Security of employment, Protection
from danger and deprivation, Security of family,
health, and property

Physiological Needs
Breathing, Food, Water, Sleep, Shelter, Warmth, Sex

Maslow theorizes that as each need is satisfied, beginning at the bottom of the pyramid, we seek to meet the needs of the next level. In a simplistic way, this astute analysis shows the evolution of the human species from its prehistoric existence into the modern social animal that we are today.

You will also see as we touch on a few of these "social scientific" concepts that they can be categorized into two broad camps. One group of concepts has a rational scientific basis, and as such exhibits enduring qualities and attributes. These concepts, when looked at today, still show remarkable logic and soundness. The other concepts, while equally rational and useful, when looked at today still have merit, but also exhibit a sort of dated quality about them. I look at Maslow's Hierarchy of Needs and see as much logic, relevance, and freshness today as the day it was originally espoused.

Maslow's pyramid and the sequential implication that it creates also begin to show clearly the evolution of "excellent" companies and how the Corporate Culture evolves within them. It also exemplifies how we are only just scratching the surface when it comes to enterprise and the potential of the human contribution.

It's easy to see how for thousands of years through the early existence of humankind, the bottom three elements of Maslow's Hierarchy were the only elements of significance. The first needs encompassed the very fundamental requirements of survival. Without a mix of food, rest, shelter, and warmth, there was no survival. Without the element of procreation, there was no continuation of the species. Step one: meet the physiological needs.

This first step quickly led to the next step where the safety and protection needs had to be met to allow for survival beyond the physiological. Security from predators, deprivation, and threat became an essential to sustain the day-to-day existence.

The very existence of the first two steps on the hierarchy, once secured on a reasonably sustainable basis, would then lead to the next element, social needs. It's interesting to speculate on the many thousands of years that may have elapsed before the next step was routinely embraced and became part of the fabric of daily existence. Undoubtedly for a select few in privileged positions, the concept of autonomy was available, though not necessarily at an objectively conscious level, but more at a "fight to the death to defend" level.

Once knowledge and competence were recognized beyond the immediate circle of the survival cell, we can deduce that self-esteem and self-confidence would grow, and with that growth would come the status that went beyond the survival cell. A generally recognized concept suggests that the distance that can be travelled in one day largely circumscribes a person's sphere of influence. If that is true, one can picture people living in the Middle Ages exerting their influence over a relatively small domain. For the working people the sphere would not likely have extended beyond the immediate village or part of the township in which they lived. For the more affluent, the area would have been larger, since on horseback a person could travel perhaps 50 to 80 kilometres in a day. Only the very wealthy such as royalty could extend to regions or perhaps a country since they would have had resources to sustain them and their staff for travel over extended distances.

In today's world, the sphere of influence has not changed much from the distance travelled in one day. But today that distance is almost the world. In saying that, it is obvious that the speed and reach of modern communication also very significantly affect the size of this sphere. People are recognized and respected for their contribution and knowledge over vast areas of the globe to a level unheard of just a few centuries ago.

All this becomes very important in the concept of Corporate Culture. Beyond esteem and ego needs is the very real and fundamental need for self-development and maximizing of one's own potential. Once achieved, this leads to a level of self-fulfilment that is a critical success factor in the successful evolution in all persons ideally, or more normally those persons who are lucky enough to have achieved this or know it is theirs to achieve. The more clearly and fully any individual in an organization feels fulfilled by virtue of their contribution, the more powerful that contribution becomes and the more sustaining it is. I have observed and experienced that this becomes an almost

74

self-sustaining cycle. The more fulfilled you are, the more confidence you have. The more confidence you have, the more powerful you feel your contribution can be. If this level of fulfilment can be accomplished for the majority of people in the organization, then the benefit and power it unleashes is quite incredible.

The power of synergy, empathy, and self-confidence

Imagine being part of a large cross-functional team of technical, sales, and marketing types who have a major project to launch a new product in a difficult market that already has a lot of competition. The difference is that the product you have is dramatically better than the competing products in the market. Plus, your product is not only cheaper and better, the improvement is so obvious that the prospective consumer cannot help but notice. It hits them right between the eyes—it's that obvious. In addition, you are part of a team that has not only the right players making their contributions, but each of you gets along just perfectly with all the other team members. You have never been on a better and more productive team. How does this make you feel? Empowered, self -confident, self-assured? Your team colleagues also feel this way. Can you imagine the power that you collectively unleash? When market success follows, imagine how empowered you feel. The word might be omnipotent.

One of the outcomes of a strong, coherent, and effective Corporate Culture and a very important element in the ability to sustain that culture is based on the fact that a large majority of the employees (or participants) are fulfilled. You can easily identify the organizations that have achieved such status by the almost religious fervor with which the people involved speak about the organization and how they act within the organization. This fervor is contagious within the organization and, provided the catalyst (the leadership source) can maintain the cultural elements in balance, the process will continue to feed and develop. The Walt Disney Company provides a good example from the "Culture" section of their web site:

"From the beginning, starting with Walt Disney, we have had five things that make me proud to be part of this Company: high-quality products, optimism for the future, great storytelling, an emphasis on family entertainment and great talent, passion and dedication from our Cast Members."

- Marty Sklar
Vice Chairman and Principal Creative Executive
Walt Disney Imagineering[8]

As we explore organizations in Chapter 20 we will also touch on what I call overkill organizations—those where the culture is overwhelming to the point where only the dedicated can thrive and the rest tend to get rolled over and ploughed under.

It is worthwhile to explore some of the other "social science" outcomes that various experts have developed and documented in the quest to describe organizational management.

Theory X and Theory Y

Douglas McGregor was another early theorist of the evolution of how people responded and grew under different management approaches. He studied the human being in the context of management and the organization. In his 1950s his book, *The Human Side of Enterprise*,[9] he expounded a very logical theory that at that time was revolutionary. His concept became known as "Theory X and Theory Y". The logic was simple and still stands the test of time, though today we largely take it for granted. The rationale was that at one end of a continuum was the traditional view of management commonly accepted in the nineteenth century. That assumption he called Theory X.

Theory X
- **People have an inherent dislike of work and will avoid it if they can.**
- Because of this characteristic of dislike of work, most people must be coerced, controlled, directed, and

76

threatened with punishment to get them to put forth adequate effort toward the achievement of organizational objectives.

- The average human being prefers to be directed, wishes to avoid responsibility, has relatively little ambition, and above all wants security.

The alternative at the other end of the scale McGregor called Theory Y.

Theory Y

- **The expenditure of physical and mental effort in work is as natural as play or rest.**
- External controls and threats of reward and punishment are not the only means for bringing about effort toward the organizational objectives. A person will exercise self-direction and self-control in the service of objectives to which they are committed.
- Commitment to an objective is a function of the rewards associated with their achievement.
- The average human being learns, under proper conditions, not only to accept but also to seek responsibility.
- The capacity to exercise a relatively high degree of imagination, ingenuity, and creativity in the solution of organizational problems is widely, not narrowly distributed in the population.
- Under the conditions of "modern industrial life", the intellectual potentialities of the average human being are only partially utilized.

McGregor went on to articulate his theory as a continuum, characterizing the Theory X as "autocratic" and Theory Y as "participative". At the Theory X end of the scale, the Manager makes all the decisions. The further along the line one gets to Theory Y or the participative side of the continuum, the greater the contribution from employees and to the organization. As the organization evolves the Manager progresses to "selling" his ideas, then advances to inviting contributions, moves to a consultation mode, progresses to taking advice, and finally at the point of Theory Y is in a consensus mode.

McGregor's rationale was developed in an era where his views and his theory were ahead of their time. His words convey much of the state of enterprise and organization at the time of his writing. In today's environment we take most, if not all, of the Theory Y for granted.

Today our starting point is often the basic elements of participative management. The question is more about how well the mechanisms are developed and exercised than whether they exist. That doesn't mean that autocratic management is dead and buried; it merely means that it's more disguised than it was before. Autocratic management, while generally not appropriate in contemporary western organizations, is still flourishing and has its place in the needs of society. A good example of this is military service where unquestioned obedience to the line of command is essential.

Argyris on Motivation
Subsequent to Maslow and McGregor similar threads of organizational logic were addressed and created by a number of other social scientists. For example, Chris Argyris, a Professor of Administration Sciences at Yale University during the 1950s and 1960s, and subsequently Professor Emeritus at Harvard University, wrote extensively on organizational effectiveness, and consulted to many North American and European organizations. His approach can be traced back to the logic we have already reviewed.

Argyris claimed that problems of worker apathy and lack of effort are not a matter of individual laziness. Rather, they are often a healthy reaction by normal people to an unhealthy environment—an environment created by management policies and approaches to the needs of the organization.[10] Argyris went on to state that most adults are motivated to be responsible, self-reliant, and independent. These motives are acquired during childhood from the education process that surrounds them. They come from the family, from books, television, and radio.

Yet the typical organization confines most of its employees to roles that provide little or no opportunity for responsibility, reliance, or independence. On the contrary, **most jobs in an individual's day were designed in ways to make minimal demands on that person's abilities and place most of the decision-making requirements on the shoulders of his or her supervisors.** The obvious reaction to such a structure from the employee is apathy, lack of interest, indifference, and withdrawal.

Argyris suggested that both workers and management had missed the main point with regard to motivation. They had largely concentrated on matters such as income, security, and fringe benefits. While these are necessary in the organization they are not motivators (we will see shortly how a lack of these is a de-motivator).

As a foremost behavioral scientist, Argyris created a bridge from the early contemporaries to later leading names in this field. One can still read between the lines to see that while organizations had evolved, they were clearly only at the early part of this evolutionary path. Argyris' behavioral observations and his emphasis on what can be done portray a clear picture of the typical management styles of the day.

McClelland and Self Motivation
Another leading theorist, Professor David McClelland, at Harvard University and subsequently as Distinguished Research Professor of Psychology at Boston University, described methods for measuring motives, the development of motives out of natural incentives, and the relationship of motives to emotions, to values, and to performance under a variety of conditions.[11]

McClelland's claim (from his studies as a social scientist) still exhibits a lot of contemporary logic. He posits that most people have a motivation to be successful and to achieve something. However, only about 10% of the population has a highly developed motivation. His analysis suggests that there is a measurable tendency in strong achievers when not required to think and asked just to relax and let their mind wander, to still think about ways to accomplish something difficult and significant.

He identifies three major characteristics of self-motivated achievers:

- **Self-motivated achievers like to set their own goals.**
- **Self-motivated achievers tend to avoid extremes of difficulty in selecting goals.**
- **Self-motivated achievers tend to prefer tasks that provide some form of early feedback or measurement of progress towards the goal.**

McClelland goes on to confirm that many supervisory practices are ill-served by this type of person since they will rarely set goals or timelines that they cannot easily achieve. And, in most cases, the imposed expectations are often a disincentive since they do not capture the commitment of the participant.

Further on in the book we will see elements of the significant fundamentals of Corporate Culture emerging from the earlier works of these highly regarded and skilled practitioners. These pioneers each speak in terms that start to imply that **openness and candid communication along with involvement of people is a key success factor in any company. I contend that this is essential for an "excellence" company**.

We also see bridges that span to the foundations of the best management practices of today.

Likert's System 1 and System 4

Rensis Likert, who was director of the Institute for Social Research and a professor of both psychology and sociology at the University of Michigan, also did a lot of work in areas of human relations and in the study of organization. In the mid-1960s he published several books including *New Patterns of Management* and *The Human Organization: Its Management and Value.*[12]

Likert expressed the view that when organizations are faced with a need to economize, the most common reaction is to cut expenses and tighten up operations. Hierarchical pressure from the top is transmitted through the management ranks into every department to work harder and spend less. (Does this still have an all too familiar ring to it fifty years later?) **When the results are measured by ordinary accounting procedures, they usually show that more cash is being generated than before. The usual interpretation is that management has made the organization profitable again.**

Likert disagreed with this interpretation. He conducted many behavioral research studies in many organizations. He points out that money is not necessarily profit. Liquidating assets can generate money and that is exactly what happens in most cost-cutting programs. **Traditional accounting fails to measure (indeed is not capable of measuring) what happens to the human assets of the organization, *i.e.* the skills, experience, loyalty, and know-how of its employees.** (Interesting to note that loyalty is an important factor, something that is much less common today.)

Likert went on to say that if damaged, the organization may show more cash on its balance sheet but it will be less capable of operating efficiently in the long term. The result, he suggested, is the same as failing to keep the plant and machinery in good operating condition. A short-term gain has been achieved at the cost of the longer-term earning power.

Likert's studies indicate that cost cutting is frequently applied insensitively. That is, when management adopts a tough "take it or leave it" attitude the reaction is likely to run through three steps:

- First, the employees become resentful, hostile, and distrustful of management.
- Second, as a result of these attitudes, employees are more likely to submit more grievances and complaints than usual. They may work carelessly and wastefully, and restrict production, as well as leave to work elsewhere. The latter, Likert noted, is more likely to occur with the more able managers and the more highly skilled workers since they are more easily re-employed. The effect of their departure is to lower the overall competence of the organization.
- Third, the cumulative result of all of these manifestations of employee resistance is measurably reduced efficiency and the probable onset of the next financial crisis, the next cycle possibly being worse than the one that the original plan was intended to cure.

In the context of Corporate Culture, Likert developed a number of variables that allowed him and the affected organizations to predetermine the potential impact of change. Amongst these attributes were the leadership styles that characterized the organization, such as the freedom or lack of freedom that the employees felt about communication with their superiors and the degree of competence and trust which the employees felt their superiors had in them.

Likert developed a four-point scale that expressed the prevailing management characteristics in terms of several key variables. The one extreme, "System 1", he described as arbitrary, coercive, and highly authoritarian, which, even in his day, was noted as being rare in its pure form in business. The other extreme is "System 4", which he described as based on teamwork, mutual confidence, trust, and genuine respect for the individuals that compose the organization. (Note the similarities with McGregor's Theory X and Theory Y.) Systems 2 and 3 were the intermediate gradations, which he went on to fine tune into more sub-categories. He noted that in his day the pure form of System 4 was also relatively rare.

One of Likert's most significant findings is that the closer a company gets to System 4 style of management, the more likely it is to experience sustained high profitability. One of the challenges that this style of management faced then as it does now is the time factor. The System 1 approach can generate short-term results in terms of profit, but at a long-term expense which is not usually apparent for sometimes years afterwards. The converse is also true for the System 4 type of company where the short-term financial picture can get worse due to the increasing investment in people before the results start to get better. Likert's findings then (as now) have repeatedly shown that the System 4 approach builds steadily towards a flexible, responsive, and responsible team approach that can achieve and sustain high profitability.

Moreover, System 4 companies can in emergencies cut cost and improve productivity quite readily through a co-operative and concerted effort. Under these circumstances, Likert's research found that the leading variables that could be identified as the key points of difference were motivation and attitude. Likert cites many examples where the management style as it relates to motivation and attitudes is the most constructive barometer of management's potential success in harnessing the productive power of the company.

Converting an organization to System 4 requires massive re-education and training of all involved. The most notable distinction between the extremes of the two Systems characterizes the one as continually having to keep the organization under control versus the other of harnessing the productive power of the organization.

The System 4 style relies on four basic principles.

- Utilize modern principles and techniques of motivation.

- Maintain supportive relationships and deal with people to enhance their feelings of self worth to meet their needs, desires, and values, *i.e.* building on people rather than destroying them.

- Build the organization into tightly knit, highly motivated teams or work groups that are committed to achieving the goals of the organization. These groups should be linked, with overlapping memberships in two groups or more to maintain cohesiveness.

- Set high performance goals for the company via senior management commitment and clearly communicated expectations of the employees.

Herzberg and Hygiene

The last of this generation of behavioral scientists that we will touch on is Frederick Herzberg, who was at the University of Utah and the Professor of Psychology at Western Reserve University in Cleveland. Two of his most notable and pertinent books were "The Motivation to Work" and "Work and the Nature of Man", originally published in the late 1950s and mid 1960s respectively.[13]

Herzberg contended that human beings have two qualitatively different sets of needs in the context of the work environment. According to Herzberg, the traditional approach to motivation (at that time) only concerned itself with the environment in which the employee operated, *i.e.* the circumstances that surround the employee and that which they are given in exchange for work. Herzberg considers the concern for the environment a never-ending necessity for management, but said it was not sufficient in itself for effective motivation. Effective motivation, he declared, required another set of factors, namely experiences, which are inherent in the work itself. **Herzberg's assertion that the work itself can be a motivator represented an important breakthrough in behavioral science thinking**.

It is easy to connect a common thread amongst Herzberg and his peers and contemporaries. But Herzberg probably became more

84

widely recognized for his work and his thinking than his peers, helped by the high-profile companies that adopted his philosophies, most notably Texas Instruments. Texas Instruments spent a number of years successfully totally immersing itself in a culture substantially shaped by Herzberg's approaches. Up until that time it was considered necessary for management either to coerce people to work with threats or to entice them by means of rewards.

Herzberg's view was that the potential motivating power of the work itself was obscured by the fact that most jobs were not at all stimulating; therefore some kind of pressure either positive or negative was needed to sustain the required effort. Many companies of that era found that by reorganizing jobs to provide more satisfaction or personal growth, a powerful new motivating tool was created.

Herzberg took no exception to the apparent conflict between the environmental approach to motivation and the approach through work itself. He did however distinguish the environmental elements into a group that he termed "hygiene factors". **The term "hygiene" was used to describe the collection of preventive measures that management needs to sustain in order to maintain the status quo. (Examples include work conditions, supervision, company policies, and salary.) These hygiene factors, when maintained, removed sources of dissatisfaction from the environment, just as sanitation removes potential health threats from the physical environment.** These were inherently limiting in contrast to the job motivation factors, which were demonstrated to have larger and more lasting effects.

His research showed clearly that when any of these factors are deficient in the organization, employees are likely to express their displeasure in ways that hinder the organization, through actions such as grievances, decreased productivity, and even strikes. When the deficiencies are corrected, productivity may return to normal but is unlikely to rise from that level. In other words, **an investment in hygiene factors may eliminate a deficit but will not create a gain.** Another important fact to emerge from this research and its applications is that the **hygiene factors are not enduring. With the passage of time, the feeling of deficiency returns.** Herzberg was very clear on the fact that hygiene was a necessary but thankless task for management. **A fully developed and efficient hygiene program will not motivate and sustain employees to higher levels of productivity and a deficient program will lead to inefficiency.**

He chose the term "motivation" to describe the feelings of accomplishment, of professional growth, of professional recognition that are experienced in a job that offers challenge and scope for the employee. He chose this term to define the factors that are capable of producing a lasting increase in satisfaction, and with this a lasting increase in productivity to above-normal levels. He found this to be true and applicable in a wide variety of business settings. It is important to note that **Herzberg had a very specific definition of the word motivation. He applied it only to those experiences that produced sustained satisfaction and he did not include in its meaning "influences that have less lasting effects".**

Herzberg went on to focus his attention on job design. At that time, most jobs were either unconsciously designed or not designed at all. Those that had some element of design in them were usually created from a standpoint of operating efficiency and economy. These types of job design took the challenge and the opportunity of creativity away from the worker and therefore contributed to the de-motivating effect. His research indicated that apathy and minimal worker effort was the natural outcome of jobs that offered only a pay cheque and a decent place to work. Herzberg's work clearly demonstrated that continued investment in the hygiene rapidly reached a point of diminishing returns.

Herzberg went on to deal with job motivating factors that he termed as "job enrichment" as a means to increasing sustainable worker input and effort. Do not confuse "job enrichment" with the term "job rotation"—a very different tool. I have come across several examples where companies think that the variety of work created for an individual by "job rotation" is a direct alternative to

86

"job enrichment". Job rotation means that you do one job over a period of time—and the job can be complex, interesting, and diverse, but it is one defined job. Within a fixed time period you rotate into another equally interesting job for another period of time and so it continues. With "job enrichment" you actually analyze the detail of the job and the scope and continually improve it, expand it, add to it, simplify it, and expand it further. In other words you have the freedom and opportunity to continually expand the role and contribution that you are making.

Two very distinct summaries of the "Hygiene" factors versus the "Motivating" factors provide a simple summary of what Herzberg saw and proved.

- **The "Hygiene Factors" are potential sources of dissatisfaction, and include issues like company policies, supervision, working conditions, the work environment, the coffee, the cafeteria and the good food, parking spaces, the social perks, inter-personal relationships, money, status, and security.**
- **By contrast, The "Motivating Factors" are potential sources of sustained increased productivity, and include a sense of achievement, recognition, the job itself, responsibility, accountability, and professional growth.**

Peter Drucker and The Workplace Revolution

Peter Ferdinand Drucker is probably one of the best known and most enduring of all management gurus, if indeed he is not THE best known. While he died in California in 2005 (just shy of his 96th birthday), he was still active and contributing to the vast domain of management knowledge that his long career had generated.

He is probably best known for creating the phrase "knowledge worker", which, when he first conceived of that idea in 1959, was a novel way of looking at what people do in business and how business has evolved and changed over the decades. Whether or not he unknowingly created the "knowledge economy", he certainly popularized the term as a chapter title of his book *The Age of Discontinuity*[14] (1969).

Drucker was a man with a fertile mind who called himself a social ecologist. He constantly focused on the interrelationship among business, government, and the worker, as well as society as a whole. His prolific writings were often regarded as the leading edge in the current state of modern day management (beginning in the 1940s, and continuing through to his last published works in the 2000s).

He is credited with authoring 39 books (not all of them on management) and countless articles.

Basic truths that Drucker espoused included[15]:
- A company typically functions best when it's decentralized (as opposed to using a command-and-control model).
- Employees are assets and not liabilities (and should be treated as such).
- The central mission of any business is to create a customer.
- An organization has the best chance of success when it adheres to "management by objectives".
- An enterprise has to constantly do two things: innovate and market—or it will waste away.
- "Knowledge workers" are the essential ingredients of the modern economy.

There was a constant yet evolving theme to his management books. Following is a summary of the ideas that run through most of Drucker's writings: [16]

- **A profound scepticism about macroeconomic theory.** Drucker contended that economists of all schools fail to explain significant aspects of modern economics.

- **A desire to make everything as simple as possible.** According to Drucker corporations tend to produce too many products, hire employees that they don't need (when a better solution would be contracting out), and expand into economic sectors that they should stay out of.

- **A belief in what he called "the sickness of government".** Drucker made ostensibly non-ideological claims that government is unable or unwilling to provide new services that people need or want—though he seemed to believe that this condition is not inherent to democracy.

- **The need for "planned abandonment".** Corporations as well as government have a natural human tendency to cling to yesterday's successes rather than seeing when they are no longer useful.

- **The lasting contribution of "the father of scientific management", Frederick Winslow Taylor.*** Though Drucker himself had little experience with the analysis of blue-collar work (he spent his career analyzing managerial work), he credited Taylor with originating the seminally important idea that work can be broken down, analyzed, and improved.

- **The need for community.** Early in his career Drucker predicted "the end of economic man" and advocated the creation of "a plant community" where individuals social

---

* Frederick Winslow Taylor lived during the early years of the industrial revolution and was mostly known for his contribution to organizing work into minute elements so that every task could be analyzed and documented. Thus repetitive activity could be measured in time and rated in effort. His view was that workers needed to have jobs broken down into the simplest of repetitive tasks to ensure uniform speed of output and accuracy. His view was that workers were not equipped to think about such things and that the thinking was management's job. Needless to say, over time his views were not always shared, particularly by the unions who he thought had no place in the work place. It was his structured approach to work measurement that led to his being credited with the founding of the term "scientific management".

needs could be met. He later admitted that the plant community never materialized, and by the 1980s that volunteering in the non-profit sector might be the key to community.

- **He wrote extensively about management by objectives.**
- **A company's primary responsibility is to serve its customers—to provide the goods or services that the company exists to produce. Profit is not the primary goal** but rather an essential condition for the company's continued existence. Other responsibilities to employees and society exist to support the company's continued ability to perform its primary purpose.

Influencing organizations as diverse as Google, General Electric, and the United Farm Workers, Drucker often said that the toughest decisions are people decisions, and very few companies are good at making these decisions. He noted, "Executives spend more time on managing people and people decisions than on anything else, and they should. No other decisions are so long lasting in their consequences or so difficult to unmake and yet, by and large, executives make poor promotion and staffing decisions. By all accounts, their batting average is no better than .333. At most one-third of such decisions turn out right; one-third are minimally effective and one-third are outright failures. In no other area of management would we put up with such miserable performance."[17]

In response to the above quote, Tim Brennan wrote:
> In sampling of management workshop participants, we asked, "Do you agree with Drucker?" We found that most do agree and they provided an additional, important insight: just because the hiring decision turned out to be a mistake does not imply that the person hired left the new job. Although in many cases, the new hire falls short of expectations and should never have been hired or he or she requires too much supervision, often they remain on the job because (for managers) accepting poor performance is easier than finding a replacement![18]

In the context of Corporate Culture, the thinkers and theorists of the mid-twentieth century contributed very significantly to a dramatic shift in management approaches to work and its organization. The principles that were revolutionary in their day are considered today to be very much part of the fabric of the everyday working world that we take for granted. There are still a lot of management dinosaurs out there today, but almost all of them at least understand the basics of the management principles as laid down half a century ago.

Chapter 5.   What Kind of Boss are You? Individuals and the Impact of Management Style

What would you say if your top employee came to you and said, "I want to take six months off without pay to work on my novel"? Or, what if she said, "I think our company should be supporting more charitable works. How about sending one of our employees to work at a food bank for a month"? Perhaps your employee might say, "I think we can do better on our production goals, but we'll need to get rid of certain people and hire new ones." What would your boss say to you if you went to him or her with any of these propositions? The immediate response can tell a lot about a person's management style.

There are almost as many management styles, as there are people in management. Every time two people interact with some form of outcome or end goal in mind, the personality of each person is involved. Who they are, what they are, where they are (not physically but in the evolution of their life), and how they got to this point in their lives has an influence on how the conversation unfolds. When focused on the contemporary business world, each person brings with him- or herself a posture and a set of characteristics that influence the proceedings. Whether it's two peers speaking to each other or a boss and a subordinate speaking together, each person brings a set of characteristics in the form of values, attitudes, expectations, and beliefs to the process. Within the context of an organization, these characteristics are strongly influenced by the cultural standards in the company.

Management styles

The boss's management style or approach can be characterized into one of a few general classifications:

- Autocratic/dictatorial
- Assertive and democratic (facilitative)
- A middle ground mixture of several of the above: the compromiser.

- Abdicating/*Laisser-faire*
- Paternalistic: the good guy

This is based on the Managerial Grid Model, or the Blake Grid (also called the Blake Mouton Grid), discussed below.

Most bosses fit somewhere into a matrix implied by the above range of characteristics. Over the past decades these characteristic groupings have been explored and packaged by numerous management consultants who have attempted to put some structure and definition around these elements. Rensis Likert, mentioned earlier, was one of the early pioneers in characterizing these management styles into some sort of structure. He described the management styles as System 1 and System 4 and implied that the other two (System 2 and System 3) were largely gradations on the scale.

More recent formats of this approach placed these elements on a matrix. Notable in this area were Robert Blake and Jane Mouton, two social scientists who developed and then spent a number of years actively promoting a management philosophy based on what they called the Managerial Grid Model, or the Blake Grid.[19] The Blake and Mouton model plots "concern for people" on the vertical axis and "concern for task" on the horizontal axis.

We will refer to the Blake Grid again but its approach is quite universal and builds on the foundation created by the earlier industrial and social scientists of the past.

The general classifications mentioned above paint a very simple picture when placed into a matrix as shown below.

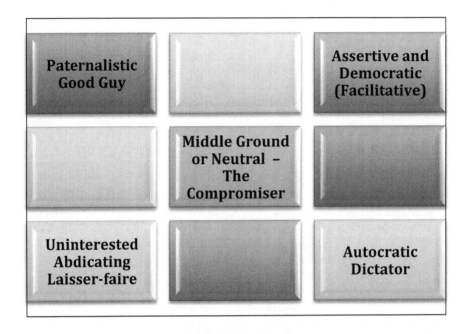

As we explore each of these types in a day to day working context, we will see how so many management styles can be simplistically grouped and why almost all of them fit somewhere onto the matrix.

Using a grid approach to classifying management styles, we will be expanding on the five key styles implied in the grid. In today's environment management styles have become progressively more refined and the extremes at the lower, bottom left (less desirable) parts of the Grid tend to be much more rare (though dinosaurs are not yet extinct). The best style tends to be more in the top right of the grid. Below is an expansion on the various styles, with an emphasis on the upper right (more desirable) styles referred to as "facilitative" and "democratic".

The Autocratic Manager (Dictator). This is the "my way or the highway" type of manager who rules with an iron fist. This style of management often fosters an atmosphere of fear and trepidation. This type of manager is usually hard-nosed and aggressive, caring little for the people aspect of the process. Orders (yes orders) come from the boss, with no allowance for discussion and often little dialogue and feedback. All activity is focused on the objective and the results. People are almost irrelevant, more a necessary evil required to get the job done. People are a tool to be deployed under direct orders to get things done. Meetings are often influenced by the mood of the boss. It is not unusual for people to be asking each other "what sort of mood is he in today" before they go in to see the person. (I pick the gender-specific "he" since the majority of this style of boss are male). This individual usually has all the answers to all the questions since there is only one way to fix any and all problems and that is their way. No discussion, no questions, no consensus. Just do it. Do as you are asked and do it immediately. This person often trusts no one since, from their point of view, no one can handle what needs to be done as well as they can. Often, they ride herd on the process and involve themselves in every facet of the problem to drive out a solution. There is no pleasant conversation, there is no to-and-fro for clarification, just a plain "get on and do it—if you can't then someone else will".

The staff working for this style of management is often unmotivated and wishing they were not here or not in this job. This style imposes a higher level of stress upon the staff than do other styles, with people often dreading aspects of their work. For example, getting up to go to work is not the most motivating thing for all people. (A recent study in Canada indicated that one third of employees disliked what they do and another one third dreads getting up on Monday morning to go to work). So, the work environment for the employees and the style of the autocratic manager certainly has a negative impact on the majority of this group.

This autocratic style has a number of variations that need to be distinguished.

The Aggressive Manager—not quite the Dictator who rules in a "perform or perish" type of environment, but still very assertive. **This person is a somewhat toned down version of the true "Autocrat".** They still tend to use people as tools or disposable chattels but in a less harsh way. The boss is still of the opinion that people are lazy and have minimal competence and need to be driven, coerced, watched, and controlled. A key motivating tool is pressure—pressure from short time lines and hard to achieve goals. The style is often short-term focused leading to more pressure when longer-term needs create a change in priority. Aggressive managers often create hostility around them and bring resentment upon themselves. Eventually, this style of management burns out the people who work under the Dictator.

The Assertive Manager: The Power Manager is often an individual more worthy of respect. This manager has risen above most of the peers on the Grid. **This individual walks a fine line between the Dictator and the more highly regarded Facilitative Manager but tends to be more of the facilitator.** The Power Manager often uses authority in a forceful way. In the process they may shift between various positive approaches to managing mixed with a variety of negative methods as shown in the table below.

Positive Methods	Negative Methods
Access to approval facilitating decision making	Perceptions of "bucking the system"
Hiring and promotion	Firing and demotion
Gentle persuasion	Pulling rank
Constructive coercion	Threats

The **Truly Facilitative Manager (the extreme practitioner)** rarely operates in any extreme management style. The Truly Facilitative Manager will use an extreme style from time to time, but always in a controlled and thought-through way, a way that is intended to give a pre-determined outcome. The Facilitative Manager knows how to walk the fine line to always get the best out of their staff.

96

The Facilitative Manager. This manager is often one of the best to work for since they know when to encourage, when to stay back, when to lead and when to sympathize. They have a unique style and approach that is most often right for every occasion. These managers usually exercise an interesting mixture of all styles with no extremes in any one area. They are strongly driven by consensus management and the need to get the very best and most complete solution on the table, without taking excessive time to get to the point. They have a very real and sincere empathy for their people, a trait that is appreciated by the staff. They know how to drive the decision process and make their people feel as if the decision was that of the subordinate. They know how to get their staff to feel as if they are accountable for the delivery without having them feeling stressed by the demands. They know when to stay back and let things evolve just as they know when to put their hands back on the wheel or step on the brakes.

They are usually very well connected to the issues that matter and know how to communicate them effectively. They are usually highly regarded by their employees and most other junior staff. Their employees are often asked "what's it like working for ----?" or they are told "You are really lucky to have her (or him) for a boss". In most cases, they interact well and constructively with their peers.

Synergy is a word that comes to mind when this style of manager moves processes forward. They are often quite humble and not usually given to boasting about their accomplishments. They are sensitive and know just how much is enough on personal matters. They show a genuine concern yet do not allow it to become intrusive. They know when to be a hard-nosed autocrat and when to be a pussycat. The bottom line with this style of management is that they usually do the right things in the right way at the right time and for the right reasons—the four R's.

The people working for this style of manager are often focused, motivated, and due to the role model, know how to take on the responsibility and get things done. They know what to report and when. They know when to get help and how. (Usually the boss already knows what is coming up and what needs to be done). Many of the staff are happy in the work environment and often talk about a sense of accomplishment and a feeling of satisfaction with their contribution.

The key thing, which differentiates this manager and the management style, is the almost uncanny knack of the individual to be in the right place at the right time with just the right amount of the right advice. All this, and the employees still feeling as if they own the process and the deliverables.

Facilitative managers often employ a technique referred to as "purposeful rounding," where they walk around to each employee daily. How are they doing? What are they working on? It gives the manager and the employee the sense that they are engaging their staff in conversation on work-related topics. They may ask other questions such as "What challenges are you facing with that project?" "Do you have the resources you need?" "Do need to other help to move things forward?" "Are there barriers or obstacles that I (the manager) can help to remove?" A Manager that takes an interest in their employees' life outside of the office also has an impact. "How is your family?" or "Any vacation plans for this summer?" It's about engaging employees and making a connection. But remember to be sincere, be brief, but do not to be too intrusive.

This style of management is very much like our 20% good drivers—almost everyone would like to think of himself or herself as being in the group, but hardly anyone is. In this case, the truly capable and totally facilitative manager is a rare person. One of the characteristics of this manager is the fact that their management style stands out and makes them memorable. Over many years in business and in many different industries, and in dealing with literally thousands of managers at every level, I can only name a small handful that fit the description. One of them would be Brian D., the person covered in the opening anecdote in this book. Another is the person I recruited into a factory turnaround situation, which you can read about in Chapter 13 under Participative Management.

Of the above five management styles it is apparent one stands head and shoulders above the rest in terms of its potential effectiveness and its opportunity to contribute to the maximum extent possible. The Facilitative Manager creates a prospective synergy or harmony that is difficult to imagine happening with the other less complete styles of management. All the logic of the evolution of management and all the research, wisdom, and experience that all the behavioral scientists have brought over the past decades all point to the same conclusion. **A well-developed facilitative management style is the most effective and complete style that any manager can bring to any process in any organization.**

We will see as the book unfolds that all management styles have a clear impact on the organization. The Corporate Culture is very dependent on the style and characteristics and all that senior management brings. The values, attitudes, expectations, and beliefs that are intrinsic to each of the senior managers are the essence of the Corporate Culture. The Facilitative Manager merely adds more to the process by virtue of the fact that she or he brings a more complete style and approach, which most of the employees look up to. It is this more complete style that stands out as the distinguishing feature. The people working under this style of management and those connected to (but not necessarily working for) the individual often hold a high regard for the manager in question. This individual becomes the disproportional influence on many of the positive aspects of the Corporate Culture.

The presence of the facilitative management style in an organization is a key factor in distinguishing the truly excellent companies from all of the rest.

Corporate Culture is the product of the characteristics of all of the people that are disproportionately influential in the organization. It is always the mix of the values, attitudes, expectations and beliefs of the key players. The distinguishing feature that sets apart the excellent companies from the rest is the presence of the influence of the facilitative management style in key parts of the company.

Characteristics of the facilitative and democratic manager include many factors.

Facilitative and democratic managers:
- Are assertive while maintaining respect.
- Consistently ensure that others know the needs and expectations of the organization.
- Exercise communication skills that motivate through respect and enthusiasm.
- Create meaningful work and work requirements.
- Recognize and act as if all employees are important and not just a variable cost commodity.

Their style is to:
- Be dedicated.
- Be supportive.
- Be visible.
- Be worthy of respect.
- Be trusted.
- Allow others to learn from mistakes.
- Balance the individual's needs and rights with those of the company.
- Develop ethical relationships and business practices.

They bring excellence because they:
- Focus on results not activities.
- Design "flat" (non-hierarchical) organizations to maximize involvement, discussion, and feedback.
- Plan more.
- "Do" less - delegate more.
- Keep a clear focus on the purpose or the goal.
- Spend time with others (over 50%).
- Build networks.

- Have many short conversations every day with many people.
- Are friendly, open, approachable, and business-like.
- Ask open-ended questions.
- Are active listeners.
- Set attainable goals.
- Allow their people to set their own sub-goals.
- Keep a mental score card and remind you of your "wins".
- Create a positive self-image.

Change is not always a comfortable process for many people, so, to be successful at it, the Facilitative Manager's approach must be as an agent of change.

As an agent of change, the Facilitative Manager will:
- Work from facts.
- Encourage diagnosis.
- Build a desire to achieve.
- Create expectations.
- Make demands constructively.

Ultimately, the facilitative and democratic leader has confidence in people, and by involving them as much as possible the manager succeeds in motivating and obtaining the highest performance from the staff. **This leader believes that people are motivated and challenged by responsibility and that the staff seeks to be involved.** This leader believes that people do not need close supervision. This leader knows that good performance does not require intimidation, continual pressure, or constant scrutiny.

The Facilitative Manager is often assertive but not aggressive. There is a delicate balance and a fine line between the two as we explored in the autocratic management section.

The Neutral Manager - the Compromiser. This manager always sits on the fence or takes the middle ground, never strong in any opinion one way or the other. They are generally easier to work for and to work with. Indeed, along with the

Aggressive Manager, a large proportion of the average management styles fits somewhere in the general area created by these two style groups. In the Neutral group, most managers have a reasonable degree of empathy for their staff and enjoy a certain amount of dialogue about the peripheral aspects of their work. They often also have an appropriate ability to focus on the priorities and the deliverables and ask the questions necessary to ensure some form of progress. Meetings are business-like and generally somewhat productive. Correspondence is equally focused in general. People are respected for their input and dialogue, and compromise decisions usually follow. Unlike some of the extremes covered in the paternalistic and autocratic groups, there are usually no real extremes to note. Nothing usually stands out as exceptional. Difficult and challenging issues or unusually stressful situations are solved by compromise, though sometimes something bordering on consensus does emerge. The manager participates and influences the process towards the conclusions required and the employee is often an equal partner—a classic compromise. Consensus is rarely achieved and compromise will be the norm when decisions are complex.

The Compromiser participates to a reasonable extent and looks for above average and better than median and similar trade-offs. A modest amount of conflict is to be expected. The prospect of maximizing potential is not usually present. Modest energy is spent on solving problems. Human needs are attended to, as are the productivity requirements, but again not to a challenging degree. Employees are pushed, but again not too hard. Interestingly enough, these managers often see themselves as great mediators.

For the most part, the staff working for this style of manager are generally motivated and focused on the contribution that they make to the process. The balance between the social interaction and the need for clear business decisions is reasonable and the staff feels as if they have a role to play and a contribution to make. They are not usually under unusual stress (certainly less often under relationship stress than the subordinates of the autocrat).

102

The Uninterested, Abdicating, or *Laisser-faire* Manager. This style of manager is literally not interested and contributes little, stays out of the way and certainly does not make decisions. They often tend to be introverted or at a minimum unmotivated. They are often people who are in positions of responsibility when they do not want to be there. This could be someone who inherited the business, or more likely someone who was promoted above his or her level of competence. Sometimes they are people who excel in other areas but not in management and not in dealing with people in an organizational hierarchy. These people are often specialists who have a passion for their specialty but not for the people responsibility that sometimes comes with the process. They do not seek involvement—indeed they are happiest when not challenged and allowed to exploit their specialty. They contribute when pressed but would rather not be disturbed.

The staff working for this style of manager are often not motivated themselves since they get no stimulation from their leader. They can be somewhat lost, lacking in purpose and direction.

One could characterize this management style as abdication and withdrawal at its most practiced. Conflicts are inevitable since those who see their role as contributors to the organization are never able to make their contribution effectively. This in turn tends to preclude good relations between the boss and the subordinate. The boss has the view that problems are never solvable, and no one does things properly anyway, so why bother?

It is evident that a person in this position is not a leader, merely a titled figurehead.

The Paternalistic Manager. This manager is very much someone who cares too much for their people almost to the exclusion of what the business requires. They often focus disproportionately on the people aspects of the organization, particularly their own part. They tend to be sociable, chatty, and always concerned about your health and well-being (constantly feeling the need to take care of others). They often inquire about your family and friends and about the things that happen in your life. They often share similarly what is important in their life. Their interest and concern is well meant and is often genuinely motivated by empathy and sympathetic feelings. Sometimes, their interest is motivated by their own fear of involvement in having to make more difficult decisions. The game of golf, the football result, the well-being of your spouse, your family, and your life are all on the agenda. The work is almost secondary and you are left with the impression that it is almost less important to them. When necessary, the work-related decision is often dealt with incompletely since more of the concern focuses on the people needs than the business needs.

The staff working for this style of manager are either happily moving ahead with what they need to do (though often not with a clear priority and mandate), or they are frustrated by the lack of breadth and scope that their direction provides. The staff are often adequately motivated since the approach taken by their manager is not de-motivating. Things get done, often in a friendly way and often without the sense of priority and urgency that may be required. This type of manager tends to take full responsibility for all plans and results. In spite of all the chatter and talk, when it comes to necessary communication, workers are kept in the dark and viewed as a tool to help management do their job better. Workers often end up suspecting management feels they are not to be trusted, are lazy, and need continual monitoring.

This type of manager is often concerned with how things are perceived and the image that is portrayed. Style and comfort are key elements in the hierarchy of concerns for this manager. In the process of trying to please everyone, the resulting compromise outcomes often fail to please anyone. The view held by the manager is that by knowing people's many needs, and by being nice, you can influence the required progress. Pushing too hard would create conflict and would therefore be avoided.

At the start of this section I noted that over time the "upper tiers" of the Grid have become more refined and the "lower tiers" were less frequently apparent. As I practice my consulting profession I often come across toned-down versions of the Grid style extremes noted above.

Facilitative Management - points to consider

A few points to ponder on constructive management, whether you are a manager or an employee:

- In a facilitative organization, employees need mechanisms that allow them to solve personal problems that may impede the effectiveness of their day-to-day work. Many companies use a confidential wellness counselling process. This discreet service is free to employees and acts as a safety valve for both personal and organizational problems that the employee may have. A skilled counselling professional can also provide management with a barometer of issues that may be emerging within the work place.

- As people get promoted into management positions, they often lack the necessary skills that are acquired through experience. Newly promoted managers must be given basic supervisory training. Often people are promoted because they are good at their job and generally have better than average communication skills. This does not make them good managers. A new manager who fails to meet expectations will often require an organizational re-alignment to get them out of the management position. If this is poorly handled then the company can suffer two losses. One is the failed intended manager and the second, a returned and disenchanted employee. Unfortunately, failure in this mode may require the removal of the employee. While this is a last resort, removal can also send a very positive cultural message to the remaining employees. In the case of a re-assignment if well handled and openly communicated in a positive way by both the management and the affected employee, it can display a level of constructive organizational humility as well as a level of maturity in the employee. (However, a culturally effective organization does not usually get itself into this mess in the first place.)

- If an employee's perspectives match the culture of the organization many positives continue. If an employee and the culture are out of step, the positives are fewer and destructive negatives can emerge. By providing direction, incentives, and support to have them change their attitudes and expectations, management can keep the employee and the culture in step with each other.
- An employee's influence on the organization culture is proportional to his or her seniority—the more senior the more the cultural impact.
- Many individuals resist change since for many people change is not a comfortable place to be. However most people will respond positively if the change is part of a team-oriented decision-making process.
- People perform to the standards of their leaders.
- In the absence of a significantly traumatic experience, individuals tend to behave similarly to their prior performance to date.
- Mentor relationships (with appropriate senior management support) add to the refinement of management skills.

Discussion Climates

A Facilitative Manager is very aware of and sensitive to the environment in which a discussion is held.

The discussion can be a one-on-one or a meeting of a group (formal or informal). A Facilitative Manager will give thought to the room (be it an office or a meeting room), the layout, the positioning of chairs and table or desk, the lighting, the privacy (both visible and audible) and where they expect to sit when conducting the meeting.

In a group meeting you will no doubt see the shift of the "power position"—the place where the meeting leader chooses to sit. The old-fashioned power position was at the head of the table at the end, away from the door. The contemporary power position is usually in the middle of the table across the room on the opposite side of the door. Modern managers have made the shift away from the "holding court" set-up where the leader/boss looks down on the individuals participating. At the head of the table the leader/boss can keep an eye on everyone and everything, while the modern power position promotes a feeling of inclusiveness.

Color and lighting have an impact, although in most settings one has limited control over them. Putting this into a corporate context, the room choice often sends a signal. A meeting in the boss's office sends one signal (one where the boss has more control, influence and power). A meeting in the subordinate's office sends a different signal (one where the perception of the employee is one of reduced formality and perhaps a more open expectation). If the meeting room is the "corporate boardroom" then (depending on the type of meeting) that too sends a signal about formality. If the meeting is in, say a lunchroom, clearly there is a less formal intention.

Beyond the need for confidentiality, the door open or the door closed sends the clearest of signals. Furthermore, the more important the meeting, the less likely it is that phone interruptions will be acceptable. Courtesy demands that cell phones be set to silent for meetings of any level of formality.

The Facilitative Manager will have considered the topic, the focus of attention, and the concentration of issues and on the tone that will be set at the start of the meeting. If required, the rapport, the relaxing comments, the easing of prospective tension will be part of the introduction.

The discussion will range around a series of open-ended, non-directional questions. They will be designed to verify facts and by questioning, will explore the context. The Facilitative Manager does not jump to conclusions; she or he waits to accumulate all of the information necessary to further a decision. The use of silence is a key tool. It's amazing what silence can do when the other party thinks there must be some input or some more to say.

Silence is golden

Think of a situation where you have been in charge of a significant project, which so far has been going well until one of your most trusted lieutenants has apparently done something wrong and in the process upset several important people. You have had the feedback from the "important people" and now you need to decide what to fix and how.

You bring your lieutenant in for a closed-door meeting. You ask open-ended questions once you have both established that the lieutenant is here to discuss this particular issue. Open-ended questions should get all the facts on the table, based on the lieutenant's perspective. "Tell me what happened from the beginning." "Were there any events prior to this that could have contributed to the problem?" "Can you expand on your observations regarding what you just told me?" "How do you think X and Y may have received that?" "If you had the opportunity and with what you know now, would you have approached this issue the same way?" "Do you think that X or Y may have misunderstood what was intended?" "How might you have done this differently?" "Do you have any suggestions on how to fix the problem?"

Each of these questions is open-ended and non-directive. The individual can answer as much or as little as they choose. If they answer only a little, you can be reasonably certain that you are still not getting the whole story. If they answer fully (as you would expect from a trusted colleague) then you can be surer that you are closer to the facts.

The value of silence is clear in this situation. With each open-ended question the key is not to interrupt as the lieutenant answers, for each interruption pre-empts the fullness of the answer. This is where silence can be a powerful ally. Let the explanations flow and just sit quietly—

making notes if needed, but without saying anything. When you think that current part of the explanation is finished, continue to sit quietly. Keep the body language open and approachable—but keep quiet. Let the quiet roll on for as much as 20 to 30 seconds. Now, that doesn't sound like a long time but in the context of a conversation 20 to 30 seconds is a long time for silence. What it allows (and sometimes forces) is that the person being questioned will think of more to say. This added information will add valuable reinforcement if they are telling the truth and it will also have them digging holes for themselves with more statements if they are not telling the truth.

The Facilitative Manager knows how to use tone of voice, the level, the pitch, and the speed to deliver the message.

We've already seen the importance of body language. The position of the leader in the room speaks volumes. Across the desk says I'm in control here; on the same side of the desk as the participant says let's work this out together. At a small meeting table (or the power position at the side of a bigger table), positioning the body to be visible rather than shielding the lower body signals openness and a desire for a collaborative situation.

The "Commodity" Chronology
At one point in my career I was in the unfortunate position of having been manoeuvred into a senior management position working for an autocrat. This individual, who was already known to me, was the head of a sister company supply organization. I had had several bad experiences with him and in my experience, having been "short changed" by him on several critical supply situations; he was not always the most straightforward of operators.

At this stage of my career I was the Technical V.P. of a major food manufacturing facility, and was being promoted to become the Technical V.P. of a major commodity processing facility. This required a transfer to one of the newest factories, a state-of-the-art facility, strategically located to receive the several thousand tons a day of the incoming raw material and well positioned to serve its customer base.

My biggest challenge was the new President, "Don", my nemesis from the supply chain part of my previous job. In addition, one of the major problems with the organization was that it was a joint venture. Joint ventures themselves are rarely a problem. The challenge arises when a joint venture is a 50-50 partnership between two giant international companies—the perfect split for neither corporation to take ownership of the really difficult decisions. This in itself is not an insurmountable problem, but it does rely very heavily on the key figurehead to be a sincere, honest, and a straightforward diplomat. How I got here is another story.

Don was the president of this joint venture and was the typical autocratic, superficially pleasant, and apparently friendly manager—but when pushed, his true colors showed. His management style was "my way or the highway". I remember very clearly an incident in the first few weeks of my joining. We were in the monthly executive meeting, a very small group since the business was relatively simple in spite of its size. We had just reviewed the financial results that were to be presented to the joint venture shareholders the next day. We were about 60% through the year and the results were close to plan with some upside potential as we were just approaching the key time of year for the commodity crops. The remedial steps were reviewed and the action steps noted for follow up.

All seemed routine until the V.P. of Finance produced the second set of books. This set of numbers showed that in reality we were about 20% behind plan and that the remedial steps were far from deliverable. The meeting drew to a close fairly quickly with no clear conclusion or remedy. I went in to the V.P. of Finance's office and asked about the status and the prospects, and was promptly told that I should talk to Don since he called the shots. (Autocrats like Don know only one style—control. Even though my colleague was the Financial V.P. with full authority for how the financial things were—or should have been—handled it was the autocrat that called the shots, even in the detail of the V.P.'s work).

So, off I trot to see the President only to be told that I should mind my business and go and run the factory making sure it could meet the required demands. I was told that we were in the commodity business and that as soon as the new crops were harvested we would be back on track with the required results.

I have a sarcastic sense of humor, and couldn't resist a cutting comment. I asked why the Joint Venture had just spent millions and millions of dollars on this state-of-the-art processing plant when to run the business all we needed was to be tied into the continental commodity exchange.*

With a couple of live screen links and the telephone system we could run the total business from his office and we would have no need for a $55 million investment.

You can see that this was a conversation that was going to go nowhere and that it would only be a matter of time before one of us was terminated. The inevitable happened—I left (actually whisked away to corporate HQ) just before he was fired.

---

* The Chicago Board of Trade or The Chicago Mercantile Exchange is a trading board, much like a stock exchange, where dozens of traders take phone/data message instruction from commodity traders from all over the world and buy and sell commodities—most of which end up as product ingredients at the processing factories that make our food and other products. The sellers offer their goods—crops, animals, processed bulk materials—for sale and the buyers offer to purchase either now or for later. The brokers facilitate the deal for a small commission. The exchange allows for contracts to be bought and sold for future transactions. By doing this advance purchasing and selling skilfully one can make a lot of money—and lose a lot too.

Chapter 6. Management Styles and How to Cope

Leadership Qualities

In this technological age we love to survey and analyze just about everything. Survey data from many sources often give us insights into management issues and opportunities. The following are some examples of items from a variety of surveys and other sources. Treat them as nothing more than interesting snippets and see how they compare with your own opinion. How does your management style or that of the managers in your company compare with the qualities listed here?

- North American Leaders are promoted for abilities to "bring in the numbers", make tough decisions and create strategic plans – "Leadership forecast 2005 / 2006 Best Practices for Tomorrow's Global Leaders" by Paul R. Bernthal and Richard S. Wellins, Development Dimensions International (DDI). 2005.

- 35% of new leaders fail according to research from Development Dimensions International Inc. (DDI) because of poor people skills.

- Many leaders are often promoted first for their technical, marketing, or financial skills.

- How do leaders acquire their skills? By observing others, guidance from mentor or current manager, reading/research, advice from others/peers, trial and error, formal training.

- 35% of first level leaders consider returning to previous position—front line leadership has become (and continues to become) more stressful.

- Those leaders at top level have better work/life balance than those who are still in the middle.

- Overburdened new leaders work harder to prove themselves and justify their promotion to self and others.

- Middle leaders are often willing to give up more personal time to succeed.

- Leaders with good work/life balance will give up more personal time to climb the ladder.

- For a leader to succeed they need to maintain drive and passion for the new role as the leader—and they need to continue to learn and grow and not become complacent.
- Leaders who succeed bring out best in others, learn from others' mistakes and respond positively to feedback and accept change.
- Leadership indicators: passion for results, adaptability to change, receptive to feedback, a learning ability, motivated and driven, culture fit, thinks "out of the box" and is genuine.
- Leaders fail because: lack of experience, unable to get results, poor culture fit, lack of motivation, poor people skills/lack of regard for others, lacking strategy, and unrealistic expectation of job/role.
- Leaders must build trust: show to be working for everyone's best interest and not just their own, must be a team player and be fair, consistency in what they say/do, be confidential where applicable, give respect to others and share their thoughts/feelings (both positive and negative).
- Leaders must have highly developed interpersonal skills to be successful—meet the criteria of needing to belong, need for personal recognition and support.
- Find balance between tasks and people—power with people *vs.* power over people
- Leaders should have the ability to grow a replacement.
- Willingness to listen and ability to express what needs to be done, listen to empower people and be dedicated to respond to and implement ideas.
- Leaders should be pursuers of progress and developers of people. Set expectations levels/goals and willingness to model behaviour expected from others.
- Leaders must have the ability to deal with problem team members.

Work Group Perceptions (Workers *vs.* Managers *vs.* Unions)
The following is from an article by Oliver Tynan, *"Change and the nature of work: Some employment and organizational*

problems of advanced manufacturing technology"[20], which was published originally in the journal Robotica in 1985. His contention was that how workers interact with the work environment has progressed from the earlier times of modern management to the position as he then saw it. The view is pertinent and while a little dated (being 1985) it still resonates as evolutionary.

His observations and my contentions are as follows:

How workers are perceived has evolved from the time when union environments were stronger and in a more traditional role. Oliver Tynan put this together as a table – listing various attributes ascribed as "workers as objects" versus a more contemporary approach of "workers as agents".

In his "workers as objects" his characterizations include comments such as workers work – managers think, the worker is an extension of the machine, the worker is a dispensable spare part, that work needs to be broken down into single narrow skilled tasks, and jobs should be broken into simple single tasks.

In the corollary his characterization of "workers as agents" parallels are: everyone can think and add improvements, the machine complements the worker by extending their skills, the worker is a unique resource to be developed, tasks should be grouped to stimulate the worker by using their broader skills,

The "workers as agents" approach is still a relatively contemporary way of dealing with people and motivational issues. The "workers as objects" approach is, today, much more idiosyncratic. What the summary further illustrates is that in most cases the worst-case scenario has improved significantly. It is rare to have to deal with the issues as described in his "objects" summary, while the "agents" summary is still contemporary and, if anything, has progressed further.

He postulated the same approach for both managers and for unions.

114

With managers the focus has shifted to managers earning respect through competence and experience, flat organization structure, participative management, work community goals are important, communicative approaches are key as opposed to the autocratic money-driven "my way or the highway" approach of old.

For unions he also is postulating cooperation, collaboration, commitment, and effectiveness, as opposed to the hard-nosed defensive stand that would be more traditional.

The bottom line is that workers, managers, and unions tend now to be more a part of the culture of inclusion rather than exclusion. This is key to a successful Corporate Culture.

In the twenty-first century unions that see the survival and collaboration imperative are the ones that are still able to attract members and make a contribution. Those that do not "see the light" risk oblivion.

Management and the Generation Gap

Two aspects are worthy of consideration with reference to "the generation gap" and "cross generation needs and expectations". One is that each generation is different and that difference is created by circumstances that were prevalent at the time of their upbringing. The other is that each generation has similar needs and expectations.

Generational Differences

Dr. Lawrence Smith, Dean for Medical Education at the Mount Sinai School of Medicine in New York was trying to clarify how and why older patients were reacting sceptically to younger doctors, often expressing concern that these young doctors cannot have had enough experience to treat them (the elderly) as patients. His summary table of generational groups is pertinent to the examination of why there is something of a generation gap between groups of people when viewed in generational clusters.

I included the Generational Profiles in Chapter 2, and repeat it below to complement the section on Generational Similarities.

Generational Profiles (based on US population numbers)[21]

Characteristic	Veterans	Baby Boomers	Generation X	Millennials
Birth years	1922 - 1945	1946 - 1964	1965 - 1980	1981 - 2000
Population	55 million	78 million	47 million	80 million
Style	Traditional	Personal satisfaction	Self-reliant	Modern traditional
Ethic	Respect, loyalty	Ambitious, political	Progressive, cynical	Loyal, conservative
Gender roles	Classic	Mixing roles	Unclear	Gone
Work	Respect the system, work for security	Respect experience, like to work	Respect expertise, work to live	Work to live
Heroes	Strong heroes	Some heroes	No heroes	Anti-heroes
Seminal event	Depression, WWII	Vietnam, birth control pill	A weak USA	9/11
Upbringing	Traditional family	Traditional family	Absentee parents	Protective parents
Rewards	Job well done	Money, title, recognition	Freedom and time	Work

I did not create the table, but offer a brief observation on its contents.

- I do not have data to confirm the population statistics.
- Ethic seems about right to me.
- Gender roles: I am not sure that there is a distinction between "Mixing, Unclear, and Gone" since each is a small evolution from the other and all three are clearly different from "Traditional".
- Work: I think I can see that.
- Seminal event: yes.
- Upbringing: yes, very much.
- Rewards: again yes, but not sure of the Millennials.

The counter to the table of differences noted above is the similarities amongst various generations. It is not that these groups are similar, for indeed they are not. What is similar is what each of us wants and expects from our work environment (and from many other things in our lives).

Generational Similarities

It is interesting to observe the similarities among the generations since it could be argued that these are very human wants and needs, regardless of age or gender.

Jennifer Deal of the Center for Creative Leadership, who spent seven years researching more than 3000 leaders, prefers to highlight the similarities, rather than the differences, among various generations. She suggests that leaders can use the similarities among generations to help "retire the generation gap" that can lead to conflicts in the workplace. The table below is adapted from her findings.

Generational Similarities[22]

Issue	Commentary
All generations have similar values	Family is cited most often by all generations. Other values include: integrity, achievement, love, competence, happiness, self-respect, wisdom, balance, and responsibility
Everyone wants respect	Older generations ask that you give their opinions the weight they believe they deserve. The younger generation tend to say "listen to me—pay attention to what I say".
Leaders must be trustworthy	All individuals want to work with people they trust. They trust these people more than their organization and the organization more than upper management. All generations expect leaders to be trustworthy.
People want leaders who are credible and trustworthy	They want their managers to listen and be farsighted and encouraging.
Internal politics is a problem at any age	All generations are concerned about organizational politics, being recognized for what they do, getting the resources they need—yet they also recognize political skills are needed to move up.
No one really likes change	Resistance to change has nothing to do with age—it is all about how much you have to gain or lose as a result of the change.
Loyalty depends on the context	People of all generations don't think that being loyal is good for their careers. However, people close to retirement tend to stay with the same organization. Time spent on the job is more to do with position than age.
Everyone wants to learn	People at all generation levels want to gain skills to move up and on. They want to develop leadership skills, their expertise skills, problem-solving skills, team building skills, and communication skills.

My observations on these findings:

- Generations do indeed have similar values (regarding those things that affect them directly).
- Respect is another facet that is important to all people. The generations may (and do) have different ways of expressing their need for respect.
- Trustworthy leadership is absolutely a given. We have already noted that trust is one of the two key cores of the whole Corporate Culture process, along with candor.
- Politics within organizations: I come across that all the time and I do not know of anyone who sees politics favorably—though most people agree that it exists due to

communication disconnects and leadership differences. As a result, politics is viewed as a necessary evil.

- Change is another facet that is typically constant with most people regardless of generation. Change is always something that people regard with some trepidation. The greater the expected change, the greater the discomfort.
- Loyalty is another factor that is expected by all generations though, while it used to be loyalty for the company and for one's own security, it now tends to be more internalized and focuses on career and self-development.
- I also agree with the learning observation though would add that it has not always been like that. I credit the change to the "information society" where you are encouraged/forced to learn or risk getting left behind (and no one wants to be a loser).

The Holistic Work Approach
The simple definition of something holistic is a system where the whole is greater than the sum of its parts. This thought can be applied (and often is) to management styles and approaches. Like many management approaches there is no hard and fast definition of how a holistic management style or approach should work, so the following is a summary of many of the elements that collectively could be described as holistic. Anyone who practices (or continuously tries to practice) the following would be considered a holistic manager.

- You understand the term "lifelong learning" – you actively seek out learning opportunities, you are open minded to new ideas, you welcome different perspectives and think critically.
- You take action from your learning to make a difference and you implement this into your life's work.
- In order to support the development of what you have to offer, your basic skills and knowledge must be complimented with understanding, values, beliefs, and creativity.

119

- With the pressures in today's society, people are pulled into so many different directions (especially if raising a young family). How do you translate lifelong learning into your world? You have to think carefully about the learning that you have just acquired and make a conscious effort to integrate it into your daily routines.

- Today's pressures often force free time to be about recuperation and entertainment—and not for learning.

- To encompass holistic learning and adoption you have find your passion and purpose by becoming more aware of your wants, needs, strengths, interests, goals, and experiences. Become motivated to work towards goals and achievements.

- You can begin to change infrastructures and beliefs when you can apply what you have learned.

- In western management you can generalize by saying intuition is ignored while rationality, reason, and science are embraced. Yet emotions are prominent when making decisions of a crucial nature. There is nothing wrong with using emotions as part of the decision making process (we are not talking about tear-jerking—we are talking about gut feel and intuition).

- The disconnect between family and work can leave a person feeling as though their soul is being torn apart— how do I cope with that?

- You must accept who you are and what your passions and emotions are in order to live a balanced lifestyle. Act intelligently and with compassion, live life with purpose. (Don't underestimate this expression, which many people throw about but rarely live up to.) Living life with a purpose is challenging and does not always make you the most popular person on the block.

- To uncover your full potential and engage the mind, find workable lasting methods to deal with those societal challenges that affect you (*i.e.* crime, poverty, abuse, narrow mindedness, racism, etc.). In other words make your contribution in the best and most positive way that you can.

- Help others believe in themselves and set expectations for life goals—become lifelong learners. Give purpose and motivation to propel others to face challenges and grow.

- Learners need to establish pride in themselves for events that have led them to what they have accomplished to date and to begin to use those to find key motivators. Identifying your own skills and knowledge with pride from previous experiences helps form a foundation of energy and perspective.

- Increase your own confidence level (and that of those around you). Accomplishments give energy to take on new challenges and allow you to feel equipped to handle them.

- Pride helps you to carry yourself forward.

- Passion for what you do consists of values, beliefs, and interests. Many people, if asked, could not tell you what they are passionate about but it becomes apparent when the conversation turns to something that touches that person. Tap into your own passion and use it to your advantage.

- Recurring pattern of values, beliefs, and pride occur when you examine your accomplishments and pride experiences—these are all small elements that continue to reinforce and build on your experiences.

- Your passion demonstrates what sustains you and makes you continue what you are doing or work on what appears to be wrong. Work and learning goals are nourished by passion for what you do. It is reflected in your work, which results in overall quality of your life and your family's life.

- You often hear others refer to work and life as too stressful, lacking meaning, or that work can interfere with family and personal life. How do you cope with that?

- The answer is to find purpose. Set small goals as a starting point for finding purpose—smaller goals are less intimidating while working through the learning experience.

- Add to that performance. Skills and strategy support effective action—get things done now and in the future (immediate movement).
- Learning becomes second nature when passion and performance are linked to learning.
- You get better at what you do when you see results in your own individual performance. Self-confidence increases, which leads to more pride experiences.
- You need to continuously obtain new tools, techniques, and motivations to perform well.
- As you walk this path you will realize that lifelong learning encompasses all parts of your life—family, work, community, and self-needs. Those who possess these beliefs can help others attain this as well.
- Work should connect you to learning, growth, and contribution.
- Success is not measured by job status or income but by how eager you are to learn and help others (the material aspects of success tend to come automatically from your approach to life and not from the obvious status symbols that money allows).
- Accomplishments occur because of what you learn, how you contribute back to society, and how you contribute to develop the next generation.
- One of the keys is to recognize learning, build on it, support it, and act on it. Create an environment of self-awareness and a holistic view of work and life in relation to lifelong learning and positive change.
- There is a level of healing and cooperation among your intellect, mind, heart, and sources of wisdom.
- The body comes into level of balance when intellect is in line with the heart and other organs. This results in healing, wholeness, and improved decision making ability, and overall, reduces stress.

- Each individual has unique talents and gifts that fit together similar to a puzzle. You as a person can only begin to accept and understand this when you have actually experienced the learning—not just as something that happens to the mind and intellect, but also to the body and consciousness as an increase of awareness of processes over time.

- Lifelong learning and energy is a result of those who are oriented towards personal growth—as a result stress decreases.

I am reminded of the following as a part of how my life has evolved.

When I arrived in England originally, I was a little German kid who was literally dumped into the English school system in the years immediately after the Second World War. I had virtually no English language skills and remember very little of the experience except that it was traumatic.

As those early years drifted by and into oblivion (oblivion in my mind at least), I remember my stepfather often telling me "my schooldays would be the happiest days of my life". WRONG. His logic was not unreasonable from his perspective. His logic was based upon the fact that he had had his University studies not just interrupted by the war, but totally destroyed by the war. After all he was now in the post-war era with a family to support. He had to go earn a living and could not go back to finish off his University learning. He was very successful at what he did for a living—but he really intensely disliked what he did. It was that dislike that drove his logic about school days being the happiest days of my life.

I was probably still in my early teen years when I had firmly decided that I would do something for a living that I enjoyed (thanks step-Dad – you unwittingly provided me with an excellent learning model). That learning of mine was not something that I shared with my step-Dad (he was not one to listen to juniors' opinions). As a matter of fact I did not know what I wanted to do for a living or a career until I was close to graduating— and even then it was not crystal clear to me. As an Engineering graduate I stumbled into my first post university job as an Industrial Engineer. I soon got identified by what I realized later was my very first mentor. He was a not so young (at least from my perspective) American gentleman who was the General Manager of the company where I was working. This was a large American company (and this unit was based in England) with well over one thousand employees (part of an international Corporation). He initially arranged for me to be a key resource person coordinating some international assignments.

Within a short space of time I was promoted into a position that for my age and experience was totally over my head. I became the Maintenance Manager of this facility with almost two hundred employees under my direction—most of them unionized. I survived that job very successfully. While the General Manager promoted me into that position, my new boss—the company Chief Engineer who reported to the General Manager—was not happy to have me as a subordinate (but that's another story). My good fortune and my really terrific learning arose from the fact that I had reporting to me three Foremen who were in charge of the almost two hundred of my new employee group. Each of these three was old enough to be my father. Each of these three had a genuine liking for me. (I had worked with them as one of the Industrial Engineers on site—so they knew me well.)

It was at their collective suggestion that we formed a pact. It was very simple—they would manage and guide the detail under my care and have me approve what needed to be done, and I would be attentive to the needs of the departments and the unions and act as their spokesperson and the approvals figurehead. In other words they would do the practical things and I would handle the politics. It was my good fortune that they were sincere and totally honest and that I could live up to my role very successfully. The four of us accomplished a lot of good things, including the creation and implementation of the first fully integrated preventive maintenance system throughout the Corporation.

While I stayed in this role for a few years, I was head hunted and made an offer "I couldn't refuse". It was decades later before I realized that that was the start of my learning in the field of holistic management.

We saw in Chapter 4 that Peter Drucker was the first to fully identify and articulate the notion that work was moving / has moved from the "industrial age" into the "information age". The result is that workers are much more powerful, independent, and autonomous than they have ever been in past history. Back in the 19th century there was no "knowledge work" since the information age had not yet materialized. At that time virtually no one had a higher education for business reasons (some of the elite and the autocracy had "education" but this was more as an ornament than a requirement for their survival).

Drucker contended that the biggest shift of the late 20th century is the shift to the knowledge society. What follows is a paraphrased summary of his article called "The Next Workplace Revolution".[23]

All developed countries are becoming (have become) post business, knowledge societies. In the 18th century work was what you inherited from your father—if you worked the fields it's because your father worked the fields; if you worked as a blacksmith it's because your father worked as a blacksmith; a wheelwright because that's what dad did; a baker because, etc. Equally, the aristocracy inherited their wealth from the previous generation and passed it on to the next.

Then in the 19th century, the first signs of alternate labor opportunity started to emerge. This was the start of the industrial age. At this time, work was available and delivered with the muscle of the man and the sweat on the brow or the diligence of the woman at a weaving machine, often delivered 12, 14, and 16 hours per day, six days per week. This phenomenon really started to expand and mushroom in the 20th century. It expanded for two key reasons—one was that serfdom had expanded into the beginnings of the "business society" where work now came from factories and thus started to create worker mobility (at a microscopic level). The second reason was the First World War where the men fought, and many gave up their lives, and the women started to work in the factories (instead of the men). After the war the relative "new found freedoms" that the working society had discovered by being able to earn a wage without sacrificing their entire waking lives turned the tide in favor of the beginnings of the knowledge worker. It was here that an education started to give the possessor the opportunity to do something more meaningful than toil in the factory.

Knowledge workers expanded as the education system expanded. Drucker comments that at the start of the 20th century there were fewer than 10,000 college teachers in the US, and that this grew to over 500,000 by the mid part of the 21st century. Knowledge workers expanded at a similar rate. Suddenly there was a need for accountants, managers, and a variety of business functions that developed into professional skill sets required by the expanding business interests. It was this evolution of business that led the worker slowly but surely out of the grinding poverty that had been the lot of the poor and the "lower class".

It was this expansion that has evolved into the mobility and continuing autonomy of today's knowledge workers. It is the evolution of the factory labor system that has created the unquenchable appetite that business has for more and more specialized skills at ever increasing rates. For it is these skills that produce the business wealth that accumulates to the benefit of the individuals who bring the skills.

It is the production of this wealth that leads to today's relative affluence. For not only is the economic growth expanding at a tremendous rate, but so is personal wealth. This translates into other benefits such as shorter workweeks to accumulate the same degree of affluence. In the late 19th and early 20th century the workweek consisted of as many as 3,500 to 4,000 hours per year for the individual worker. Today's average is in the range of 1,800 per year in the developed world with places such as Germany and some Scandinavian countries as low as 1,500 hours per year. And all this with still more wealth being generated.

What makes knowledge workers the new plutocrats is that their knowledge is vast yet deep (in their own speciality). In the 19th century, the worker had to retire after 30 years (if they lived that long) because they were physically worn out. Today after 30 years the knowledge worker is fresh, current, and up to date, and ready for his or her next career (even if that is now in a smaller business or in volunteer work that utilises their skills and experience).

What makes the knowledge workers the winners in this long race? It is the fact that they have choices. They are no longer tied to the business unit since the knowledge skill they have is totally mobile. It is immaterial to the computer specialist if she serves her trade in a hospital, a university, a government agency, an accounting office, or a larger food conglomerate. What matters to the knowledge workers is the opportunity to be satisfied with how they can pursue their ambitions (money, status, recognition, satisfaction, etc.). They want to know, "Is what I am doing leading edge for me, is it on the best equipment, is it in the best environment?"

A knowledge worker who takes his craft seriously is the new wealth generator. The challenge that business has is how to motivate and retain these new plutocrats. For much of their motivation comes from their own success in their chosen field.

The business leaders' challenge is how to capitalize on these individuals' goals and aspirations and yet still retain them and focus them for the greater good of the company.

Drucker wisely argues that this has to be done by offering clarity of purpose (what is the win/win for the individual and the company?) and giving the individuals the freedom to make a meaningful contribution within the needs of the business. This opportunity comes from having the individuals leading semi-autonomous work groups across several different projects. In this way—through matrix management—the individual practices her or his special skills in an environment where they are a (or the) key player responsible for the delivery of the overall success of the assignment. The follow up challenge then becomes how do you manage this structure. It is like a hospital organization there are the doctors and specialists (the task leaders) and the hospital administration structure (the management group) where neither is in charge yet both must be (within their fields).

Drucker makes the point that this is a problem. He also argues that the equally important problem is how do you train senior people to become the top managers of tomorrow? How is this training accomplished? The analogy is relatively simple – the leaders who emerge from these group processes will progressively become the more senior leaders of the larger units as time and experience builds their skills. It is somewhat like having the leaders of the baseball farm team progressively moving into the similar role in the major league team.

The real challenge continuing into the future will be the ongoing shift into the information-based business, for if you consider where we are going, the next decades will continue to belong to the information businesses and not to the functional conglomerates. He who will control information will control outcomes.

Management best practices

Get Leaders involved: get their buy-in in order to better motivate staff. Share materials beforehand to better prepare leaders for questions or concerns with which they may be confronted.

Make sure it's a product or idea that leaders believe in. They won't/can't sell something they don't believe in. Allow time for discussion and answer period in case some leaders are disapproving or shell-shocked.

Engagement is critical. Factors that contribute to engagement—competitive compensation and benefit packages, reward and recognition programs, working environment, performance management systems. Most important is the behavior and attitudes of leaders.

Behaviors' and attitudes that need to be displayed: openness and honesty, accessibility of leader/manager, communicating business goals/initiatives, passion for performance, build excitement for business/goals, meet business challenges head on, show respect for others, respond to employee concerns/questions, show appreciation of work done at all levels.

Chapter 7. Decision Making

There are a number of ways to define decision making such as:

- The process of selecting from several choices, products, or ideas and taking action.
- A position or opinion or judgment reached after consideration.
- Choosing between alternative courses of action using cognitive processes such as memory, thinking, and evaluation.
- The cognitive process of reaching a decision.

No matter how you phrase it, life is filled with decisions. Some are minor and others can be life altering. There are good decisions and there are bad decisions, and then there are those that never get made or get made too late.

I can think of a decision I made shortly after a significant promotion to the head of engineering and facilities in one of the larger research labs of an international food conglomerate. When I arrived, I was immediately bombarded with many complaints about the poor reliability of the site steam supply systems. It frequently broke down and often delayed and even destroyed many of the science experiments and the production experiments.

After a short investigation, the solution was obvious to me. My predecessor was budget conscious and had contracted to run the steam boilers on (cheaper) heavy grade fuel oil. The types of burner systems the boilers used were not designed for this heavy grade oil and would frequently clog and shut down. Within 24 hours I had the systems cleaned and changed to a light grade of oil (closer to a domestic grade) and the problem just disappeared. Within the first week I had made my mark and was the site hero.

Great decisions happen at the right time with the right circumstances. Some might say that luck plays a part in their personal decision-making or that other decisions are simply mandatory, not leaving them a choice at all. For example, having to sell your house because you can't afford to live there any more could be considered mandatory, but buying a car and choosing what color to purchase wouldn't be.

When in the position of having to make decisions, big or small, there are a number of things to keep in mind that can assist with decision-making. It's important to put ourselves first and be conscious of those around us and how they may also be affected by the decision. Don't compromise your own/family values, beliefs, or expectations. There should be a work/life balance that you and your family should benefit from in the short and long term in regards to the choices you make.

Don't let others run your life and don't give others the control to do so. It's essential to make our own decisions based on the information and knowledge we are provided with. If we allow others to sway us or make those critical decisions for us, we aren't in control and may end up uncomfortable with the outcomes, especially if things don't work out. We are fortunate enough to live in a country where we have the freedom to make our own choices, but we also need to be prepared to accept the consequences of those decisions. To make effective decisions, we need to be confident in ourselves as well as our abilities. Should the outcome not be what we anticipated, we can learn from those errors and consider what we could have done differently next time. Ultimately, others will respect you for it.

When implementing a decision, it's important to take steps one at a time and expect the unexpected. However, once a decision is made, evaluate how things are progressing and clear up any uncertainties that are not conducive to the desired end results. One almost always has the ability to change a decision that is not working effectively.

Decision Making Styles
There are many different decision-making styles and at one time or another, we have all crossed paths, personally and professionally, with individuals who utilize any one of these approaches. Here are a few of the decision-making styles, followed by a description of each type of decision-maker.

Agonizing
This person agonizes over a decision and spends a lot of time over-thinking the options and possible outcomes. This is necessarily a bad trait, especially if the decision is one that is of great importance such as choosing a career path, dealing with financial situations, or handling family or relationship problems. If a decision ultimately impacts the individual or those around them to the extent where it will have long term or lasting effects, it's logical to take all precautions necessary and progress through the decision making process with care. On the other hand, if the decision is not one of huge importance, don't waste a lot of time dwelling on the options such as deciding on what social activities to partake in or what restaurant to eat at.

Avoidant
Avoiding making a decision doesn't make it go away—it only prolongs the inevitable. People who find themselves in a difficult or uncomfortable situation may avoid making that decision for as long as possible but eventually it has to be dealt with. The longer it takes to make that decision, the more it may cause others to be affected by the outcome. Therefore, gather all the facts and information in order to determine the best possible decision. Those who feel they fall under this category may want to seek advice from others or use a group decision-making methodology to assist in the process.

Autocratic
One person or a leader/manager makes autocratic decisions. This individual does not seek out the opinions or input of others and takes complete responsibility for the outcomes whether good or bad. Being an autocratic decision maker can have its advantages, such as being able to make decisions quickly using one's own
132

internal perception of the situation. This can also create challenges by making others feel as though their opinions and ideas don't matter. In a work setting, this can decrease morale and commitment.

Collaborative

A decision that is made collaboratively involves the input, opinions, experiences, and abilities of others in a group setting. Most people involved in this method of decision-making are accepting of their responsibility for their role in the decision and understand the ramifications of the end result. Collaborative decision-makers enjoy sharing information that is pertinent to the decision.

Compliant

Compliance is allowing someone else to make a decision for you rather than taking responsibility and ownership for that decision on your own. At times, it may be beneficial to be a compliant decision-maker when you aren't necessarily confident in your ability to make the right choice based on the information you have been provided. On the other hand, when it comes to life-changing decisions, such as deciding which job you should take or what city you should live in, the last thing you want to do is leave these choices to others around you. You may wish to consult with family and friends, but who wins in the long run if someone else is always making the decisions? You or them?

Consensus

Decision making that is completely left to a group of individuals rather than the leader is considered to be a consensus. Complete buy-in and commitment must be obtained and the whole group must be in agreement and take full responsibility as a team for the outcome. This type of decision making can help build relationships among team members or groups and provide a sense of security in knowing everyone has involvement in the decision making process. Although it can be a productive method, it can also be slow and time consuming, and it may be difficult to get everyone in agreement.

Consultative

With consultative decision-making, others typically share the process and often the decision is not adaptable to change once made. Often the decisions are of a sensitive nature and those involved in the process need to have full understanding of the issues or concerns. Someone of authority and knowledge of the topic makes the overall decision. A lot of research is recommended in order to make a final decision.

Democratic

Democratic decision-making is left to the group to decide upon the issue with a majority vote rather than the leader stepping in to dictate the outcome. This approach can be fairly quick and involves a certain amount of participation from others involved. However, the team may lack a feeling of responsibility for the decision when things don't go well and may even claim it wasn't what they voted for.

Directive

Directive decisions are made by those of authority and are not typically open for discussion or debate. This type of decision-making is ideal for policy and procedure implementation, staffing decisions, handling confidential issues and other concerns of a sensitive nature. It gives tight control to those involved in the decision making process where others who may have knowledge of the situation or expertise in the area are not asked for their input or feedback.

Flexible

Decision-making that is flexible can also be referred to as "going with the flow". It works best in a situation where there is little to no risk regardless of the outcome, and where there is little concern about the advantages or disadvantages of choosing a particular option. One disadvantage of this approach is that is someone may choose to go with the flow and follow others when it isn't the wisest choice, and they could suffer for their choice either personally or professionally.

Impulsive

Impulsive decision makers spend little to no time thinking about the possible options before deciding on one and simply respond to the circumstances that surround them. This is ideal when dealing with emergencies such as rescuing someone from a burning building. There is no time to consider other options; therefore it's best to react impulsively. Acting impulsively can be a positive approach to decision making, especially in a social setting where someone may find himself or herself reacting in a spontaneous manner, such as getting on a plane and flying off to Vegas for the weekend (although, of course that could be proven a bad decision too). Impulsive decision-making is not normally appropriate in a business setting—unless your building is on fire.

Logical

Decisions made by someone who is logical are choices that are defendable—all data and resources have been exhausted prior to that decision being made. Logical decision makers will ask themselves questions such as "Have we considered all options?" or "Do we have enough information to make a sound judgment call?" Decisions are made on specifics without guessing at what the outcomes may be. There is a clear understanding of the reason behind the choices made. The best decision is made based on the available options.

Participative

Participative usually involves a leader as well as team members where all are encouraged to provide their perspectives and discuss openly the various options based on the knowledge and expertise of those involved. The leader maintains complete control of the final decision and is solely responsible for the outcome of the results. Group participation is valuable, resulting in personal commitment and involvement. It can be a fairly slow process when a large number of people are involved, but decisions are legitimately made by the team's efforts.

Proactive

Proactive decision makers like to have lots of information made available to them before making a final decision. These types of individuals are not so much restrained by data as they are focused on exploring the possibilities prior to there being an issue or a need to implement new ideas. They create images and express themselves artfully and often consider global options before coming to any conclusions. Therefore, they will see a potential problem before anyone else and begin formulating a list of options prior to its becoming a larger concern regardless of the situation.

Procrastinator

As we all know (sometimes too well), the procrastinator will put off making a decision for as long as humanly possible. While there are similarities with the Avoidant style, Procrastinators don't usually agonize—they just put off the decisions. People may resort to the Procrastination style when the decisions can be challenging or even life altering, or when concerned with the overall outcome and how it will affect not only themselves but also those around them. This is not an effective decision making style when urgent decisions need to be made. Prolonging the decision doesn't make it go away—it simply makes it more agonizing in the long run.

Personal Decision Making *vs.* Group Decision Making

The following table compares what happens in individual decision making *vs.* what can happen in group decision making.

Personal Decision Making	Group Decision Making
Determine all factors and information gathered to evaluate options. *(Gather the facts.)*	Create problems through insensitivity of others. *(Agree on the problem and the facts.)*
Build confidence and learn from previous decisions. *(Previous experience is a great guide.)*	Serve own interests by leading group. *(Who is driving the bus?)*
Options compatible with own values, beliefs, and expectations. *(Confirm the basis of making the decision.)*	Lack of response by members of group. *(Engage them if you need them - or move them out.)*
Decision made based on emotion, other influences, or left up to fate. *(Be clear on your reason for the decision.)*	Authority rule by voting. *(This is a cop out —see next box.)*
Plan decisions when important or complicated; have deliberate approach to choose from. Takes time and energy. *(Develop the detail so it can be executed.)*	Decision by consensus—no better way. *(Requires detail discussion and buy-in to get a final consensus.)*
Support from family, friends, coworkers. *(What help is required to make it happen?)*	Brainstorming. *(Use this if consensus is elusive.)*
Number of desirable options. *(Evaluate, select, and move forward.)*	Nominal group technique—rank order a set of options. *(If you are here then you still have not got consensus. Re-cycle the process.)*

If we look at decision making in general, certain characteristics do appear (not always in all cases, and such generalizations can be misleading)—BUT: In group decision making, women are more likely to be altruistic and tend to be concerned with wellbeing of others while men in groups tend to be motivated by self-interest and prefer competitive solutions. Women also want everyone involved to benefit, therefore having a significant impact on decision-making and the process of reaching that decision.

Steps in Decision Making
1. Identify the problem. Figure out what the issues or concerns are that need to be dealt with.

2. Clarify the problem. Ensure all of those involved understand the issue and have the same or similar views.

3. Determine the cause. Dissect the issue and come to a consensus as to what the root of the concern is.

4. Find alternate solutions. Whether making a decision as a group or an individual, come up with options to correct the situation.

5. Select alternatives. Determine the advantages and disadvantages of each option and what the possible outcomes may be.

6. Implementation. Look at the details of the problem and each solution as suggested and assign responsibilities and duties to others when group decision making is required.

7. Clarify the direction. In a group decision-making effort, ensure all those involved understand the solutions and the desired outcomes.

8. Create an action plan. Keep records of the events that unfold and how all is progressing in order to accomplish the overall decision making goal.

9. Provide accountability. Look at duties and responsibilities of each person involved in the decision making progress.

10. Set into play and evaluate progress. Ensure follow up with any items or individuals that are involved in the final outcome of the decision.

Decision-making is as complicated or as simple as we deem it to be. We can't always be 100% certain that the choices we make will be the best option, but putting off making that decision due to uncertainty is not the best choice. Not making any decision could ultimately be the wrong decision.

Women and Decision Making
This may be the biggest can of worms we can open in a book on Corporate Culture. If you look at the global picture, women having been making life critical decisions for hundreds of years— long before recorded history. From ancient times we have

extensive documentation about great women leaders. Yet in today's society the equality question and the balance of power question never dies. As the author, I see nothing wrong with that and certainly nothing to get overly wound up about. I take it as a fact of life.

Again, we may be criticized for some gross generalizations, but while this snippet is not directly about Corporate Culture, the roles of males and females are different within a Corporate Culture. The fact that they are different is a strong positive and the culture forms around those differences, most noticeably when the corporate head is female versus male. The tone of the culture shifts. That is neither good nor bad—it just is and needs to be accepted as such.

Even in this day and age, many cultures only permit men to make certain types of decisions, and even though in North America and most of Europe (as well as many more developed countries), women can now make their own decisions, there are still many countries out there where women have little or no say. Yet even here there are many exceptions: Indira Gandhi (India), Pratibha Patil (India), Janet Jagan (Guyana), Corazon Aquino (Philippines), Joyce Banda (Malawi) to name a few (though there are still many countries that are not even on the map when it comes to women in leadership roles).

Although the Canadian government continues to work diligently with many associations and organizations to level the playing field between men and women (or at least tries to have us believe that), countries like India and Guyana, although improving, still struggle to allow women to make decisions.

In South Asia, women are becoming role models for the younger generation by speaking out and making choices for themselves and their families whether it be personal, economic, or political. Yet some still believe that women who are in a position to make decisions are classified as "proxy women" meaning they are still controlled and manipulated by men in their family and still have no real voice.

139

The least developed countries still lack training and support for women to implement changes that would increase their ability to freely make decisions and be heard in a predominantly male-dominated decision making hierarchy. (We just need to look at some of the repressive regimes that insist on denying women's education.) In Guyana, for example, women are more likely to make decisions in the private sector versus men who make decisions for both the private and public sectors.

Even today in North America, relatively few women hold high-level decision making positions in spite of apparent relative equality. Those who have made it to the top are well noticed and get added press due to their role. It is to be hoped that as time progresses and government agencies intervene, the status of women making decisions across the world will improve to ensure full, equal, and effective participation at all levels, be it personally or politically. Everyone can benefit from the diverse experience, talents, and capabilities of those around us, regardless of gender.

Left Brain vs. Right Brain
Within the sphere of decision making, the physiological make-up of the human brain is worth bearing in mind since each of us is exactly that—we are the product of our genetics and our environment, and how our mind works is THE critical and essential factor in our small part of the makeup of a Corporate Culture.

Very early work in this area can be traced back as far as the middle of the 19th Century. More developments were noted in the 20th century, but the much more detailed research and investigation that led to a more detailed understanding of Left Brain vs. Right Brain phenomena was not well documented until the middle of this last century.

It has long been a common misconception that this phenomenon means simply that the two different sides of any person's brain are responsible for different manners of thinking. That is not strictly true. What is clear is that each side of the brain does have different approaches to the situations that arise in a person's everyday life but it is the blend of the two that deliver the person's final reaction and next step to the outcome of that situation.

Most people have a somewhat distinct preference for one style of thinking over the other and they do process information differently. It is, however, extremely rare that anyone has a distinct one-sided dominance. Over the centuries there has been much research on this topic, and the best current thinking suggests that while there are two distinct hemispheres in the brain (indeed a very clear cut left brain and an equally clear right brain). However, the two halves both work in parallel to provide a person with the reactions and next steps to what they choose to do regarding the circumstances that they have been presented.

The old adages of right handed people are left brain dominant and left handed are right brain dominant in also not true—though a large proportion of motor skills preferences can relate back to brain dominance.

In general there is a strong bilateral symmetry in both the structure and the function of the brain and the simplicity of "logical for the left" and "creative for the right" is exactly that—an over simplification. While research continues, there is little evidence to support the "modularity" or specialization of the two brain hemispheres. There is clear evidence that suggests that if one side of the brain becomes damaged and is significantly reduced in function – the other side will pick many of the required skills that may have been observed to be modular.

There is however no doubt that these left and right brain differences can affect communication.

After having opened the thoughts from the above that there is no clear dominance of one over the other – it is clear that some generalizations can be made that do have an impact on how people behave and communicate. At the risk of over simplifying (or perhaps, more correctly, "over compartmentalizing"), we can assume:

Left Brain tends to be:	Right Brain tends to be:
Logical	Random
Sequential	Intuitive
Objective	Subjective
Rational	Holistic
Analytical	Synthesizing
List makers	Visual
Analysts	Conceptual
Detailed	Imaginative
Methodical	Sensual
Likes rules, facts and certainty	Dislikes rules, facts but creates own reality
Detail oriented	Big picture oriented
Present and past	Present and future
Math and science	Philosophy and religion
Safe	Risk taker

So, as we have discussed above, people are not exclusively one or the other but usually a mixture of the two with one being the more predominant. Scan the list for yourself and determine which is the more dominant in your thinking process. Successful cultures have many shades of both in their hierarchy and even have healthy mixtures of both in the various functional areas. You can imagine that marketing and sales people would likely gravitate more to the right brain headings whereas the manufacturing, engineering and technical types would have more left brain characteristics.

In determining how people fit within a particular Corporate Culture, these characteristics are important but more so in the functional sense (do the characteristics suit the management style and is the blend providing synergy and harmony?). The real value in the determination of the Corporate Culture is still focused on Values, Expectations, Attitudes, and Beliefs.

142

Chapter 8. Delegation and Follow-Up

The word delegation is frequently used with many professionals not really understanding the true concept behind it. Managers may choose to delegate for development purposes such as to stretch an employee to maximize their capabilities, or to see how teams work or don't work together, and how, as a group or individual, they handle the failures and learn from their successes.

Fear of Delegation

Delegation is more than just telling someone what to do, and there are plenty of reasons why people don't delegate at all. Hans Finzel outlines some of these reasons in his book *The Top Ten Mistakes Leaders Make*[24]. All credit to Mr. Finzel – his book is a worthy read.

- Fear of losing authority. If the employee ends up knowing more than their manager, it may be perceived that the employee will want to leave the organization and move on to better things once they know they are capable of so much more.

- Fear of work being done poorly. Management doesn't want to take a risk that a task won't be done on time or that the end results will be poor. Employees have to be given the trust and authority to try their best.

- Fear of work being done better. If the employee can do a better job, management may fear that those higher up will see the potential the employee has and the manager will not get any recognition for the end results. It's okay to let others get some recognition.

- Unwillingness to take the time. It's perceived by some that in the length of time it would take to show someone else what to do, well, they could have just done it themselves. Be patient and allow others to take on tasks when appropriate.

Some managers just aren't good at delegating. Perhaps they aren't sure how to approach someone or ask without sounding as though they just can't be bothered with the task, and so are passing it on to someone else to take care of.

The more experienced and reliable an employee is, the more responsibility and freedom she or he can be given to complete the required tasks. The more critical the task is, the more cautious management may need to be in extending that responsibility and freedom, but the opportunity should still be granted.

How to Delegate

There are various methods to use in approaching someone when delegating tasks. It's all in the way the request is phrased and communicated to the individual. Telling someone to "look into this and get back to me on your findings" is asking for investigation and analysis without having the individual actually making the final decision. Asking someone to "decide what needs to be done for this task, take action on your findings and keep me updated" provides more freedom but at the same time, keeps you in the loop should their decision prove to be an error prior to putting something in place.

Delegation is about freeing up time to allow the shift in focus from certain tasks to other areas such as developing new ideas and finding ways to be more efficient and profitable.

Delegation is based on trust with minimal management controls and is recognized as a way of tapping into detailed knowledge and information of other individuals or teams. Management can't know everything nor do they need to. Employees and teams can be utilized effectively when they know enough to assist in other areas as required.

Steps in Delegating:

- Define the tasks and confirm that it is suitable to have delegated to someone else.
- Select the person who will take on the task.
- Ensure that the person is capable of doing the task and they understand what needs to be done.
- Explain why the task is being performed and what outcomes are expected/goal is to be accomplished—where it fits in with the overall scheme.
- Let that person know what the desired results are and how you intend to decide if the task has been accomplished.
- Discuss and agree with the person what resources they may require—location, people, equipment, money, etc.
- Determine when must the job be finished, what are the deadlines and why. How does it affect other people or activities if deadline is not met?
- Communicate with others who need to know what is going to take place and that the task has been delegated to someone else to perform.
- Get feedback prior to the deadline and follow up with the person to make sure they are on track so you can deal with any problems that might occur.

Employees need to be given the authority and resources to act on a task that is delegated to them. Management also needs to make them accountable for the results. There should be minimal interference from management to allow employees the freedom to use their talents accordingly.

Theodore Roosevelt purportedly once said "The best leader is the one who has a sense to pick good people to do what he wants done, and self-restraint enough to keep from meddling with them while they do it."

VALUE-ADD JOB

"I'M BUSY, SEE IF JOE'S TIED UP"

Chapter 9. Responsibility, Accountability, and Authority

Responsibility, accountability, and authority are terms that are frequently confused and often used incorrectly.

We should start with some clear definitions.

The Oxford dictionary defines these words as follows:

Responsibility: "Liable to be called to account (to person for thing); morally accountable for actions, capable of rational conduct. Being the primary cause for a result".

Accountability: "Bound to give account, responsible (for things or person)".

Authority: "Power to enforce obedience: delegated power (to do or act); personal influence especially over opinion; a person who's opinion is accepted (subject expert)".

Funk & Wagnall's Standard Dictionary defines these same words as follows.

Responsibility: "The state of being responsible or accountable. That for which one is answerable. To act without superior authority and guidance."

Accountability: "Liable to be called to account, responsible."

Authority: "The right to command and enforce obedience. Delegated right or power; authorization."

The reason we need to be clear on the definitions is to ensure we have clarity of intent and purpose whenever these terms are used. The terms are NOT randomly interchangeable, though they do have complementary meanings, which is particularly obvious with responsibility and accountability.

Think about the applications of these terms in your organizational environment—how often do you see or hear these three words used and never really give a thought to "is that the correct term for what is requested or expected?"

To clarify these three further – we need to look at them sequentially as they may be applied to any appropriate work place situation. The first step is that someone (the "boss" or someone with the required authority) will delegate responsibility for a series of actions or tasks that are expected to deliver an end result. As these activities unfold and the series of actions comes to a conclusion, the person to whom the task was delegated (or who accepted the task) would be asked to give an account of the activity, the outcome, and the conclusion (often in the form of a report—verbal or in writing, and sometimes in the form of a presentation). The authority aspect has everything to do with the power to influence the outcome of the "responsibility" and to put that outcome into action. That step is often not part of the "responsible" person's "accountability". The responsible person was the tool that gathered the information that allowed the end point decision to be made so that the outcome could be turned into action, based on the authority to create and allow that action.

Responsibility is the first step in this chain of events. Assigning responsibility is the "please will you do this, prepare that, organize the other, find the—whatever?"

Accountability is bringing back the completed task or action for review so that a higher "authority" can decide upon the suitability of the information and the resulting outcome and therefore upon the applicability of that information—confirm that it should be used or implemented.

> I recently provided consulting project management work to one of our clients on a project that had "gone wrong". The project was now very late (the window of opportunity for the work to be executed was a shutdown period that had occurred and was missed several months earlier). The

project was way over the allocated budget (about 60% projected to overspend) and the second deadline for its completion was fast approaching (and that deadline was an immoveable date).

I was asked to step in and take over the control of the project, get it back on track with a revised plan for the execution dates and the required budget.

While the project was technically very complex and took a lot of detail planning to get all the stakeholders agreeing how the program can be put back on track – the complexity is not the point. The point is how the difference between responsibility, accountability, and authority played out in this project.

In this case the clarity is helped by the fact that I was the consultant in the role of the client's project manager. The rules are very clear. I had total responsibility to do anything that was required and using any and all of the assigned resources to "get it done". As the process unfolded and the various activities got back on track I was accountable. I was accountable to the stakeholders and the technical group that owned the project (who were also the group that failed to execute the process the previous time). I was also accountable to the senior manager who needed to know what was going to be done and when it was going to be completed. That accountability was discharged by regular meetings with the stakeholders, the project group, and the senior manager responsible.

The point is that I did not have any direct authority. What I mean is that I could not execute or implement decisions that were outside the defined scope of what the project needed to successfully deliver the required results. I could not approve expenditures since I had no financial authority. By virtue of the position that I held as a service provider I had no real authority—but I actually had a lot of "implied authority" since the executive who was overall in charge made it clear to the group involved that they were taking direction from me and that he would endorse my decisions.

So, the sequence is clear:

A person is given **responsibility** for an activity, an end result to be achieved, or a task to be accomplished.

That person is **accountable** in that they report progress and outcomes to others (usually more senior people involved and peers with a direct interest).

The **authority** is that which is exercised by the senior management from the outcomes noted above.

PART III: CHANGE TOOLS AND CATALYSTS FOR CHANGE

This section of the book provides an extensive review of change tools and change processes. After all, you cannot walk around in a dream with a vision of wanting excellence. You need to make it happen with a "boots on the ground" strategy, tactic, technique, or tool. Many of these tools are ever present in contemporary organizations but even in today's' highly "connected age" several of these tools are still very valuable in shaping and locking in a Corporate Culture. Several of the tools are still front and center in many key companies. In other cases, the revamping of one of these critical tools can become the current catalyst of change. This then is an overview of tools that have made a difference in the past two decades.

Chapter 10. Culture Change Mechanisms

There is no best, right, preferred, or only way of undertaking a Corporate Culture change process.

Catalysts to Corporate Culture Change

To significantly shape (or shake up) a Corporate Culture any one of three momentous events will do it for you without the intervention of a change tool process.

- Imminent or prospective bankruptcy of the organization in question.
- A merger, acquisition, or takeover of the organization.
- An organizational disaster such as a major product or service failure in the marketplace, an accident that takes away a significant portion of the leadership team, a complete and irreparable failure of a significant part of the business (total failure of all data systems, collapse of a significant division).

The change of the figurehead of an organization can also shake up a Corporate Culture, but this event is more under the control of the shareholders, the owners, the Chair or the Executive Committee— but if used wisely by selecting a figurehead that is a catalyst of change, a culture shift can be effectively engineered.

Choosing and Using Corporate Culture Change Tools
In this section of the book you will see a large variety of change management tools—some very current, and others that have been around for a quite some time but still have value. Each of them has a summary of what they can deliver and a comment on their individual value (why would I use that tool?).

Not every tool in the manager's tool chest is appropriate to change the culture of an organization. We will expand upon each tool, what it does, how it works, and how it can be used to shape a Corporate Culture.

As you move through this section, two very important standards must be considered and remembered.

One: Any organization of reasonable size (hundreds of people and upwards) must have a well-established stable of four essential tools—either in place and fully working or actively being implemented and improved upon (or expanded). These tools are:

- **A way to manage the quality of the delivery.**
- **A fully integrated set of operational data and information based on single source, real time and interactive (what systems don't deliver that these days?).**
- **A mechanism for maintaining this process in a constantly changing environment with some form of continuous improvement.**
- **A mechanism that makes time the essence of delivery, *i.e.* Just In Time (JIT))**

In the context of a manufacturing or a service organization, these elements would be:

- Quality Management focuses on "right first time" production requirements, or the focus would be on "right first time" processes that deliver the service objectives of the organization.

- The information technology aspect is be a fully integrated database that covers all facets of the business, from the integrated service delivery needs (that meet the client objectives of the organization), the communications needs (both internally and externally), the financial needs, and the customer service objectives.

- The maintenance process is the mechanism that that keeps all the systems linked seamlessly and functionally and continues to not only keep them current but also secure and relevant to the fast changing needs of corporate computer systems.

- The Just in Time element relates to delivery of the service expectations to both the client and the internal organization in a manner that is expedient and timely in the delivery of all the essential features and needs of the service that is being delivered.

In the framework of these essentials - we can look to Toyota as an example of a company that constantly strives to "do it right".

- "Lean" is a buzzword but also more than just a buzzword – since it really reflects the process that is the Toyota approach—kaizen (literally "improvement" or "change for better"), which started from Total Quality Management (TQM) principles dressed up in contemporary western language. More on TQM and kaizen further down.

Comparing the essential tools between a manufacturing organization and a service organization presents a challenge. With the manufacturing organization the focus and delivery of the four key points is almost totally internally focused since each of the elements either serves the internal audience or is directly measured by the internal audience and the results are tangible and in real time. For the service organization the delivery is far less contained. Here the delivery is much more indirect. The delivery has to be measured and gauged by way of customer service feedback. This requires continuous dialogue with the recipient of the services being provided, as well as a mechanism for recording and assessing the effectiveness of the service and a mechanism for measuring and charting the outcomes.

We'll expand on the Corporate Culture change tools below.

Two: The second important thing to remember is that the change management tool must be:

- **Large enough in its impact on the organization to span a broad spectrum of that organization.**
- **Compatible with the Corporate Culture characteristics exhibited by the senior leadership group.**
- **Sufficiently sustainable and enduring that it will survive in the organization through the gestation, birth, and maturity of the tool.**

If these elements of characteristic compatibility are not present, then don't waste your time and your shareholders' money.

Even in these cases, the success or failure of the Corporate Culture element in delivering lasting change is still disproportionately impacted by the successor leadership and how they act to move forward from the "traumatic event".

Six critical success factors
Six critical factors affect the success of any corporation or large organization:

- **Total support, commitment, and ownership by the CEO (the leader), the top team, and the key managers.**
- **A clearly articulated mission (goal) and strategy.**

- **An unwavering desire to have people make the difference.**
- **An open communications environment.**
- **The ability to identify the core process factors that deliver ultimate customer success.**
- **A widely communicated succinct set of performance measures based on outcomes and not on scorekeeping.**

What do these six critical success factors look like in a successful company? I am reminded of a very successful piece of Corporate Culture evolution that arose from the same set of circumstances that gave rise to the "Merger Mania" anecdote noted further below.

Success factor leadership in action

I was directly involved in a major acquisition and merger process a number of years ago (one of several I have been involved with over the years). At that time I was one of the executives of an international consumer products company that had a long and successful history of excellent products, good brands, good quality, and good results. I had been with this company for a couple of years, having left a similar (but even larger) international company in related areas of business to join this business. Unusual but perhaps not unexpected, my former international employer choose to make a semi-friendly takeover of our international business (the one I had joined).

A couple of years after the original merger had been completed and most of the initial "teething problems" of the newly integrated organization had settled down, a successor president was put into the organization. This individual brought with him a unique and very personable style of leadership. He was open and straightforward. He said what he thought, welcomed comment and dialogue, and strove to manage by consensus decision-making.

He took the time to create a vision and a mission for the company that reflected what he saw as the market needs—

155

but he did so with many inputs before locking in the end expectations. He sought inputs from key customers (regarding the strengths and weaknesses that they (as customers) perceived. He canvassed the employees at many levels and in most places (around the many locations that the company operated). He worked closely with the Executive group at his disposal to refine the various inputs and feedback provided. He canvassed the key suppliers for their perceptions. Then, with all this in place he distilled the collective information into a relatively simple summary that provided a vision statement that was consistent with the market expectations and a mission that was not only easy for the employees to understand but was simple enough to be memorable. These were then tied into a simple set of performance measures that, while not totally all-encompassing (some areas/departments had only fringe involvement) were comprehensive enough that most people in the company could see where their responsibility fitted into the bigger picture and how each of them could make a difference.

So what did this leader accomplish in this initial phase?

Total support, commitment, and ownership by the CEO (the leader), the top team, and the key managers.	**CHECK**
A clearly articulated mission (goal) and strategy.	**CHECK**
An unwavering desire to have people make the difference.	**SEE BELOW**
An open communications environment.	**CHECK**
The ability to identify the core process factors that deliver ultimate customer success.	**CHECK**
A widely communicated succinct set of performance measures based on outcomes and not on scorekeeping.	**SEE BELOW**

This leader's management style was a very open, approachable, pleasant, friendly style. He had time for everyone who needed it without making himself a slave to every demand that was made. His office door was "always open" to quote an often used cliché—but in this case it was for real. While he was "protected" by the proverbial executive secretary that separated him from the rest (of the employees), even she was coached (and filled the role admirably) to be supportive and err on the side of admitting people and not excluding people.

Under his regime we created a simple series of measures that related to a few key business success parameters such as quality management, customer service, cost effectiveness. We undertook a TQM program as the focus to involve and engage as many of the employees as possible. The fact that he was there, visible, present, and always interested made the difference. His commitment generated commitment and enthusiasm in others on a consistent basis.

So—how does the six-point score card look now?

Total support, commitment, and ownership by the CEO (the leader), the top team, and the key managers.	**CHECK**
A clearly articulated mission (goal) and strategy.	**CHECK**
An unwavering desire to have people make the difference.	**NOW ALSO CHECKED**
An open communications environment.	**CHECK**
The ability to identify the core process factors that deliver ultimate customer success.	**CHECK**
A widely communicated succinct set of performance measures based on outcomes and not on scorekeeping.	**NOW ALSO CHECKED**

So, I ask again—what do these six critical success factors look like? There is no mould that reproduces this scenario each time you want to create one. Having said that, I will describe how I go about assessing these factors in the context of a typical corporate assessment session.

I begin with a "management by walking around" exercise. The first part of this is just based on observations. As I walk around and meet the top executives, every step reveals to me many attributes of the senior management group. Who are they? How do they interact? Where are they? How do they communicate? How are their offices set up? Are they accessible to their staff? What meetings do they attend? What is their contribution at those meetings? What hours do they work? How much formal versus informal communication exists? What is the decor of the work environment? Are the offices open-plan or closed? Is everyone in one location? If not, how do the other parts of the organization stay current with the head group? How much autonomy do the leaders in the satellite groups have?

From this set of observations, I already have an early but clear picture of what to expect when I start asking questions. My questions are pretty standard and are designed to probe the six critical success factor points noted above. I have each executive tell me about the strategy, about how they have people making a difference, about the communications environment, about customer delivery and performance expectations and finally, about how they measure and keep track of it all. From this process it quickly becomes clear who are the "movers and shakers" in the group. As each gives me detail, it is how the detail is given that tells me much more about the individual, their role, and how their contribution affects the business than what they actually say.

As I then gradually work my way through the organization and down the hierarchy, I continue to get a picture of everything that connects coherently with the senior management's articulation and, more importantly, the items that do not connect. The disconnects always tell me more than the connected items. The disconnects refer to items that less senior managers may comment on that are clearly out of step with the CEO.

158

How long can the processes of changing a Corporate Culture take?

The fastest way to create a culture shift in any organization is to focus on the leadership team and determine the cultural compatibility of all the key players. The more quickly these can be harmonized, the faster the change. BUT Culture change is not a quick process and is certainly not "a quick fix" for all that troubles you.

While there are no hard and fast rules, the process may take some time unless there is a corporate event of the "significant emotional experience" kind noted in Chapter 2 under Changing Corporate Culture.

In a small organization (50 to 100 people) the culture shift process can take one to two years depending on the tools used and the reason for doing it. Why so long? Because the culture needs to be absorbed by all the people involved for it to be enduring and consistent.

In medium organizations (100 to 700 people) the process can take one to three years, again depending on the tools and the reason.

In large organizations (800 people and up), two to four or five years will be needed.

If done internationally with a multi-continent conglomerate the time can be even longer.

Again, remember—the process can be started very quickly BUT to be enduring and durable, all the tools employed to make the Culture change shift need to be constantly nurtured and reinforced.

This is why in my cynical opinion the CEOs of so many North American companies change so frequently. Changing the CEO is one of the quickest ways to change the Corporate Culture. Unfortunately, most of the people who initiate the change do not recognize why they select this change mechanism; in other words, they do not select the change to initiate a change in the culture—if that happens it is mostly luck. They are normally driven by the short-term need to improve the bottom line and to ramp up shareholder expectations. I refer to this phenomenon as "the toilet seat syndrome" (raise it, make a contribution, flush—and move on).

The process never quite finishes, since every addition of another person has an impact on the Corporate Culture. The more senior the individual, the more the impact will be. Hence the need to have a clear view of the Culture as it exists and a vision of what is desired. There is always room for improvement and the wrong leadership style introduced at a critical time can create a setback or a reversion.

Corporate Culture Change Management Tools
Below is a table of 33 different tools that can be used by management to effect Corporate Culture change. Most of the tools are not black and white in their categorization, although they fall roughly into three types:

- A: Clear major change catalysts
- B: Key contributors that can be shaped into catalysts
- C: Tools that, though useful, are not catalysts.

We'll briefly discuss each of these tools in the next three chapters.

Four Basic Corporate Change Management Tools	A	B	C
A company wide "Total Quality Management" program	X		
A dramatic company wide systems re-vamp (such as installing SAP)	X		
A far ranging cross functional maintenance tool (more applicable to machinery oriented industry sector compamies)		X	
A time is of the essence program - service delivery becomes the critical focus (courier companies for example)		X	
Key Stand-Alone Corporate Change Management Tools (Chapter 11)			
Mergers and Acquisitions	X		
Kaizen (Continuous Improvement)	X		
Business Process Reengineering	X		
Six Sigma	X		
Important Culture Change Contributor Tools (Chapter 12)			
Mission and Vision Statements		X	
Customer Service		X	
Zero Based Budgeting		X	
Productivity Review		X	
Strategy Development		X	
New Technology/Philosophy		X	
The Creation of a Communication Culture		X	
Quality Circles		X	
Greenfielding		X	
Complexity Reduction		X	
Activity Based Costing		X	
Benchmarking		X	
Hazard Analysis Critical Control Points (HACCP)		X	
ISO		X	
Manufacturing Requirements Planning/Enterprise Resource Planning (MRP / ERP)		X	

Useful Tools or Techniques to tackle Specific Problems (Chapter 13)			
Visualizing Techniques			X
Training			X
Participative Management			X
S.W.O.T. Analysis			X
Anonymous Key Weakness List			X
Succinct Measurements			X
360° Employee Feedback			X
True Colors™			X

Column A denotes key stand-alone culture change tools.

Column B denotes important contributor tools but ones not usually powerful enough to stand on their own in the context of culture change.

Column C denotes useful tools or techniques that can be used in isolation to tackle specific problems or opportunities, but these would likely never be anything more than contributory tools.

Four basic tools: What in the world are these all about?

Any company of any significant size needs a number of systems-based tools to operate effectively. Once you are beyond a few hundred people and a few tens of millions of dollars, there has to be some control structure in place. I'm not implying that smaller companies do not need control, but smaller companies can often afford to be less formal in how their business structures operate and integrate.

I'm also taking for granted that all companies (other than the lone operator) have some form of accounting system in place. Therefore I have not added that to my acronym-laden summary since its existence is almost mandatory.

To deliver a successful, sustainable, and growing business of any reasonable size, the following tools are required:

162

The Quality Management based process
Six Sigma (see further below) is a specific example of this.

This is a tool that delivers quality. It is any of the quality management and quality improvement tools that exist in almost any company. It is a tool (and a methodology) that engages many levels of the company and many of the people to constantly strive to do better, more quickly with fewer resources. It is a tool that drives constant improvement.

At the end of this chapter is my perception of the Toyota quality management story.

Integrated Systems capability
The company wide installation of an SAP (Systems, Application and Product) platform is a specific example of this.

This tool links the production or service provision process (that the company supplies) to the control and measuring process that plans and monitors the delivery of the end product (or service) that the company provides to its customers. At the very basic level it is the planning tool that allows customer demand to be translated into the action that delivers the goods or service that the customer has requested. At its most sophisticated level this activity has grown into very large integrated software systems that are referred to as Enterprise Resource Planning tools (or ERP, also referred to as Enterprise Requirements Planning tools). These tools are now so far advanced and well developed that most larger companies have an integrated data tool fully operational. Some smaller and medium sized companies may well not be there yet. SAP has over 28,000 systems installations worldwide and is one of the leaders (if not the leader) in this area of integrated technology. To express this capability in their words "all the data, all the time" and I would add "anywhere".

"SYSTEM BE DAMNED – ALL YOU NEED IS A GOOD MEMORY!"

The Maintenance tool (or Total Predictive Maintenance)
More useful in machine oriented manufacturing environments.
This tool is used to ensure that whatever it takes to keep the supply and delivery of the customer's requirements is in good working order so that reliable delivery is assured. While more applicable to industry where machinery and equipment is used to transform materials into goods and services, it is the tool that keeps the wheels turning and (physically) keeps the lights on.

Time is of the essence
Couriers live and die by this credo.

This is the tool that keeps the delivery time of the goods or service just as short as it can possible be. Ideally, if the customer wants one banana now, that banana should have arrived at the store literally just a few moments before the customer asked for it. If the customer wants a new car to this specification and in this colour with these options, that car should ideally be the next one off the production line and be available for almost immediate delivery.

So, why these four basic tools?
- The quality tool is the first essential.
- Systems based tools allow you to plan exactly what is required and when, AND keep control of all the detail that is essential to run the business.
- The maintenance tool allows you to be sure that whatever you use to create the value added to the materials you have purchased or the service you are providing does so with the utmost reliability.
- The time-based tool ensures that your total service delivery cycle time from receipt of the customer's requirements to the delivery of the goods or service to that customer is just as quick as it can possibly be.

All these tools are supported by a process to ensure total quality and continuous improvement.

Total Quality Management (an earlier part of Toyota's development)

When used to its fullest extent Total Quality Management (TQM) can become a Culture Change tool.

As the name may imply, TQM is less of a quality process and far more of a quality management philosophy. TQM is a people focused management system that is designed to constantly improve the quality (or service) offering of a company while also consistently reducing the cost.

ISO (the International Standards Organization (see Chapter 12) has defined TQM as "a management approach for an organization, centred on quality, based on the participation of all its members and aiming at long term success through customer satisfaction, and benefits to all members of the organization and to society".

As noted in the introduction to this section, TQM is one of the four organising principles that, when coupled into a coherent management program, can deliver all the power and consistency that any company could require in the day to day delivery of its mandate and its business goals. Therefore, TQM is a solid foundation for a Corporate Culture.

Toyota is a good example of how various critical management tools are organized into a coherent program that is designed to deliver excellence. Toyota called it "TPS" (Toyota Production System), which subsequently evolved into "Lean manufacturing". It appears that TPS is a carefully orchestrated hybrid of very rigorous quality programs coupled with Continuous Improvement (*kaizen* in Japanese) and the related business needs of data-driven information. This system allows for a fully integrated approach to the day-to-day and even minute-by-minute delivery of consistency in everything.

166

It is clear from an outside observer's perspective that Toyota has managed to create and maintain a Corporate Culture that is structured around Continuous Quality Improvement. The critical factors to the success of all and any businesses are essentially what I see that Toyota uses. If you don't have quality, you don't have anything worthwhile. They have taken TQM to the highest level and made full use of it coupled with the continuous improvement process of *kaizen*.

The other elements of TQM include Computer Integrated Manufacturing (CIM—the data side of organizational success), Total Preventive Maintenance (TPM—the maintenance part of the process), and JIT (doing everything on a "Just in Time" basis), all part of an all-encompassing philosophy that has long been the Toyota Culture.

As a management philosophy TQM is one of the few tools that can be described as a Corporate Culture change tool.

Corporate Culture is not one single thing that you can select from a textbook or that you find in the latest management magazine. As shown by Toyota, it is a "way of life" within that organization. It is an enduring and constant approach that not only keeps everyone and everything focused, but it also allows (and strongly drives) the process of continuous improvement. Furthermore, unlike so many programs and processes in North American businesses, the program and the process is not a "flavor of the month" approach to management. The longevity of the program and continued clearly defined purpose never goes away. It gets modified, it gets improved, but as managers come and go over time, the program and the process endures. No "toilet seat syndrome" here—just focused and long lasting consistency.

Fifty years ago Toyota was like most (if not all) Japanese companies—in the quality doldrums, trying to recover from the ravages of the Second World War. "Japanese Made" was synonymous with cheap and inferior goods and services. Yet today Toyota has become the world's most formidable auto manufacturer. Several years ago they surpassed GM as they top-selling automaker in the world. Is this accomplished flawlessly? No—as they get bigger and bigger, they too have quality and growth problems. But one senses that they know better how not to introduce the "quick fix" and try to patch over the problems in the hope that the next/new CEO (or whoever) will get it fixed (if that person is allowed to stay there for long enough to get it fixed).

Chapter 11. Key stand-alone culture change tools

This chapter discusses the clear major change catalyst tools categorized as "A" in the Corporate Culture Change Management Tools table above.

Mergers and Acquisitions

One of the many places where Corporate Culture diagnostics and the management of change-control are of benefit is in the merger and acquisitions process. Research indicates that up to 70% of mergers and acquisitions either fail or under-perform relative to the in-going expectations. The reason is often very simple to diagnose but very difficult to pinpoint, rectify, and reverse. Incoherent culture mixes are what undermines most mergers. Management often fail to recognize that this is what is wrong. If the company were to use the culture process after the merger, they would significantly improve their chances of a successful integration.

Why is this so?

In a merger or takeover process, the buying side often over-expects and over-anticipates the positives. After all, they need to sell the proposition as a good deal to their shareholders. Because the time to accomplish the full due diligence process can be limited, they usually also fail to see some of the lumps that have been swept under the rug.

The selling side (if they want to sell) often over-represents the many positive elements of the acquisition in the realistic expectation that the due diligence process may not catch the questionable item. Equally (if they do not want to sell—a hostile takeover) they will carefully hide positive things under the edge of the rug hoping no one will trip over the item. The selling side will also "fail" to reveal everything since it is not in their best interest to over-equip the buyer.

As the acquisition process unfolds it usually has several key people leaving—and it is often the best of the group that leaves (since they are the mobile ones with transferable skill sets that can readily find their next opportunity).

Once the acquisition is consummated and the new combination is moving forward, it almost always takes longer than planned to regain the momentum in the market to make the gains expected because there are always some unexpected aspects that have to be dealt with. It usually costs more to implement than expected because of the time and the added unexpected items. The synergies expected do not deliver to their full and anticipated potential.

Merger Mania

You recall that I was directly involved in a major acquisition and merger process a number of years ago (see the "Success factor leadership in action" anecdote above). My former international employer made a semi-friendly takeover of our international business (the one I had joined). The process was not long since the takeover was not hostile as such. It probably took three to four months before the serious conviction "we are now one—let's coordinate and cooperate" started to become the daily norm.

Both companies had a lot of independent brands, all with widely recognizable brand names. Both companies also had a lot of "competing" brands that needed to be maintained since each had its own strong consumer following. Both also had a complete organization and operating infrastructure. As the merged businesses started to move forward as one unit, two good examples of what can undermine the level of expected improvement became very obvious (these were two of many).

It is important to note that the newly merged companies now operated as a multi-billion dollar business—not small change, and large enough that a larger executive group was not the end of the world.

In one example the Executive Committees of the two companies effectively became one just by giving all the senior managers a part of the job that normally would have been done by one of them. For example, instead of one marketing head, we had two, each split on some sort of product group basis. I was the executive in charge of Operations (manufacturing, distribution, customer service, etc.) in the company being acquired. My counterpart in the acquiring company had a similar role. The decision in the end was that my counterpart would handle the manufacturing role for the new company and I would handle the distribution, customer service, *etc.* role.

This meant that out of fourteen executives (the original number when the executive group from both companies was added together) thirteen were used to form the new Executive Committee. The only person lost was the President of the acquired company who choose to move on (and then into a competing area—but that's another story). It took the better part of three years before this unwieldy committee was progressively streamlined into a much smaller self-contained executive group.

In the other example the new company had a very major systems crash about three months after the newly integrated business became active. In both companies the systems specialists each had a totally different computer infrastructure with which to run their "old part" of the business. They had worked hard to come up with a foolproof systems integration strategy. The heads of the systems groups had created a plan that would have two very different legacy hardware technology platforms working seamlessly as one.

On the day of the switchover to an integrated system the inevitable happened. Both systems crashed—not just crashed, but irrecoverably out of action. Nothing worked. We could not take orders, we could not create invoices, we could not purchase, we could not ship, we could not plan production, we could not track inventory, we could not even monitor cash flow. Everything just did not work. It became my job with one of my executive colleagues to fix this. First, everything went back to pen and paper. We hand wrote orders, we hand created picking documents, we hand created sales documents, we hand created invoices. We did inventory by hand, we planned production by hand, and we controlled purchasing by hand documentation. We went back to basics and continued to run the business entirely through manual documentation. Remember, we are talking about a company with several billion dollars in sales each year.

By day two we had terminated both of the heads of the systems groups and started immediately to design new operating platforms and planned for new hardware on which to run the new systems. It took us about four or five months to recover from this disaster and get the new systems into operation. We succeeded and we did not harm ourselves in the market place. We did not lose sales or lose control— thanks to a lot of dedicated and hard working people who put in long hours and lots of extra effort. Without great people rising to a challenge like that, you can only imagine the disaster that could have occurred.

Two points stand out from this experience:

The first point is that the focus that the systems disaster created became the defining element that rallied all the employees and galvanized them into the new company. Long gone was any implication that this person or that activity was part of the legacy of one of the old companies. The "crash" was so fundamental that it shook the business to the core and became the defining moment for the new business unit. Back to my point at the start of this chapter—there is nothing like a disaster to help shape a common bond and forge a new Corporate Culture. (Note—I am not recommending this as a suggested approach to shaping a new Corporate Culture, though I know it works.)

The second point is that the very occurrences in this merger that were unexpected (the systems crash) or just poorly handled (the amalgamated and initially top heavy Executive Committee) were exactly those things that undermined the original goals for the merged business to deliver the stellar results and performance that the merger plan had projected. Had the systems disaster not

172

happened, I am absolutely convinced that the performance objectives of the merged business would never have been met.

In spite of some of the drawbacks, a merger process is one of the most powerful catalysts that you can use to bring about a change in a Corporate Culture. But it needs to be handled with care and forethought. The senior people involved in the process must be sure that they have a sense of what they are about to accomplish. What will the new culture look like? (You cannot pick the required Culture in advance—you can only shape it knowingly from the circumstances and the leadership that is present). Who will be the leader? Who will be the senior executives? How will this group act? How will the organization be moulded? What will be the key goals and expectations of the new company? What values and beliefs will the new company have or require? There are literally dozens of questions, most of which cannot be answered up front—just when you need them answered. That becomes one of the challenges of the new company. You just don't know up front who and what will be required. That only comes much later. At the launch of the merger process, you often know what you would wish to have happen, but wishes do not deliver, and the detail of what is available only emerges much later in the process.

In spite of this, the change that is forced—yes forced—upon the organization in a merger is tremendous and is one of the most fundamental catalysts available to shake up the status quo.

Kaizen **(Continuous Improvement)**
The word "Kaizen is Japanese; it stands for "change for the better". Over time and with common usage in the English language the word was adopted as a descriptor for the management technique that was created in Japan, and it has become more regularly referred to as "continuous improvement" as it became adopted in the western world.

In the context of a management tool it is also often referred to as "The Toyota Production System" since it is Toyota that has been the world's largest and most consistent proponent of Kaizen as an all embracing philosophy that they use to run their business on a global basis.

In the context of Toyota, it is difficult to comment on how you introduce the Kaizen process since it is a totally ingrained philosophy to the point of being daily life in a Toyota environment.

改善 Its existence in Toyota actually relates to the culture change process, since the development of Kaizen arose from the ashes of World War II when Japan was a country in ruins, struggling to get back to some semblance of a manufacturing economy.

In those early post war years the term "Made in Japan" was synonymous with cheap goods and poor quality with no durability or reliability. In the 1950s the goods from Japan were so inferior that an urban myth sprang up suggesting that the Japanese had named a city in Japan "USA" so that they could declare goods as "Made in USA". This myth has since been disproved (the district of Usa dates from at least the 8th Century), but it shows how widespread the perception of inferiority was.

At that time two American consultants, Edwards Deming and Joseph Juran, who had in depth skills and knowledge in job improvement methodology and in statistical analysis and reporting respectively, were not getting the ear of management in the US. So they choose to go to Japan. Japan was ripe for the introduction of their skills and relatively quickly the Japanese approach to business and the skills offered by these two experts became the fermenting pool that has led through several generations to a Japan that is now without doubt one of the consistent world-class producers of almost anything they choose to do.

The tool is relatively simple and straightforward. The process is highly structured and effectively engages everyone at all

174

levels. The basic premise is that any person can stop any process at any time to correct a problem or a defect. There is a requirement to initiate the improvement or remedy. This becomes the first step in the Kaizen process. The outcome of the remedy or solution is a new standard for that defect elimination. This then leads to a cycle of improvement where you:

- Standardize.
- Measure the related parameters.
- Gauge the measure against the requirements.
- Innovate to meet the requirements.
- Increase productivity.
- Standardize the new and improved process.
- Continue the cycle repeatedly.

There is also a non-operational or management approach to this same activity. Business coach, consultant, and motivational speaker Tony Robbins preaches this approach when he refers to his "Constant and Never-ending Improvement" (CANI) methodology.

Business Process Reengineering
One of the change management tools that became very popular in the 1990s was called "Business Process Reengineering" (BPR). This was a powerful tool that was expounded upon at length and very effectively by its authors Michael Hammer and James A. Champy. They define BPR as "... the fundamental rethinking and radical redesign of business processes to achieve dramatic improvements in critical contemporary measures of performance, such as cost, quality, service, and speed."[25] As management tools evolved, this was (and still is) one of the best. To over simplify, it tables every single process step throughout the business and determines if it adds value, if it is duplicated or if it can be eliminated—the business structure and people roles are "re-engineered" to deliver simplification. Unfortunately it had a relatively high failure rate (some reports as high as 70% to 80%). The failure rate is not from the tool itself (it is an excellent tool)

175

but from the people and organizational components that interact to deliver the intended result. The anecdotal example below will show why the failure rate is so high.

The process was born from a simple premise that being that information technology should not be used to automate and make faster processes that did not add value to the company goals and market place objectives. Before automating and speeding up processes companies should carefully and in detail examine the work to be automated and eliminate any and all that was not value add. In other words, if the elimination of a task, a function, a work activity or whatever does NOT have a detrimental impact on the ability to deliver on time, on standard, goods or services to the end user, then it needs to be eliminated.

Identify Processes

Review, Update, Analyze As-is

Test and Implement To-be

Design To-be

Delivering BPR can be set up relatively easily and can be accomplished with a dedicated focus on the big picture of what the company needs to achieve in the market. It requires some experience-based facilitating which is often best done by an impartial outside expert who can organize the internal resource groups into delivery teams and ensure that the simple repetitive question is asked and fully answered, "What does this process step (operation, function, activity, etc.) do that adds value to the customer delivery outcome?" This is followed up by the corollary question, "What stops or fails to get done that is still important to the customer delivery outcome if we stop doing this?" These two questions are repeated for absolutely everything that every single person in the organization does.

When I handled this process – I used the following methodology to guide my actions.

It is important to have an open architecture systems process with a single source relational database driving the systems technology area of the business. This means that all information is current (real time) and comes only from one source, which is the only accurate source. The data is captured only once and from the correct and most accurate direct source. This is today's business systems architecture and therefore is the basis of the information required to drive the process.

As you move through the process it is important to organize the outcomes around the results required and not the tasks that get you there. The task that gets you to the outcome is just that—a task. It may have no value in the process of delivering the end result. (If you organize by task you will never eliminate the redundant steps.)

It is important to have the people engaged in the process own the results that are generated. Ownership delivers engagement. Engaged people deliver results because they feel ownership and responsibility.

Put the decision-making where the process is controlled and have those people who are directly engaged make the decisions regarding what is required and how to proceed.

It is important that the people engaged in the change process are treated as independent, customer-focused decision makers. Again it is this aspect of ownership that drives success.

Finally, build control into the process—partly so that it does not regress into the previous way of doing things, but also to ensure that the re-engineered aspects link together coherently.

I was personally involved with Business Process Reengineering on two occasions, both times as a management consultant. On both occasions I cautioned the management involved that success would only come if two things were categorically clear from the outset. One is that all the "risk of failure" factors that are noted in the book on the subject are clearly noted, observed, and acted upon pre-emptively. The list of almost two-dozen prospective failure items is, by and large, obvious, and must be part of a clear and unwavering commitment from the senior management.

The second caveat was that the process must be used for redeployment of resources and not for downsizing, which, unfortunately, is often the possible end result due to the very powerful nature of the change process tool. As soon as this potential outcome starts to become obvious to the participants, two things start to happen. One—the people that are driving the process at the execution level start to de-rail the process since it is often several of their (and their colleagues') jobs that are on the line. Two— it starts to become obvious to management that they have failed to anticipate from the start of the process that downsizing has had a detrimental impact on the contribution employees are prepared to make.

I personally found this process to be a disappointment since in both cases of my experience, the companies involved could easily have planned for an alternative to re-deploy staff and as a result, lost out on significant possible benefits from the program.

To clarify this point—in one case I was directly involved with the teams that had been selected to deliver the BPR process steps. I was the outside facilitator. There had been extensive discussions with senior management regarding the prospective outcome from the process that we were about to start. Management was fully aware that we had selected the best resources, had defined and were focussing on the best opportunities, and were engaging significant sectors of the employee groups to initiate and enact the program. We had even discussed that the process would release a lot of employee talent and experience by virtue of the fact that the process would eliminate a vast amount of non value-added work activity within the business (this was a service business in the logistics sector). We were projecting that as many as 15% of the employee work force could become spare and available for redeployment. Now, in many companies this in itself can be a bigger challenge than opportunity since many companies cannot realistically re-deploy that number of staff. They do not have the alternative business area available to absorb so many people. This was not the case with this company.

This company was one of a group where there were two other operating divisions in related business areas (able to use the similar skill sets) both of which were in their infancy and expanding. Both had growth plans over the next two years, which would readily absorb these people.

It didn't happen. As the process started to deliver the expected results, the people that I was facilitating were starting to ask the questions (for as you move through this process the outcome becomes crystal clear as you get about two-thirds through the process). At that time senior management did not step up to the plate and make clear to all staff involved that there was an alternative plan and that redeployment was a certainty. The end result was inevitable—some of the participants drew back from the process and the expected results became diluted. In addition, some of the key talent within the company decided to look for greener pastures. The process delivered some of its results, particularly in the IT simplification area. But the end result was a mere shadow of what was available.

Six Sigma

Six Sigma is one of these powerful tools that can be used to drive a culture change process. Indeed. It did just that for Motorola who were the instigators of the process and the methodologies. At a cynical level it is both easy and very rational to argue that Six Sigma is little more than an enhancement of the many long established quality programs including the simple (almost old fashioned) "quality control" (it used to be a department before it came out of the closet and became mainstream in almost all businesses), Zero Defects, TQM, and a host of related activities.

Six Sigma takes the conventional quality approaches to a higher and more focused level of statistical quality control. Six Sigma is commonly defined as a process that produces defect levels at a rate of below 3.4 occurrences per million opportunities. Six Sigma is registered by Motorola as a trademark and service mark, although numerous organizations and businesses use it freely. There is a complete philosophy attached to the process including training and graduation hierarchies that emulate the levels found in martial arts programs—with yellow belts, green belts, and black belts.

There are several methodologies in the Six Sigma arsenal with the two primary approaches being called DMAIC and DMADV. It is commonly considered that both (and therefore Six Sigma) were inspired by Edwards Deming's approach to quality management, which is the repetitive cycle system of "Plan – Do – Check – Act".

DMAIC is the process improvement variant of Six Sigma and has the following five steps in its methodology:

1. **Define** the process improvement goals that are consistent with the customer requirements and the strategy of the organization.
2. **Measure** the current process and collect relevant data for trending.
3. **Analyze** to verify cause factors, determine what relationship exists, and ensure all relevant related factors have been considered.
4. **Improve** the process based upon the analysis.
5. **Control** the process improvement and correct any variances before they become defects—and continually measure.

DMADV is the design variant of Six Sigma and in turn follows these five steps in its methodology:

1. **Define** the design activities that are consistent with customer requirements and the strategy of the organization.
2. **Measure** and identify the critical qualities, product capabilities, process capability, and risk factors.
3. **Analyze** and develop the design alternatives to create the highest level of design and design capability— and select the best.
4. **Design** the details, optimize, and verify (use simulations if required).
5. **Verify** the design through pilot runs, and then implement the process.

Since these founding approaches were developed by Motorola in the mid 1980s there have been a number of sub methodologies developed. But all of them are variations of the same theme.

Six Sigma requires the following:

- Continuous effort to reduce variation in process outturns.
- Manufacturing processes that can be measured, analyzed, improved, and controlled.
- Commitment from the entire organization to achieve sustained and constantly improving quality control standards.

While it can be argued that Six Sigma is little more than the structured quality control techniques that have evolved from the Second World War, there is no doubt that the intense focus that the Motorola organization brought to bear has raised the bar significantly.

There are two aspects of including Six Sigma in this summary–. First, if the tool had not developed into something as structured and as all-encompassing as the Six Sigma technique, it would never have made the grade as a change tool. After all, many of the long established regular quality control techniques have not made the grade. But "dress it up" as an all singing and dancing Six Sigma (and don't misunderstand my intent), and it becomes a very potent tool to deliver some excellent results when needed.

Additionally, it also demonstrates that even tools that I have listed as being too simplistic, too dated or superficial to be change tools can always be developed and enhanced, and with enough senior management backing, any one of them can become the "tool of the decade".

Chapter 12. Important Culture Change Contributor Tools

This chapter discusses key contributing tools that can be shaped into catalysts. These are categorized as "B" in the Corporate Culture Change Management Tools table above.

Mission and Vision Statements

These are less significant change tools these days.

Everyone has to have them. Just a couple of decades ago the development of mission and vision statements was all the rage. Now everyone has them, and in too many cases they have become relatively meaningless. In their prime, the very creation of these statements was a mechanism to get many employees involved in the conception and clarification of the "mission and vision". This process, particularly when well handled (on a broad and cross functional basis with lots of input and involvement), had a tremendously useful impact on the business, particularly as it gave everyone the opportunity to get engaged with the process of developing the words and the meaning. People got excited and were pleased to be involved and to understand exactly what management had in mind by the words that were chosen to express the desire. Having gone through many of these exercises, both as a company executive and as a consultant, I can attest to the painstaking thought and detailed discussion that went into picking one word as opposed to another to ensure the meaning was captured "just right".

Employees find it easier to place trust in company that has clear vision. It creates a degree of trust and loyalty. A clear vision is one that encompasses the corporate strategy, is simple to understand and remember, and is short enough for people to internalize and adopt. The mission statement must also be able to be understood and internalized.

Vision must state clearly the attainable stretch goals (usually many years forward or often timeless) and emphasize importance of employee contribution and buy-in.

What are the key features?

Vision and Mission must be clear and concise since they will have an impact on the organization and give direction to everyone. It takes time to write and get it right.

A vision statement outlines what the organization wants to be, gets employees on the same page, and paints a picture of the organization's ideal in the future. The vision is a short statement about what the organization wants to accomplish. It needs to address people, culture (values), and product/service. In order to effectively write a vision statement, you must know and understand the organization's core values, and show how you plan to govern the company in the future.

The mission statement outlines what the organization is now. It identifies the process and states level of performance expectations. It describes the overall purpose of the organization—what you do, how you do it, why and who you do it for. It sets boundaries of current activities.

Both the vision statement and the mission statement should be reviewed periodically. During the review processes, structure, staffing, and resources can all be assessed. By involving the employees on a wide and cross-functional basis, the value of employee engagement and buy-in really adds power to the process.

Talk to employees and see how they perceive the work they do. Talk to them about the strengths/weaknesses. What about the opportunities and threats? See how they feel about where they are and where the organization is. Do they fit in? Is there a match of their expectations and those of the company? Define core competencies and use core elements to write out a statement that describe the organization and get feedback and input from others.

184

Where do the Vision and Mission Statements sit today as a change management tool? Well, they really sit nowhere. Today they still have a purpose and they are still very conspicuous to remind everyone what was and still is expected. They also help with new recruits in the orientation process to ensure that there is at least a basic understanding of what was intended. But realistically, the "punch" has gone and the value is limited to the marketing and public relations purposes.

Mission and Vision Statements—what's next?

Some companies are moving slowly away from Vision and Mission statements and are adopting a new approach. The summary of choice is fast becoming a document that effectively condenses the Corporate Strategy into a single page. This is often a challenge for senior management—since the strategy document is generated from weeks of hard work, much soul searching, and a lot of consensus-building discussion and compromise. This is not easy to condense back into one page. When completed however, the feedback we have received suggests that this summary is very powerful in that it gives all employees a clear, concise, and brief picture of what senior management expects and wants to achieve, needs to achieve, and is trying to accomplish.

The process of preparing a one-page summary from an extensive document requires intense and careful thought about what the one page communicates. After all, if the strategy document generated a summary report of dozens and sometimes a few hundred pages, how can you possibly condense that into a one-page summary? The truth is that it's not easy, but in the process of doing so you have to weigh carefully what gets removed versus what remains. What remains is the very essence of the absolute key priorities that are critical to the success of the business over the coming year or so.

A typical strategy document will review the various goals and key deliverables of each major department, the financial expectations,

185

the sales and marketing plans, goals and expectations, operations goals, systems goals, human resource goals, etc. The document will review and assess the market place, the competition, expansion, consolidation and downsizing, the supply implications, the customer service and delivery implications and on and on. There will also be a carefully thought-through section regarding the company's strengths, weaknesses, opportunities, and threats. It is not hard to see why and how these documents are large and complex and take a lot of time and detailed effort to develop. (See Strategy Development below).

Imagine then—after all that work—you now have to leave out 98% of the words, yet capture 100% of the intent. This is not easy, but a focused day of effort by the same team (the most senior management members) can get to an agreement on what the major elements must be and what they must communicate.

Customer Service
A significant change tool—if used correctly.

While at face value it appears that this tool only delivers to the "outside" customer, this is not necessarily a limitation. It is very possible (and many companies have done it very successfully) to engage the whole organization in a "customer driven" approach. After all, everyone in the organization has an internal customer— each and every department and each and every employee has someone somewhere in the company who uses their services (or makes use of what they provide). So to engage everyone in the concept of Customer Service—be it internal or external—is easy to do.

What follows is a summary of the facets and requirements of good customer service intended to satisfy the external customer. **But as you read it—and if you want to use this as a change management tool—think about each item in the context of the internal customer.** Once you get past the very next paragraph the whole concept is as applicable to the inside as is implied for the outside. Keep this point in mind as you read.

186

Customers take the time to find your business and show an interest in what service or product you provide. They spend time researching all about your organization or perhaps have even paid money for previous services or products. Do whatever it takes to keep them as customers. It's been said that more customers leave due to poor customer service than for any other reason (including price or quality).

Memorable customer service can be rare. To create memorable and good customer service, organizations need to go beyond what is expected of them. Good experiences live long in the minds of customers, and behaviors influence the network of associates in doing business with you again.

Customer service excellence starts with leaders. They set the standards for others by listening to their employees and customers, and remain consistent in their personal quest for service improvements. Top executives must continue to provide top service levels to set the example. Dealing with employee issues that can affect customer service negatively if not handled immediately and correctly can make the difference of an employee having the ability and right attitude to approach and respond to customers.

Delivering good service needs to be an integral part of a business. The employees that are serving those customers should have a positive attitude and approach to the way they conduct business. After all, they are representing you and the organization.

Successful customer service can increase revenue but it also provides personal benefits as well. Customer-related jobs can be more enjoyable than technical or production line jobs. Customer service can provide a continuous challenge and ongoing success can lead to better job security and opportunity for promotions. Customer service roles are more demanding when employees have to remain positive at all times. Customers want to be treated as special so personal attitude is as important a job skill as product or service knowledge.

Employees who do not enjoy their role in customer service will appear depressed or angry. These may be people who would rather work alone or with technology, they may prefer to work at their own relaxed pace, and must have things happen in an orderly and predictable manner. You do not want these individuals representing you on the front line.

When establishing the customer service level your organization wishes to portray, determine what the characteristics of service are that you provide. Is it oriented towards people service or tool/technology service? Where is your location? Do customers come to your site or do your employees go to them? How often is the service provided and required? Is interaction in person, over the phone, by email? What training might be required to ensure successful employees and growth? What education level or areas of expertise do employees require? Is supervision required?

Establish rapport with customers and make them feel welcome. Employees and leaders should be sending a positive message to others with their tone of voice, both in person and over phone/email, with their eye contact, personal appearance, body language, and in staying energized. Smiles and gestures can go a long way when being approached by customers. Even remembering someone's name and addressing him or her accordingly can have a lasting impact on a customer.

The difference between effective and ineffective service is sensitivity, sincerity, attitude, and human relations skills. Customer service is about relationships, and customer trust builds over a period of time. If employees feel trusted enough to personalize customer service, then this feeling of inclusion in the process is passed on to the customers.

Quality customer service is important for growth of the service industry and to ensure repeat customers as well as attracting new ones. A greater understanding of consumers can give an organization an advantage over their competitors.

The key here is to identify your customer's needs. Employees need to know what the customer wants and needs. It's as though they need to anticipate their customer's feelings and what they are thinking. Customers should be made to feel welcome and comfortable. Service should be timely and the customer should be listened to. To ensure effective listening, don't talk over the customer and avoid distractions. Concentrate on what the customer is saying, then summarize and repeat it back to them to ensure you understand.

Know and understand your customer's expectations and maintain an up-beat positive attitude through every interaction—positive thinking and behavior is a choice we make even when dealing with conflict.

Being proactive is a critical point of customer service which means staying in touch with the customer and knowing how they are feeling. This will assist in solving problems before they turn into disasters.

When problems do arise, solve the issues effectively and efficiently. Speed and quick accurate results are what customers want—it's critical. So work with the customer to resolve the concern and then take whatever steps you need to get the end result. Don't ignore customers—return calls and emails and deal with the complaints. If a customer is not happy, they will rarely report it to you yet will tell others of their issue with your product or service. It costs anywhere from six to thirty times more to get new customers than to keep the ones you already have.

When working through a concern or conflict with a customer, show empathy and express that you understand their feelings and/or frustration and that you are going to do all you can to rectify the situation. Steps to deal with customer concerns:
- Listen carefully and repeat back to customer what you understand the issue to be to ensure clarity and eliminate any misunderstandings.

- Use words that are easily understood by the customer, and not industry terminology or codes or slang that only those working with the organization would understand.
- Explain what action you are going to take and thank them for bringing this issue to your attention.
- If necessary, follow up a verbal message with a written message to facilitate effective communication.

Remember to watch the tone of voice when communicating messages whether written or verbally. Good employees should also keep their supervisor and other co-workers informed of the situation. If the employee who originally took the complaint is not available to that customer next time, at least others will be aware of the issue and can step in to assist.

It's important to recognize the types of different customers such as the angry, nasty, or obnoxious customer. There are those that talk non-stop and are indecisive. Some can be very critical and demanding. Some customers operate from a base of insecurity and are expressing a need to communicate their concerns. They aren't necessarily upset with you but with the issue at hand, so don't take it personally, remain calm, and listen carefully. Focus on the problem and not the person.

So how do you know if you are providing good, effective customer service? Service success shows in the positive attitude and cheerful outlook of the employees. People who genuinely enjoy working with people have an ability to put their customer's needs first. These employees have high energy levels and are flexible to allow customers to be right. Thriving businesses have loyal employees, which can result in loyal customers.

Any experience can make or break loyalty with customers. How they are made to feel when dealing with your organization and how issues are handled will determine if they will be repeat customers for you. Loyal customers use your service or buy your product and are willing to pay more for it and will refer others to you. Loyal customers understand your processes and tend to be

190

more forgiving when mistakes are made. Just because a customer sticks around doesn't mean they are loyal though.

One method to ensure you are providing good customer service is to conduct customer satisfaction surveys as a means of staying in touch and showing you care about what your clients are feeling about your organization and the products or service that is provided to them. Customer satisfaction surveys can enhance customer service at all levels but before implementing, you must define the goals and reasons why the survey is being conducted. Is it just to stay in touch or to focus on particular areas of concern?

Surveys can be conducted through email, regular mail, newsletters, and web sites/Internet. Once the reason for conducting the surveys is determined, decide what types of questions you need to ask to get the answers that will assist you in moving forward. Keep questions and surveys short and ensure they don't cause concern for privacy matters. Most of the time, multiple-choice questions are the more effective route to go, but be sure to leave a box for customers to write any comments.

Select customers to complete the survey who will help accomplish your objective of why you were conducting it, and once completed, collect the results and compile the data. Review the results with supervisors and employees and put into action what you need in order to correct any concerns that have been brought to your attention. Survey results can also be a great coaching tool with employees.

Providing quality service can be challenging. To ensure you reduce the risk of unsatisfied customers consider what contingency plans your organization may need to put into place if you experience foul weather, loss of power, equipment failure, or find yourself understaffed. What if there is a fire or health emergency? What if climate controls malfunction, you have exhausted supplies and don't have enough to provide to the next customer, and if there is a breakdown in delivery?

Make sure your customers return. Be pleasant and welcoming. Remember to smile and handle complaints professionally. Go above and beyond what the customer expects each time by providing helpful suggestions and explaining features and benefits of service or product.

But just because you are in business doesn't mean you have to take on every deal. You need to know when to draw the line with difficult customers who may be abusive or lying. Or perhaps you have a customer who doesn't pay your invoices in a timely manner. The customer is always right but not all customers need to remain as customers.

Zero Based Budgeting

A very useful change tool but not powerful enough to be a culture change catalyst.

Zero Based Budgeting is a highly focused and disciplined management tool that can have a tremendously useful impact on the cost of doing business.

Most companies have what I call a reiterative process when it comes to setting the annual budgets. The process tends to look at what was required and planned to be the budget during the past year (and often also the year before) as well as how the actual year compared to the earlier forecasts. Trends are examined, inflation factors are calculated, expansion (growth), diversification, and downsizing are considered. All this information is then spread incrementally among departmental managers and related key staff so that they may extrapolate what the next year may bring in terms of the cost of doing business.

Almost invariably the budget numbers that come back from this process are too high to be acceptable and the projected sales numbers and revenues are too low to be acceptable. Everyone is then sent back into the detail of the process to find ways of achieving the required cost reductions and the increases in revenue. When all these numbers match the shareholders' expectations (and it is not usually the shareholders' expectations but the interpretation that senior management has made of the shareholders' expectations that drive this process—after all the senior management needs to look good to preserve their jobs and satisfying the shareholders is always key), the budget can get approved. As the new budget year unfolds the status is reviewed monthly or quarterly to manage the actual results against the expectations and redirect as required.

How is Zero Based Budgeting different from the above process? The key difference is that it assumes nothing and does not allow for the simplistic projection from the previous year. The starting point is $0—that is the budget. The other half of the picture presents what it is that is required to be produced (or the service to be delivered). So now you know what you need to accomplish (make, serve, deliver) and so far you have a budget of $0—zero dollars. The question then becomes: how can the goal (product or service) be accomplished to the same or better standard with the least possible cost? This process requires every single element of the delivery process to be challenged and, if required, put into the budget summary as one of the essential cost elements to deliver the goal.

To do Zero Based Budgeting well every element of the required end goal must be known and understood. If something is being manufactured or assembled, then every element of the end product needs to be known and assessed in detail. The questions are varied and almost incessant: why does that need to be spent? What would happen if we did not spend that? Does that add value to the goal? Does the customer really want that? Can we simplify that? Can we do this more smartly? Can we do it with fewer people? Can we reorganize the people so that we can get/accomplish more with less? Is this a must have or is it a nice to have?

The process works by using a constant barrage of questions about every single element of the cost (fixed or variable) at every single stage of the process about every single element in the process (or product).

Sometimes this process is used to examine a Division within the business unit. In this case while the questions above remain in the process, other questions are also required to provide a complete picture. These include questions like: What business should we be in? What are the emerging markets? Are we equipped to meet these markets? How do we need to organize to meet those needs/markets? Are there items in our product range that do not need to be there? Does a Pareto analysis (a statistical technique that is used for selection of a limited number of tasks that produce significant overall effect) show us information regarding delivery of value, cost and benefit of what we are doing today? What can we simplify while still delivering the same or preferably better quality? The questions are relentless and unending.

Two final points regarding the use of this tool:

1. It is not essential that this tool be used in isolation – it can often be linked with other tools (such as Greenfielding, Visualization, Strategy Development, Productivity Reviews, etc.) to get even better results. (See below for more on these tools.)
2. The tool is best used when NOT under the pressure of tight budget deadlines. The tool is best used from a position of strength when time is at your disposal. In other words use it to rejuvenate the business unit or area and use it as a preventive tool rather than a curative process.

Productivity Review
A good change tool but not powerful enough for culture change.

Productivity Review can be an excellent focus tool but tends to work best in high staff, labor, or service industry environments. A Productivity Review can be used in one of two major ways. One is to create a focus and deliver a higher return on the investment in the business. The second is that it can be used to encourage a climate that is receptive to change. The reason it is not easily used as a culture change process tool is that it is often task force related—that is assigned or delegated to a group to resolve some specific cost effectiveness issues.

The process works by assessing many elements of the business and their cost effectiveness. Quality and quality delivery, value, service delivery, organization effectiveness, scrap rates, reject rates, write-off levels, idle inventory, absenteeism, and labor inefficiency. In addition a variety of functional activity should be reviewed in the process including: budgeting, controls, financial indicators, information technology platforms, capital investments, and various aspects of how the staff is used and directed through a review of policies and procedures.

The key is to have an independent and objective management team who can identify and diagnose the causes of problems and create opportunities.

It is quite common to use outside consultants to help with this program. Indeed there are companies that specialize in the delivery of the outcomes. Many of these companies provide their services for this type of activity "free". Well, not really free— their fee is generated from the savings that they create and can prove to have delivered. Often the fee is a contingency of 50% or more of the first one to two years of savings. This can be a bargain for the company that is seeking the help since that is found money and has not been an incremental cost. For the consulting company it can be very profitable also. There are few companies that I have entered and with whom I have worked that do not have some big cost effectiveness opportunities to capture.

To make the process work it is smart to have some senior people and a number of high flyers involved.

There are a number of parallel tools that can be used including quality circles, time management, and organizational effectiveness surveys.

The final delivery is a highlight list of the crucial factors that challenge the current approach and philosophy of the senior

195

management. The senior management should challenge this in return and in the process reinforce their own beliefs and values regarding the critical success factors that emerge.

Strategy Development

An essential tool in the tool chest of every well-run organization—but not a key tool for changing culture.

Make sure that your company has this process of Strategy Development in place. Any organization of any reasonable size (multi-million dollar turnover and staff into the hundreds) must use this process on a structured and consistent basis. Not doing so is to do a disservice to the company, the leadership, and the employees at large.

Ideally, this process should be done every two years and should project four to five years forward. With a cycle like this the previous four or five year plan gets refreshed and updated every two years. Experience has shown me that an overlapping cycle of two years over four allows for short-term focus on key goals and deliverables along with the opportunity of a series of "mid-course corrections" as the program intent and the plan unfolds. In today's fast moving and sometimes volatile business environment, even a two-year gap can sometimes be too long (but that is what contingency plans are for).

The process of Strategy Development needs to be carried out by the leadership team of the business. It needs to be the complete leadership group, for if some are missing, either they do not have a significant role in the organization—and perhaps are surplus— or the end result can be skewed and therefore potentially misleading. In addition, by having the full leadership team engaged you also have the leadership team commitment and ownership of the outcome of the process and therefore the expected deliverables.

Preparation for the Strategy Development process comes in two parts. The first part is the development of all the pertinent business data that reflects where the business is and how it has progressed along the path set by the previous strategy. This requires both the internal and external data to be assembled in clear summary formats. The internal is all the key reporting that allows everyone to know exactly where the business stands day to day, while the external is all the marketing, sales, competitive, and economic data required to determine where the business is today in the context of the outside scenario. The second part is the assembly of the viewpoints and opinions of all the senior people about where the business is and what state it is in given all the data that has evolved from the first part.

The strategy is usually best delivered with the help of a facilitator. This ideally is a neutral outsider who has enough business experience and depth to understand all of the business and also all of the functions of the business. This person would oversee the assembly of the data and facilitate the interviews that precede the actual Strategy Development session.

With regard to the data, this needs to be a business status analysis—an economic summary of exactly where the business stands at this point in time. A snapshot of some of the sorts of questions that need to be answered include:

- What are the current financial results?
- How have these tracked against the previous strategy expectations?
- What does a detailed market analysis tell us?
- What is the status of our products or services (fresh, new, old, stale, outdated)?
- What/how is the competition doing? (Be specific and cover all the key contenders.)
- What are our delivery mechanisms (do they meet or exceed our consumer's expectations)? Do we have the research to confirm our status?
- What is our status in relation to the business goals and expectations we had set in the previous strategy?
- What is our status in the context of all the external influences on the business (economic, government,

197

markets, export and import pressures, labor and employment, etc.)?

The bottom line is that this needs to be a comprehensive review of the status done in depth with all the inputs from a multi-disciplined team who know the company, the products (or services), and the marketplace.

The second part of the Strategy Development process is a retreat where the leadership team removes themselves from day to day business over an intensive one to two day period. At this forum all the above data and relative positions are reviewed with a view to reconfirming progress and direction or (more usually) to set the course for how the following two years should unfold relative to the accomplishments to date and the expectations of the shareholders. As the retreat unfolds, this process draws the analysis created at the first step into focus.

The following is a summary list of the items that should be covered and formalized into the strategic plan for action and follow up:

- Position the Strengths and Weaknesses against the analysis, against the previous strategy and in the context of the corporate expectations.
- Test and feedback within the group.
- Reassess the expectations and test again.
- Create an assessment of the Risks and Opportunities including a sensitivity analysis, which assesses the market and the customer expectations.
- Develop any refinements and adjustments to the mission statement and test that the mission statement is still totally relevant (or may need some fine tuning).
- Communicate the outcomes and reconfirm the desired Values and Beliefs (this is particularly important since some of the senior leadership may have changed and some new Values and Beliefs may now need to be accommodated in the mix).

(Note the above is mostly "strategic" in nature whereas what follows is mostly "tactical".)

- Position the products and services in the context of the market and the competition in terms of the accountability and contribution to their success of every functional area.
- Review the infrastructure and the people resources to meet the product and service goals.
- Assess all of these in the context of the budgets (can the revenues generated support the cost and will it provide the required returns?).
- Develop short, medium, and long term set of action plans (with named delegates who have both ownership and authority to deliver).
- Communicate and adjust as required—based on the feedback obtained.
- Solicit full commitment and maximum participation for effective execution from all the delegates.
- Agree on the goals, the milestones, the key dates, and the network of accountability.
- Review the path/program of execution to be sure that the work is prioritized, balanced, and appropriately distributed.

Once complete, the retreat needs to be summarized into a Strategy Manual. This summary needs one more review by the leadership team and then should be widely communicated to all the affected employees.

It must be noted that if the fundamentals of the status quo have not been strongly challenged and the identifiable opportunities have not been rigorously identified then the process will fail to meet its potential. This would be an opportunity lost.

A final but very useful step is to be able to summarize all of the above requirements and expectations onto a one-page document. This one page will ensure that the staff not only buy in and support the outcome, but also can genuinely remember all the key elements that the leadership team is trying to deliver.

New Technology/Philosophy
A useful tool but not a Culture Change tool.

In many respects this is less of a tool and more of a technique. This process is a suggested structure either for the introduction of a significant new approach to the way business is conducted or to facilitate the introduction of some broad-reaching initiative. Examples of the sort of program that would be introduced through a structured process could include Computer Integrated Manufacturing (CIM), a new set of Human Resource initiatives (new appraisal systems, new benefits systems), a new marketing initiative that goes well beyond one product group, a Total Quality Management (TQM) program, etc.

The purpose of a structured approach is to ensure that the initiative generates the widest possible awareness and gets a high degree of consistency as the message and the detail get rolled out across many divisions spread out in different places. In addition, the structured approach also provides an opportunity to build commitment to the initiative by again delivering a consistent message.

The steps are relatively logical and straightforward:

- Determine and confirm the communication intent (what is it you want to create and communicate?).
- Discuss the need and the prospective process with all the key people and get consensus on the message and the approach.
- Consider if the program or the message is of sufficient complexity that you will undertake a pilot run to test how complete the message is and how well it gets understood.
- Engage the wider audience to ensure their initial understanding and their commitment.
- Create assignments to encourage responsible participants to get involved and to stay involved (prizes, incentives).
- Develop awareness and communicate the intent to communicate.

200

- Make sure that the regions that are away from the Corporate Centre also get some special attention—some hype to ensure that they too feel that this is both special and has been put together specifically for them (the audience).
- Create a holistic presentation program. The message to be delivered should be professionally crafted and presented by one of the most credible senior staff in a format that is perceived to be well beyond the norm and of a very high calibre (almost a "Hollywood" production) that really emphasizes the message and puts it out there in clear, strong emotive terms. Make sure also that it is couched in very down-to-earth human terms that give all the recipients a sense of belonging.
- Ensure that there is a balance between the people, the work groups, the organization, and the program that is intended by the introduction.
- Arrange for the special introductions across the board and at all locations.
- Ensure that there is a follow up communication to cement the buy-in from the first round of presentations.
- Above all be communicative, receptive, responsive, and constructively directive; *i.e.* don't let people just absorb and walk away (since many will forget almost as quickly as they were shown).

The Creation of a Communication Culture
This can be a change tool but is tough to do well, being too dependent on the leadership characteristics. But if you get the right leadership to head up the action, then anything is possible.

Although Corporate Culture can be slow to change, it controls the desire and the ability to communicate. As we consider a Communication Culture as a change tool, we need to be aware of one very important aspect of this approach to Culture change: in every business unit and in every business culture there are limitations on what can be and is communicated. This is not to say that the organization is secretive or that there is blatant censorship but in every organization there is a sense of how far can you go with what you say and how you say it. This is mostly manifested by the level of sensitivity that the employees have towards their bosses. This relates mostly to critique and criticism—things that you just would not say out loud or to a co-worker only in muted terms. This restriction in communication also flows the other way (and is often perceived by employees as the "confidential" things that are not widely communicated within the company). These are the very things that feed the "grapevine".

Communication skills are no longer considered just "soft" skills but rather an essential competence in business. It is an essential element in retaining employees and assisting with reaching their ultimate goals or performance levels. There is more to communication than ensuring employees have an understanding of policies, compensation, and responsibilities.

Formal communication consists of relaying the company message of the vision statement, values, and mission. Semi-formal communication is portrayed in the management style, systems and processes, policies, and employee surveys. The day-to-day discussions that take place between employees and management are considered the most informal way of communicating.

If you want to create a "communication culture" you need to have employees who want to share information and ideas and you need to give them an environment and tools where that is effective. This is a challenge that the leadership has to face in deliberately creating an openness where criticism and critique is not only accepted but is also embraced as being healthy and thereby useful. Creating a communication culture has little to do with conventional communication—though obviously any and all communication is a key part of the process that forms and drives this particular Culture.

Communication is simply the way we share information. Direct communication takes form in the ways of speaking, listening, body language, and silence. Corporate Culture affects every conversation.

A communication Culture is one where the management has made a clear choice that the various communication channels and vehicles are open, available, and free for all to use (*i.e.* everyone is free to talk to everyone else and "this is how we expect the communication tools to be used"). In addition, management will have had to make a commitment regarding their own level of openness. They will have had to decide how much of the top level strategic "stuff" is shared and how. With the management having decided that openness is best, they then need to follow up with the encouragement of an open approach to all communication. Through training and direction, the employees are encouraged to share as much of everything that goes on and that may be useful in driving the business forward. This type of environment has applicability in many places—a research and development environment comes to mind where scientist groups work in silos (to protect their intellectual property). They may be driven by the latest opportunity to capitalize on a discovery or perhaps they are so engrossed in the work that they do not have the time to communicate (and often may not even think that there is something to communicate).

To create a communication culture, management has to be seen to be fully open and accessible and employees both need to and want to work together cohesively and be equally open. Employees need to and want to share information. Employees need to engage in the idea of better communication and be aware of how their communication style comes across to others.

We aren't asking people to change who they are or their personalities, but merely suggesting they each become aware of how their actions can affect those around them. Body language and facial expressions are relevant to any conversation and eventually, with time and practice, people will make fewer misinterpretations of a look on someone's face or will learn how not to allow another person's mood to set the tone for the entire office. This evolutionary approach is best delivered through a training program that engages many groups of people right across the company, and is often best facilitated by a trained communication specialist who can not only talk to and demonstrate the body language needs, interpretations, and gestures, but can also contrast how countries differ in this area. The contrasting helps to cement the visual images and reinforces understanding. Communication can make or break an organization. Good communication builds trust in relationships, both internally and externally with clients and/or vendors.

Leaders need to communicate about anything and everything and share the messages. What they do, how they do it, and with what frequency and consistency set the stage for all others within the company. In every case communication is an important factor in leadership behavior—sharing messages and executing on that message. Walk the walk and talk the talk. Effective communication between CEOs and managers/supervisors, and formal communication processes such as meetings, memos, emails, company intranet, employee feedback, and communication between employees and managers can all lead to communication performance success.

Productivity and motivation will improve significantly if senior management provides the openness and leadership and gives employees a "voice" through which to contribute to two-way communication with managers and a way to offer input and ideas.

Chris and Sandy (not their real names) are the principals and owners of a small to medium sized company that they run in a very open manner—a style not dissimilar to that being espoused above. There is nothing that is not on the table. The staff is encouraged regularly to challenge the status quo. They are always being asked to provide input and always being encouraged to bring their views to what senior management has said and is doing regarding any of the business situations in which they find themselves. They hold regular discussion forums where anything and everything is on the table. To the degree that senior management has not "put it on the table", the employees are invited and encouraged to ask and challenge.

Even in this environment a challenging situation emerged. One of the "rising stars" in the company came up to performance review time. The discussion moved on to salary and a range adjustment to bring this individual's salary up to the levels thought appropriate for the position and the experience. During the discussion the employee expressed concern that even though there was a generous salary adjustment being processed, the employee was substantially behind colleagues who were of similar seniority. As the discussion unfolded, it came to light that the employee had been talking to and accepting as fact (from some fellow employees) how much more the fellow employees were getting paid and that the rising star's compensation was out of line. While other employees' salaries are not for public review, there was the need for a serious discussion based on publicly available salary ranges and responsibility levels. When this discussion was complete, a number of apparent misconceptions and misunderstandings were cleared up. The closing on this saga included a mutual promise that whenever issues and perceptions arose that could undermine the confidence of the individual, that a dialogue would ensue to ensure that openness and confidence would remain. In the end, the salary was settled as originally intended.

Quality Circles

Another very useful management tool—but if used in isolation it is not powerful enough to warrant being used as a Culture Change tool unless used in the context of a higher level tool such as Total Quality Management.

A Quality Circle is a small group of people from a specific work area who voluntarily meet at regular intervals to identify, analyze, and resolve work related problems. The process not only improves the quality of the issues under review but also acts as a strong motivation to the workers whose role and importance to the organization becomes enhanced by the process that they choose to undertake.

The Quality Circles process is a highly structured and rigorous approach to the ability of the organization to deliver total and complete quality in everything that the organization does and touches.

Quality Circles originated in Japan in the early 1960s. At that time the quality of goods provided by Japanese industry was considered to be significantly inferior (almost the total reverse of how they are perceived today).

Quality Circles are generally regarded as being created by a Japanese university professor, Kaoru Ishikawa.* At that time, Japanese industry was in poor shape and had not recovered from the Second World War. With the creation of the Quality Circles methodology the movement was supported and coordinated by the Japanese Union of Scientists and Engineers. The premise that Professor Ishikawa brought forward was based on his belief that by tapping the creative potential of the workers involved in the production processes that quality could be improved significantly and that the improvement could be sustained.

It is easy to imagine several or even many Quality Circles operating simultaneously throughout many parts of an organization. When structured and organized to deliver tangible and quantifiable outcomes, the effect can be very powerful and beneficial.

For example, Quality Circles was one of the first key tools that Toyota used many years ago to start them off on their quest for quality excellence. The practice of Quality Circles has been proven and documented extensively by a number of innovative companies including several Scandinavian organizations.

---

* Professor Ishikawa was also the inventor of the analysis tool referred to as the Fishbone Diagram (due to the end result looking very much like a fishbone), also known as the cause and effect diagram.

The tool is widely used today by many companies under different names and guises. See Total Quality Management and its derivatives at the front of this section.

Greenfielding

Another very useful management tool, but nowhere near powerful enough to warrant being used as a Culture Change tool—unless the outcome is a new and totally integrated location.

Greenfielding is a "clean sheet of paper" process, which, as the name implies, has the physical aspects of the current organization redesigned from scratch as if there were nothing prior to this new starting point. To put that another way, the products, the markets, the suppliers, and the inbound/outbound distribution remain largely as is. It is the conversion process—the value added that is put under the microscope.

The process is usually applied to the re-creation of a new factory at a new location but the process can equally be applied to a larger and more diverse program (including the amalgamation of multiple locations onto one site).

The starting point of this process is to determine all the elements that need to be assembled at the new location to allow the organizational objectives to be met. This would include a detailed review of all the production lines, the service departments required to support the lines, and all the organizational staff needed at the new location to make a successful integrated unit fully functional.

As the process unfolds it presents clear and unique opportunities to re-assess the needs of the organization and how things are done currently. What does the factory need to do? What is the most basic requirement to deliver the needs of the business? Do we have the best machinery and is it configured in the best way to give least cost / best quality / highest productivity? If not, now is the time to theorize what can be done better. It may be that some new production machinery will create a more beneficial outcome but may not currently be available from the budgets. That does not preclude the new design from incorporating the requirements of the new line so that it may be installed later. As the production needs become clear we need to focus on the support activities such as materials movement and handling. How little material can be made available adjacent to the lines so that there is a maximum of "just in time" delivery (to minimize inventory cost)?

When the picture for production and local logistics becomes clear, you then need to assess the requirements for the service functions. How is the new location and all of its material needs supported? What functions need to be available to ensure that everything works smoothly and at minimum cost?

In this way, layer-by-layer, you add on each of the requirements that will ultimately provide a well-developed model for the new location that does everything that is required to deliver the goods and services from the company to the end customer.

As each of these layers is added, each presents a new and unique opportunity to challenge the process. Is this really required? Is there another way of doing this piece? Can we do something else another way? Can this aspect be integrated with another part and thereby delivered more quickly, more easily, or cheaper? The success from the process comes from challenging everything thoroughly and completely and leaving no stone unturned.

> I recently did a Greenfield strategy for a manufacturing location—actually several locations near each other, all of which were an integral part of the production process. Because the locations were in different buildings, the inevitable inefficiencies occurred. Time was lost between production steps; work in progress (WIP) inventory was higher due to delay risk between locations. More people were required to handle the process since the conclusion steps in one building required a preparatory step in the next building. There were materials handling duplications and added trucking between process steps.

208

Each of the building locations was land-locked and each had no space to expand. Only one was adjacent to another and both were at capacity.

The Greenfield exercise was developed for two options. The first was to relocate all the essential production process steps and the immediate support requirements into a new building onto a Greenfield site. The second was to take those Greenfield parameters and use them to help specify a Brownfield site (a site with a pre-existing building) that could prove appropriate to meet the need. As each of these options was developed and budgeted it became clear that the Greenfield option would prove too expensive. This was in part driven by the fact that the products involved were pharmaceuticals, which meant that the products would need to be re-validated upon relocation to a new manufacturing address. (Clinical drug products are licensed by international regulatory authorities and a new address for the point of manufacture would require the products to be re-registered and re-qualified as approved drugs—for each of the regulatory organizations that had jurisdiction.) For any major drug it costs about $750M to $1B to get to the market. Change an address on a blockbuster and you have many billions in cost and several years to deliver. For this particular manufacturer, the added cost burden proved to be prohibitive in the process.

The value that arose from the study was that the Greenfield factory brought a number of new ways of thinking about manufacturing process and its efficiency. The end result was that the factories were not relocated but—through some innovative thinking—many of the Greenfield model features became a reality by building the efficiencies that the model showed to be available into the day-to-day production process. The organization involved has now embarked on a two-part plan—one, to implement an extended program of upgrades and improvements that progressively improve the cost effectiveness of the processes, and two, a number of carefully planned on-site moves that makes creative space of the vertical footprint of the site by expanding upwards and reconfiguring the process steps vertically. This proves to be both useful and appropriate since the process steps lend themselves to some vertical flow integration. This, when coupled with the newfound production efficiencies gave rise to a solid yet cost-effective expansion plan that increased capacity several fold without the disruption of the relocation process.

Complexity Reduction

This too is another useful management tool and powerful in its own right—but again not quite powerful enough to warrant being used as a Culture Change tool. The tool can be boiled down to two words: excessive simplification.

Complexity reduction is a very structured tool that brings a lot of positive benefit to any manufacturing organization that chooses to use it. The tool is extensive and multifaceted, though not so much difficult to use as time consuming to use. The outcomes are, however, very clear and very positive.

The process is only of real value in applications where there is an extensive range of products that are manufactured (or assembled) from a variety of ingredients in a number of different formats that ultimately are delivered for consumer use in a variety of packaging alternatives. Many food products from a diversified manufacturer would fit this category, as would automotive manufacturing, where complexity reduction has been and is referred to a "Value Analysis" or "Value Engineering".

The five distinct facets to the Complexity Reduction tool:

- Random Iterative Formulations (RIF)
- Key Ingredient Simplification and Standardization (KISS)
- Range Optimization and Reduction (RO)
- Packaging Component Standardization and Simplification (PCSS)
- Operations Redesign (OR)

To make this tool effective it is necessary to have a well-organized approach with very clear summary information

210

regarding the outcomes. This requires a team who understand the process and the use of the tool, and are able to keep a clear and coherent summary of the outcomes.

Each facet of the tool can be used in isolation and generally is, since each tool is to some extent a precursor to the previous tool. The RIF process usually precedes the KISS process which itself leads to the Range Optimization step. With these well underway though not necessarily complete, the Packaging Simplification can follow, though many of the aspects of this step can operate effectively without the previous being completed. The final OR step is an encapsulation of all the best outcomes from the former steps as the whole process is delivered and enshrined into day to day operations to take advantage of the whole program and all the outcomes and opportunities.

I last used this process with very solid success with a large global manufacturer of a broad range of food products presented in various formats (dry, frozen, canned, bottled) and packaged in a variety of consumer convenient packages.

The process steps were applied to most of the manufacturing formats over a period of almost two years.

Random Iterative Formulations (RIF)
The first step is to literally play with the product ingredient specification ratios and components. By switching ingredient ratios one often comes up with another product. By expanding the use of the cheaper components you can often reduce the cost and with a little adjustment to the flavor components you can often maintain the same consumer perception of the end product with a noticeable cost reduction. Alternatively, you can expand the use of the more expensive components and create a more upscale product (or even a range of upscale products), which could command a price premium. Often companies have developed product formulations that have stood the test of time and with which no one dares to interfere. (Remember the cautionary tale of the failure of "New Coke". Less than three months after its introduction, after widespread criticism from consumers, the

company reintroduced "Coca-Cola Classic"—the original formulation that Coke drinkers had grown to love.)

The RIF process step is intended to challenge the conventional wisdoms and bring fresh approaches into the daily routine.

An example of this could be a packaged food product where one specific ingredient has "always been in the product" (indeed, early advertising used to emphasize that component) though it is now "out of date" and could be replaced with a better and more contemporary component.

> Another example of this could be a coffee formulation. To the coffee connoisseur's palette there is nothing like the taste of a pure Kenyan coffee bean that has been carefully roasted to bring out its strong and aromatic flavor. Kenyan coffee is one of the world's expensive premium origins and as good as it is, it becomes an expensive proposition to drink such a high-end brew. Also, due to its strong aromatics and equally strong coffee taste, it becomes a specialized brew for the select few.
>
> When we went through the RIF process for a particular coffee brand, we took the Kenyan base and added an equal amount of Columbian beans (Columbian are milder and very much a preferred choice to the average North American palette). The Columbian bean is also significantly less expensive than the Kenyan. This still made a strong coffee that was not for the mass market (except perhaps in Europe where they prefer their coffee stronger). We then added a really inexpensive coffee bean such as a Mexican or one from Guatemala (no disrespect intended to the countries). The result was amazing. We finished up with a product that had a classy high-end palette taste without the sharpness and without the premium cost. If it were not for RIF we would not have discovered that opportunity.

Key Ingredient Simplification and Standardization (KISS)
Having started the process through the first step, the opportunity to review ingredients follows. In this step the approach is to look at the total inventory of all ingredients, but not as discrete

ingredients but as a large scale review of all the bulk items that over the course of a year add up to a significant tonnage of a large number of components. This gives an opportunity to review and question many things, but two keys emerge. First, is the bulk implication for purchasing being used to best advantage? Second, has new ingredient technology passed us by and are we still using inexpensive bulk items where there may be alternatives that are more cost effective, offer better product (stability, quality, consumer appeal), and can change the scope of the of the cost of goods without any negative impact on consumer perception and acceptance in the market place?

In this exercise the Pareto principle lives (and thrives). This principle, also known as the 80:20 rule, states that, for many events, 80% of the effects come from 20% of the causes. The 80:20 rule can be very useful since the larger items can often be leveraged up into bulk purchase opportunities with a consolidated preferred supplier network. And some of the very smallest may actually be able to be removed from the mix or (by buying in concert with other items) can be consolidated with better delivery control and the opportunity of reduced cost. Another big advantage from this process is the opportunity to reduce (or even eliminate some of) the cost of inventory—either from the total volume of raw stock held or from the identification of slow moving and "zero turns" inventory which has sat totally unused for a year or more. The outcome is another big step in the quest for cost effectiveness.

Range Optimization and Reduction (RO)

Pareto is key in the Range Optimization step. In this step each product range is analyzed and the bottom 20% are challenged as to why they exist. This part of the product range is often disproportionately expensive to produce, carry, and deliver. It often has the smallest orders attached with the lowest frequency of fulfilment, the highest percentage of "stock outs", the highest risk of being out of date code and disproportionately large inventory relative to its contribution. In addition, it often has the least diverse distribution range finishing up in a very small proportion of the customer outlets. A real cost analysis based on true cost allocations (not averages) and looking at the time sensitivity of money for this group of slow moving products raises some serious questions as to why this product still exists.

Packaging Component Standardization and Simplification (PCSS)

The Packaging Optimization step can often be done largely independently since many of the opportunities in this area are independent of the earlier steps. In addition, as the earlier steps introduce more opportunity for packaging simplification, these simplification steps can usually be easily added. When it comes to packaging optimization it is important to look at the performance of the packaging machinery. Two factors dictate most of the pace of a packaging line.

- What is the slowest-filling component in the line? Here we ask what can be done to change that (*e.g.* a large fill of one component coupled with several other smaller fills may suggest that the largest fill be split into two or three streams and dosed for a shorter cycle simultaneously, thus speeding up the unit pace of the line).
- What does the packaging material flow onto the line do and does it adversely have an impact on the line speed? In other words, is the packaging material in a pre-assembled format that flows onto the line easily, smoothly and converts mechanically into its final form very quickly?

Another important component of this process is to assess the "up time" of the line. How many minutes per hour does the line actually produce saleable product—independent of the issues relating to fill speeds or packaging components?

Operations Redesign (OR)

The final opportunity in this barrage of techniques in this Complexity Reduction tool is to lock all the findings and good outcomes into an Operations Plan that enshrines all the learning and opportunities into a longer-term benefit while still maintaining the creativity that got everyone to this goal.

In other words—don't rest on your laurels and wait for the next sunrise.

Activity Based Costing

Activity Based Costing is a relatively simple way to raise the accuracy of a conventional variable cost of product process to another level. This is accomplished by applying the same level of detail to the fixed cost and overhead cost analysis process as would usually get applied to the variable cost process. In the usual variable cost process—the incremental cost of goods is made up of a pretty accurate total of the cost of materials, ingredients, the cost of labor, and the cost of production—*i.e.* looking at and adding up the exact cost of each incremental component including the cost of waste involved. Overheads and fixed cost are usually applied on a proportional basis. That would give a small volume production item the same fixed cost as a large volume item. In other words, each item would get the same unit cost attributed to a similar product as would the sister product.

Activity Based Costing looks in detail at exactly what portion of the overhead cost and what portion of the fixed cost each product should carry. What happens in this scenario is that a small volume item that is complicated to make and requires a lot of support attention gets attributed its "fair share" of the support costs.

This provides for two outcomes, one being that the "true cost" of the product is now better understood—so that the company can decide if the product is properly priced and if the product is profitable. The second outcome is that it allows the company to decide if the product is really viable. Should it be made in house at this cost or should it be out-sourced?

There is one snag to this process. Once the "true cost" is known and if a decision is made to eliminate that product, one also needs to consider how to reduce the fixed cost contribution that the existence of this product previously covered. After all, fixed cost does not disappear—it merely gets spread across the remaining products and each of these will now be incrementally more expensive to produce.

Benchmarking
Benchmarking is a tool that encourages a company to look at best practices and to look for best in class standards of quality and effectiveness.

What usually transpires is that through investigation and comparison the company attempts to model the highest attainable standard for a particular product or process. The company then compares its own equivalent product to that highest standard and sees what and where the differences are. In this process the "industry best practice" is often derived and used either as the target or the in house item becomes the industry standard and therefore the target for others seeking to emulate this "best practice" item.

There are advantages to being an industry "best practice" leader. It usually means that you have a dominant or at least leading position in the market with that particular product or service.

One sector where best practice is considered is the automotive industry. For example Toyota is often considered a leader in the delivery of "right first time" quality standards in their domestic vehicles. Some of their factories are considered models of worker / manager relations. Most of their factories are not unionized. Many consider this too to be a best practice capability on Toyota's part.

Hazard Analysis Critical Control Points (HACCP)
HACCP is another tool founded on quality principles (interesting to see how many of the tools of the past and current management practices are based on quality process and focus). The primary difference between HACCP and conventional quality control is that quality control (even as it evolved into quality assurance) was still a system for measuring the production of food through its

216

various process and distribution steps on its way to the consumer's table.

HACCP was developed originally in the 1960s to support the space program where the quality and reliability of food transported into space was of course a paramount requirement. In this environment and under these circumstances the food had to be assured of being in perfect condition—even after months in storage and transit. (Is there no convenience store at that altitude?) The program was commissioned by NASA when they asked Pillsbury to design and manufacture foods for use in outer space. It became the foundation of food safety programs since and has successfully migrated to pharmaceutical and personal care industry (each of which has its own stringent demands for preventive quality solutions).

HACCP is a rigorous identification and analysis of those elements of the food system supply, manufacture, and distribution that would be potential safety hazards. Through this process key actions, known as Critical Control Points, are identified so that actions can be put in place to eliminate (or at least significantly reduce) the detrimental risk.

Since its inception there are now mandated areas for HACCP application including many facets of the meat and poultry business in the United States.

The HACCP process is a systematic approach to preventive quality control. The primary steps of the process are:

1. Conduct a hazard analysis. This is where (for food industry purposes) the users determine the safety hazards and then identify the preventive measures that can be applied to control these hazards. The hazard can be any biological, chemical, or physical attribute which may cause the food to be or become unfit for human consumption.
2. Identify the Critical Control Points. The CCP is a point, a step, or a procedure in the food process at which control

can be applied and as a result, the hazard can be prevented, eliminated, or at least reduced to a lowest level.

3. Establish critical limits for each of the control points. This is the maximum (or minimum) value to which the physical, biological, or chemical hazard must be controlled at a critical point in its existence to prevent, eliminate or reduce to a lowest level.

4. Establish the critical control point monitoring requirement. This ensures that the process is under control at the point where this hazard is prevalent (or at its most accessible).

5. Establish the corrective actions. These are actions to be taken when the monitoring reveals that there is a deviation from the critical limit criteria or where a critical limit is not met. The corrective actions are intended to ensure that no product enters the consumer chain as a result of the deviation.

6. Establish record keeping procedures. The HACCP regulations require that a number of directly related documents be maintained regarding the plan, the monitoring points, the critical limits, verifications, and the handling of process deviations.

7. Establish a procedure to ensure that the HACCP system undertaken by the company using it is working as intended. This is the ongoing verification (or validation) that ensures that the plant, the people, and everything involved does exactly what it was designed to do—that is ensuring totally safe products.

Today's HACCP programs require that each of the above steps forms part of a documented process that list fully the procedures and the frequency at which the various program steps are executed and noted.

It is interesting to observe the evolution of two tools emerging in the food industry. In my opinion they build on the HACCP process and are trying to become the ISO (see below) of quality within the food business.

These two are BRC (British Retail Consortium—obvious where that started) and GFSI (Global Food Safety Initiative). BRC started in 1992 and merged with another like forum in 1998 to become the BRC of today. Some years later and originating in Belgium, GFSI evolved in the year 2000. From my very limited exposure to them, I judge these to be the early development of the ISO equivalent of "ISO for food industry needs".

ISO Certification
This can be a very powerful tool if used correctly and under some conditions it could be used as a Culture change tool.

To be used as a Culture Change tool the organization embarking on this journey has to be in bad shape from a quality perspective—thereby requiring a very significant overhaul of the total quality requirements of the business.

ISO is the International Organization for Standardization, which was established in 1947. It's a worldwide federation and is associated now with over 160 National Standards Bodies globally.

When ISO first created the quality standards that have now become almost famous, the outcome was not exactly spectacular. In the first rounds of quality standards the focus was on documentation, structure and control. The problem was that "control" was looking to verify the consistency of the documentation that was intended to ensure consistency in the delivery of quality. The outcome often became less than perfect since poor quality was almost as readily certifiable as good quality. The second round of ISO became what I would define as the real start of the delivery of quality consistency.

ISO is the world's largest developer of standards. It contributes to making development, manufacturing, and supply of products and services more efficient, safer, and cleaner. It also provides the government with a technical base for health and safety and environmental legislation as well as aiding in transferring technology to developing countries.

219

ISO is a non-government organization and is considered to be the most popular quality standard in the world, which applies to all types of organizations and industries. It is used to ensure organizations follow the path to control quality of product and services, reduce costs associated with poor quality, and to become more competitive in the marketplace. ISO standards, available for a fee, can consist of a four-page document to several hundred pages and each carries the ISO logo, which states "International Standard".

ISO standards are voluntary and are developed for those standards where there are market requirements Even though ISO is considered to be voluntary, some organizations will insist on only doing business with those organizations who are also ISO certified.

Organizations develop a quality system under one of several standards. The organization is governed by a committee of 20 people who are experts in the field of standards. This committee is of global representation and rotates with new members on a structured basis. Over 250 technical committees report to this governing group.

Numerous guidelines exist and carry umbrella designations to cover the numerous global sectors.

One primary classification is the ISO 9000 family of standards for the quality requirements in running a business. It is concerned with quality management such as what an organization does to enhance customer satisfaction by meeting customer requirements and regulations. It's about continually improving performance.

Another classification, the ISO 14000 family of standards, takes a look at environmental challenges primarily concerning environmental management. Again, what the organization does to minimize effects on the environment based on activities performed by the organization and again continually improving its performance. The term "Generic" management systems relates to the same standards which can be applied to any organization no matter what size or what product/service it offers. "Management" system refers to what the organization does to manage its processes or activities.

There are numerous other classifications to govern many key aspects of business including evolving standards for Information Technology.

Standards place a strong emphasis on ensuring an organization's alignment between quality management systems and its processes, and on continuous improvement. The end result is a higher achievement of business and customer satisfaction.

ISO standards specify the requirements for products, services, materials, systems, and managerial and organizational practice. It facilitates trade, spreads knowledge, and shares technology changes/advances, as well as ensuring ecology, safety, economy, and efficiency for all those that are part of the standardization.

From humble beginnings shortly after the Second World War, it has grown into a powerful force helping regulate the global standards.

The benefits of ISO to society are to:
- Businesses—increases productivity and minimizes waste.
- Customer—offers wider choices and benefits from effects of competition among suppliers.
- Consumers—ensures quality, safety, and reliability of products and services.
- Government—provides technology and scientific legislation for health and safety and environmental legislation.
- Trade Officials—provides a level playing field for competitors where political trade agreements can be put into practice.
- Developing countries—provides a source of technology know-how and a basis for making the right decisions as

well as raising the capability to export and compete in global markets.

ISO standards contribute to the quality of life in general and are concerned with the preservation of the environment by way of the quality of air, water, and soil.

ISO is a profitable business investment and not just a certification process. There are eight Quality Management Principles, which provide customers with a higher level of confidence that products will meet their needs and increase satisfaction. These principles focus on the customers/consumer needs, leadership, the involvement of people, the process, and system approach to management, continual improvement, factual approach to decision-making, and mutually beneficial supplier relationships.

Customer satisfaction must be monitored to evaluate that the product/service meets the needs and expectations of the consumer.

ISO standards result in:
- Dependable and reliable products received by customers.
- Increased job satisfaction and better working conditions.
- Increased ROI and profits.
- Supplier's stability and growth in market.
- Improved health and safety.
- Reduced environmental impact.
- Increased security.

In order to become ISO certified, an organization must first determine what processes are to be documented, a decision based on size of the business, type of activities performed, complexity of process and interactions, criticality of process, and available competent personnel. Processes can be described by way of a flow chart, block diagram, responsibility matrix, or the most common method, which is written procedures.

An organization must first identify their process, then implement and measure the process, and finally analyze the process and make improvements where necessary. Process may be explained as set

222

of interacting activities that add value to the organization, whereas a procedure is the way in which all or part of the process is performed.

Once a system is in place, regular internal audits are conducted to ensure the system is working properly, and that you are doing what you say you do. The certification steps are determining which ISO standards are applicable and then developing the management system that meets the standards. Internal audits are then conducted to ensure the process is accurate and being followed. Organizations are externally registered with an accredited auditor who then evaluates the effectiveness of the quality system that is put in place. If an organization passes, a certificate is issued and put on record with ISO.

PDCA Cycle stands for the following:
- **Plan** (what to do and how to do it)
- **Do** (execute the plan)
- **Check** results (did things happen according to plan)
- **Act** to improve the process (how to improve next time)

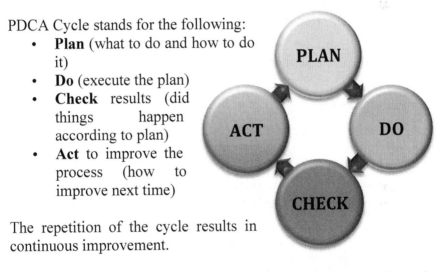

The repetition of the cycle results in continuous improvement.

A Process Owner is responsible for ensuring implementation of the ISO program, as well as maintenance and improvement of the process and interactions.

Auditors can be external or internal but either way should be able to demonstrate competence in the structure, content, and terminology of the standards and be able to understand the organization's activities and processes.

A lack of standardization can affect the quality of life. Standardized performance exists on safety requirements of equipment, allowing manufactures to design based on specific needs. Standardized symbols provide danger warnings and information, consensus on grades of various materials and give common reference for suppliers and business dealings. Standardized documents speed up transit of goods and identify sensitive or dangerous goods.

ISO enhances customer satisfaction by meeting customer and applicable regulatory requirements. Future ISO standards pertain to the environment (new program for greenhouse gas verification), service sectors (finance services, market opinion and tourism), security (freight transport, countering illegal trafficking) and good managerial and or practice (social responsibility).

MRP / ERP

The acronym MRP is often used (almost interchangeably) as "Manufacturing Requirements Planning " or "Manufacturing Resource(s) Planning". The term "Enterprise Resource Planning" (ERP) is directly related but is often used to signify a much broader and all-encompassing process that spans the total organization. The principles of all three are quite similar and all three are heavily dependent on the norms for today—a fully integrated database (certainly for ERP and the more sophisticated versions of MRP).

MRP started out decades ago as a hand-planning tool that used spreadsheets to plan production and ensure that materials (and labor and ingredients) could be in the right place at the right time. This also encompassed inventory control and mechanisms for operating with significantly reduced inventories.

There are basically three principles involved in establishing and using a fully functional MRP system:

1. Ensure that products and materials are available for customer delivery and for the production process steps on a timely "as needed" basis.
2. The system must allow a detailed view of inventories so that the lowest level of inventory can be maintained at all times.
3. The above needs are met through a detailed planning and control process.

The process functions by constantly asking and answering (through the system technology and the database) three questions:
- What items are required?
- How many items are required?
- When are they required?

Correct use of MRP gives two consistent outputs that become the focus of attention in the production execution process. One is a "recommended production schedule" and the other is a "recommended purchasing schedule".

Of the many challenges in operating a well-integrated and fully developed MRP system, the two most significant are the forecast and the accuracy of the data. Forecast variations are one of the biggest challenges in running an MRP system since forecast changes require adjustments to the planning schedules and to the materials schedules. The more these change for any reason—internal or external—the more variability the MRP process generates and the less accurate the whole process becomes. The second challenge is data accuracy, for without data accuracy the MRP system can only deliver as well as the input provided. This is one of the many areas in our data driven world where "garbage in" most certainly provides "garbage out".

Enterprise Resource Planning, as noted above, is a more fully integrated version of MRP but covers all facets of the whole organization. Here the intent is to have ALL the corporate data integrated on one database in a real time interactive mode. That means that as anyone anywhere is using the system the data that they are using is the very most current data that was updated literally the second before they chose to handle the transaction that they are handling. While this may have been a challenge some time ago, today it is taken for granted.

To be a fully integrated ERP system the MRP system must also cover all key accounting functions as well as the payroll functions. So, in addition to those items noted for MRP (manufacturing and supply chain management), ERP also has financials, human resources, customer relationship management, and projects. All of this is managed from one central data warehouse (the source of all the real time information required for the system to function).

A fully integrated MRP system and a well-implemented ERP system is a powerful tool, which can effectively be used to manage and effect a culture change program. Some current global vendors play a high stakes game to be the preferred service supplier for Enterprise Resource Planning—SAP is certainly among one of the global leaders in this field.

Chapter 13. Useful tools or techniques to tackle specific problems

This chapter discusses useful tools that can be used in isolation to tackle specific problems or opportunities. These techniques are unlikely to be used as culture change tools. These are categorized as "C" in the Corporate Culture Change Management Tools table above.

Visualizing

A useful tool used in the right context, but not a leading contender for the culture change driver.

This tool is somewhat similar to Greenfielding (described in Chapter 12). Here the key technique is to start literally with a clean sheet of paper. The starting point is "nothing". The purpose of the process is to create a totally objective, dispassionate, and detached model of what the ideal organization could be, given the implied constraints and the directional intent of the corporate mission. The process should leave absolutely nothing unchallenged.

The process requires the model to be developed in great detail using various techniques to build the ideal people structure for all aspects of the organization, the ideal information technology platform, and all the attributes that would be required for the perfect organization. Tools that assist in this process include Zero Based Budgeting to optimize the financial resources, an environmental analysis to evaluate all the best elements within the company and specifically needed for the new structure, and a S.W.O.T. (strengths, weaknesses, opportunities, threats) analysis to determine the greatest prospective strengths and opportunities along with a rigorous assessment of the weaknesses and threats with clearly defined prospective actions to substantially eliminate their influences.

As these tools start to unfold the detail of the anticipated outcome, the cultural impact and intent also needs to be shaped. For this, the style and structure of the organization needs to be planned.

- How will authority be handled (with what freedom and with how much delegation)?
- What will the organization structure look like?
- In what space and environment will it be housed?
- What sort of image would it ideally present?
- What would be the ideal job definitions, skill sets, recruiting and training standards, benefits, and rewards?
- What will be the key communication tools and the mechanisms?
- Finally, what will be the influence on the corporate mission and how will the outcome create a superior end result?

I have only ever used this tool in a limited way for a divisional structure within an organization. The tool is very much an intellectual exercise and requires careful facilitation and an extensive amount of time and thinking to achieve the desired result. Patience is a key word here, since this is not only a very esoteric tool but the outcome also becomes a very intellectually based summary of the team's expectations. Translating this into meaningful structure and actions is a challenge because the process speculates on the outcome of human interactions in a series of dynamic business situations. These outcomes rarely follow the ideals of a theoretical model.

There are two sisters to this tool. One I have used very successfully many times is the process of Greenfielding (described above). The other is Imagineering. The significant difference and the reason that the sister tools are stronger is that they both deal with more tangible things. Greenfielding and Imagineering each deal only with the "hard" structure of the organization. In the case of Greenfielding it deals with the bricks and mortar and the physical assets. The Imagineering process deals with a specific set of expectations within a defined structure—it is focused on the delivery of ideas. This makes the process much less subjective and far more objective (and quantifiable) for both of these tools.

Training

A very important tool but not ideal for change management. Every well-run company must have this staple in place.

While training today is an important tool that is widely used, it is really only an important maintenance tool—a tool that is used to orient new people and for the introduction of new things to ensure that everything is done in a consistent way. It is difficult to make training a culture change tool and we would not recommend it for that purpose

At one point, employers believed training was for new employees only but the reality is that training can be beneficial to all employees when warranted. Employee development is the responsibility of both the employee and the employer. The employer needs to ensure the support of growth and learning when employees bring to their attention areas where they feel they can use improvement. Training can build a more efficient and highly motivated team and aid in promotions within the organization when the employer is aware of the employee's potential to advance. Determining what the employee needs to be successful and grow is key to the success and growth of the employee and the organization. Benefits to training include increased productivity and efficiency resulting in higher revenues, reduced employee turnover, and decreased need for continuous supervision.

Training needs are usually determined through the employee appraisal process or performance review. To identify training needs, it's best to begin by analyzing the organization as a whole, then analyze by each job characteristic and finally by the needs of the employees. This will help in determining who needs the training and what must an employee specifically learn to be more productive and successful in her or his role. There is no point in training everyone across the organization if only a select group of employees require it. This would result in de-motivating those that don't need the training and will have a negative impact in the training sessions.

Ensure the organization is willing to commit to supporting the training efforts financially. Once the budget and training need are determined, the next step is to establish the precise content of the training, who should administer/facilitate it, where should it be held, and how long a session is required (four hours, one to two days, or more).

Prior to training commencement, make sure employees are clear on the purpose of the training. Training objectives are established based on the organization's goals and objectives and the determined skill gap of those attending. When administering training, take into consideration the location, facilities, accessibility, comfort of the room (windows, seating, and space to move about), equipment required, and timing of the training. The learning environment must be safe and informal, show respect to those that are learning as well as the trainer, and promote positive self-esteem.

The training method must be decided on, dependent on the budget and content of the training itself. Training may be on the job or off the job. On the job training is administered (no surprise) while the employee is doing her or his job. Off the job training consists of lectures, conferences, case studies, role-playing, and programmed instruction. Use the "who, what, and why" technique to determine the best method of training.

On the job a supervisor or manager usually conducts training and off the job an outside trainer provides training. In house training is the daily responsibility of supervisors who should be knowledgeable in the best training techniques in order to effectively administer good training. Supervisors should also be aware of how adults learn differently and have effective ways of communicating with the trainees.

230

Courses, workshops, and seminars can be the more cost effective approach and an experienced and qualified trainer usually facilitates a larger group. One drawback is that this method of training can result in one-way communication and it can sometimes be difficult to determine if all participants are getting the same message.

Role-playing brings realistic situations to the employee's attention and has them work through scenarios they could typically face while working. It gives real world experiences.

Audio-visual training, such as videos/movies and computer based/e-learning, can be accomplished in a shorter time span, and the same message is given each time no matter how many times it is viewed and who is administering the training. However, it doesn't allow for interaction with others or question and answer sessions. Employees can learn at their own speed and this can be the most cost effective method of them all.

Apprenticeships are also a useful technique for training. It gives exposure to different tasks/roles and this method is especially useful for production skills. The administrator of the training can evaluate what was learned and then how it's being used on the job.

Coaching and mentoring provide feedback and guidance while the employee gets to practice the new skills obtained. Usually a more senior person gives guidance to a more junior person or those lacking in the particular skill gap.

Training should be interactive by finding ways to integrate group exercise. The knowledge learned needs to be connected to real life work experiences. This can be reinforced by way of observing that what a trainee has learned is being practiced on the job.

Outside training sources are available such as consultants, technical and vocational schools, and continuing education. These organizations are well versed in training techniques and can customize the training material to the organization's goals and objectives. Disadvantages to using an outside training provider are that they may have a limited knowledge of an organization's product or service, and costs can be higher compared to in-house trainers.

No matter what method is used when administering training, know the organization's goals and objectives and the skill gap that has been established. Select only those that require the training and choose the best method of administration. Be sure to evaluate whether the end result is in line with the training objective. Ask for the participant's feedback on both the courses and the trainer.

Participative Management

This can be a change tool but is tough to do well. It's too dependent on the leadership characteristics—but if you get the right leadership to head up the action then anything is possible.

A Participative Management style is the most open, straightforward, and non-political approach that one can take within a company. The style is just as described—participative. Everyone has a role, everyone has a contribution, everyone has a say. The leadership that propagates this process is equally and totally comfortable and in tune with the requirements of this approach—and it's not as easy as it may sound.

For this style to work, the senior management has to be approachable, open, trustworthy, and prepared to be candid about anything and everything. The leadership best suited to this style is often a very aware individual—someone who clearly sees and reads well what is going on around them. They usually do not have a big ego and are often relatively humble in terms of the position and the status that they hold. They are people who will take the time to sit and talk about any and all of the issues that may need to be covered.

That is not to say they indulge in the frivolous and the time wasting detail of things that are not relevant—far from it. These people are focused and generally have their priorities and the priorities of the others that they need to manage well in sight. They are often unwavering without being dogmatic. They are usually decisive without making the decisions for their subordinates. They manage their staff without micro-managing what their staff does. They know what is going on because they pay attention to enough of the detail to have the picture clear. They listen to what they are told and advised. They also spend the right amount of time "managing by walking around". They are astute enough to be able to read clearly what is going on in almost every situation that they come across. They are smart politicians without being unduly political themselves. These people tend to be business-like in their communication yet are prepared to (and do) spend the time to listen and remember some of the key personal detail of what their staff is going through (both inside and outside the office).

The participative manager is assertive while maintaining respect. They consistently ensure that others know the needs and expectations of the organization, they exercise communication skills that motivate through respect and enthusiasm, they create meaningful work and work requirements, and they recognize and act as if all employees are important and not just a variable cost commodity.

Their style is to be dedicated, be supportive, be visible, be worthy of respect, and be trusted. They allow others to learn from mistakes, they balance the individual's needs and rights with those of the company, and they develop ethical relationships and business practices.

They bring excellence because they focus on results not activities; they design "flat" (non-hierarchical) organizations to maximize involvement, discussion, and feedback. They also plan more, "do" less, and delegate more. They keep a clear focus on the purpose or the goal, they spend time with others (over 50% of their time), they build networks, and they have many short conversations every day with many people. They are friendly, open, approachable, and business-like, they ask open-ended questions, they are active listeners, and they set attainable goals and allow their people to set their own sub-goals. They also keep a mental score card and remind you of your "wins" (note: not the losses) and they create a positive self-image.

On one occasion I was part way through the transition of a culture in anarchy at one of the production units that I had inherited when I joined this company. I needed to move this organization to the next level of control and cooperation. I needed a genuine and very capable "participative manager" to replace the hard driving disciplinarian that I had used in the two prior years to get the operating unit back under control. We had control re-established but at a different price (from the original "out of control anarchy")—we had mushroomed to eighty-seven outstanding grievances from a union who for years had had total control over the operating unit and the management.

After much searching I found what proved to be a perfect General Manager for this unit. In the context of Corporate Culture, the individual I found was a leader of stature and substance. He exemplified the style of a participative manager. He was a natural manager, a clear leader with a sufficiently outgoing personality that he became the focal point of that factory. As such, he became the icon that set the tone and the standard of the Corporate Culture for that location.

His style was distinctive and influential enough that he created a more memorable leadership role, which over time supplanted that of the nearby company headquarters (who previously tried to exert a lot of influence—unsuccessfully). The presence of the corporate senior management just a fifteen-minute drive away became secondary in the confines of that location. In the context of Corporate Culture this is not unusual. The top figures in a local operating unit are usually the ones to set the standard. The corporate influence tends to provide uniformity through policy, procedures, budgets, and reporting formality, and thereby exerts its influence. It is, however, the local leadership that shapes the local Corporate Culture. When you look at the above attributes and characteristics of leadership through a participative management style, this individual could run a scorecard and have almost every one of the characteristics checked off as a positive.

Needless to say, within another two years we had turned around a disaster (which in its history could boast the longest strike ever recorded globally for the parent company) to a unit that consistently ranked as one of the top three global manufacturing units for product quality and factory productivity. This success was indeed an enviable record. Much of the credit had to go to one of the best "participative managers" that I ever had as part of my management team.

S.W.O.T. Analysis

Another strong and very useful management tool—but again not powerful enough to warrant being used as a Culture Change tool.

S.W.O.T. stands for Strengths, Weaknesses, Opportunities, and Threats. This very effective tool has a lot of value in any organization and should be a part of every manager's tool chest. The tool is easy to use and it generates clear information with the prospect of clear (potential) outcomes being deliverable (and often deliverable relatively quickly).

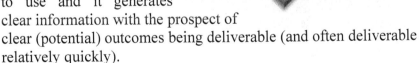

The process is based on a "brainstorming" exercise, which is conducted by an appropriate group of senior people using little more than a white board or flip chart to record the outcomes.

The people

The group must consist of any and all of the people who know enough of the detail and have enough of the "high level" picture to be the required contributors. The group also needs to have a sufficiently detailed knowledge of how their business processes work to be able to keep things in context. The group will not do well if the large proportion are from the lower to middle level management ranks since these people know the business process but often do not see the bigger picture (because they are not exposed to it) on a regular basis. The group also needs to be broad enough to cover the whole business perspective (all functions required to help solve the problems need to be represented). Finally, the group cannot be too large since the process will become unwieldy and complex, though as many as 12 to 15 people are not too many.

The process

The S.W.O.T. process requires a definition of the problem or problems that you are trying to solve. The definition must be general enough to allow far ranging and "out of the box" thinking without being too vague. For example, "our business is doing badly—what should we do to fix it?" is too vague, whereas "our business is struggling in this and that area and is strong over here" is more helpful. The trick is to make statements of fact about what you are trying to solve and not provide directive information. It is usually best if the most senior people in the group allow someone else to present the problem on their behalf (in the most neutral terms possible).

From this point of definition a classical brainstorming can proceed. The forum is open, nothing is stupid, nothing is disallowed, and absolutely nothing is explained, amplified, or challenged. It is raw brainstorming thoughts that flow and each one stimulates the next one. Ideas are categorized under one of the four S.W.O.T. headings. All four headings need to be on the board since ideas will often bounce from one heading to the other. No attempt should be made to prioritize them at this stage.

Once the brainstorming has exhausted the ideas then comes time for clarification, discussion, and prioritizing. This is a very important part of the process and often the discussion and clarification of the various ideas lead to more items that should sit on the list. This is healthy and appropriate. At this stage it is still important not to jump into the prioritization and action modes since a thorough understanding of all aspects of the ideas is essential. Once all the clarifications are noted, prioritization can begin. Often this is relatively straightforward and is also often split in part across several functions.

From the conclusion of this step a detailed action and follow-up plan can be completed and assigned for action and delivery.

Within the a week or so from the session it is helpful to reconvene the group and determine whether the "cold light of day" does indeed confirm the thoughts and priorities as correct and appropriate. Regular review at the "executive committee" meetings can keep the program and its expectations on track.

There is another variation to this process, which can be used more widely and down to a lower level in the organization.

In another forum (or one of several if the intent is to include many people from all parts of the organization) go through the same basic set up program as noted above and allow the same brainstorming process to develop. When you choose to span a larger part of the organization the detail that emerges is often slightly different. When assessing the Strengths and Weaknesses there tends to be more of a focus on the internal aspects of the organization such as people, structure, systems, policies, and procedures. The Threats and Opportunities side of the picture often creates a more external focus such as customers, suppliers, markets, products and product positioning, and competitors. In this process it can be useful to analyze the cause and effect relationships among the factors that emerge from the brainstorming process. The more objective the analysis, the more sound the cause related remedial solutions will be.

In my experience of using this tool at both levels, I have found that the senior management approach often results in a more uniform mix of internal and external factors in all four headings whereas using the tool at the lower levels often creates the sort of internal versus external focus between the strengths and weakness side versus the opportunities and threats side. In other words, senior management bring a broader perspective to each of the four headings whereas lower levels of management tend to see things from a closer perspective. In my opinion this is due to the senior group often thinking and dealing with strategic matters on a more routine basis and lower management dealing with tactical matters.

Succinct Measurements

Succinct measurements is a simple process whereby the company management chooses several key metrics that are essential to the organization's success. These metrics need to cover the essentials of what the operation makes or delivers. The metrics must be easily measured and also easily understood by the employees so that everyone can see if they are on track with the improvements and are under control.

The keys are:
- Simplicity. Do not have too many metrics—they become confusing and therefore meaningless.
- Measurability. They must be easily measured and be somewhat intuitive for the people involved. (If they are too complicated then they are not understood and it takes too long to generate useful data.)
- Readability. They must be easily displayed and put on a graph so people can see the progress (or setbacks).

The metrics often need to be departmental but don't use more than one or two per department since the amalgamation of the data becomes too convoluted and the bigger picture of the organization's progress gets lost.

Anonymous Key Weakness List

Another very useful management tool—but nowhere near powerful enough to warrant being used as a Culture Change tool.

This is a variation on the S.W.O.T. analysis with two distinct differences. First, it must be done with a larger group (otherwise anonymity cannot easily be delivered) and secondly—just that—it must be anonymous. The second part of this process, which makes it unique, is that it only focuses on the negatives. But, having put that into context, it can also be a relatively speedy process. It does not require a lot of preparation or analysis. It is almost a "back of an envelope" process that can deliver some useful insights and some interesting consensus on what really needs to be fixed (and that will make a distinct difference).

To deliver the process, each participant is asked to provide a list of the ten most pressing weaknesses, not nine or eleven but ten. They must not be in rank order—preferably a random list. A neutral facilitator who can assemble the lists into the final review summary must serve the process.

The facilitator then sets up a review forum with all the participants and takes the random and now shuffled list (so that even the random lists are not easily recognized) and puts them up for discussion and prioritization.

A lot of discussion is needed since no one "owns" the item and is therefore not speaking to the item or defending its existence. This discussion process is often very helpful since it exposes what one person sees as a problem to everyone and all get involved (or at least hear) the outcome. There will also be a large number of items on the list that will be difficult to explain since the item may not be clear in what it intends to communicate. The initiator may be reluctant to speak to the item since by doing so (depending on the nature of the item) they become identified.

After extensive discussion and when a consensus-based summary of the conclusions and prioritization has been reached, an action plan can be formulated. This outcome should be reviewed widely through the organization. This often provides quite a lot of positive reaction since—if done well—the employees will acknowledge that the list was real, had substance, and yes, senior management actually does know what is going on and is not asleep at the switch.

Once again, follow up with commitment, actions, and reviews until the desired outcomes have been achieved.

360° Employee Feedback

A 360° feedback questionnaire or survey is a process intended to assist with employee development and to improve skills based on feedback provided by colleagues. The objective of this process is to provide insight; therefore it is important that all questions be answered truthfully and for colleagues not to make the assessment more "attractive". Only a frank and fair perspective of the individual's skills will be useful, as honest feedback will provide the individual with information regarding performance and ensures the person is heading in the right direction within their job/role.

The purpose of the 360° is to measure an employee's performance, knowledge, skills, and abilities. This process is not to be used to replace any existing performance management program but to enhance the system by providing colleagues the opportunity to provide their perspective as well. The 360° seeks input from several people who have a relationship or who have regular contact with the employee being assessed. In other words, it's not necessarily colleagues from the employee's own department who may be providing the assessment but colleagues from other departments may be asked to complete the questionnaire or survey in order to provide insight from a variety of sources. Typically management is the only one evaluating an employee's performance, but implementing the 360° Employee Feedback tool minimizes the halo effect, when management is no longer the only appraiser to evaluate performance.

A 360° program can be a productive tool if phased in gradually, starting with one department and working through the kinks or errors first, then moving to the next department. The advantages of using a 360° program are:

- Increased involvement of employees at all levels.
- Direct reports and peers evaluate rather than just managers.
- Employees can better manage their career and performance.
- Reduced discrimination based on race, age, gender, or other factors.

It is important to ensure that a 360° program fits into the culture of the organization and that it isn't something the company is just doing because it's "trendy". For this program to be successful it must first have full employee acceptance. The evaluators completing the 360° survey or questionnaire are typically the employee's manager/supervisor, peers/colleagues, direct reports, customers/clients, suppliers, and/or vendors. Employees should be encouraged to actively participate but also be given the opportunity to voice opinions and concerns regarding the process and its results. It's not always easy for others to be open and frank about someone else's performance, skills, and abilities, as no one wants to hurt anyone's feelings.

Employees should be respectful and sensitive when providing feedback; therefore it is critical to have the process explained to them in full detail prior to completion of the questionnaire or survey. Only an accurate and fair perspective can be useful. Evaluators should be careful not to provide information or detail that may identify who the evaluator was in order for all results to remain confidential. The final report does not identify the evaluators as all responses are compiled into one report, which is given to the employee and manager to review together in alignment with the employee's personal and professional goals and objectives.

When implementing this program in any size organization, it must be consistent among all employees and administered frequently. Evaluating over a period of time provides employees with development benchmarks in relation to their current job and career goals.

Completing this program one time is not effective and will not accurately measure anyone's performance. Therefore, conduct this program at least three to five times a year. If the 360° is not rolled out correctly, it can cause turmoil within the organization by reducing morale, destroying motivation, and could potentially result in employees seeking revenge.

Evaluators are randomly selected from the pool of colleagues by way of email, allowing time to complete the questionnaire or survey at their convenience within a certain time period (typically 2 weeks). A summary report of all responses is provided to the employee and the direct manager/supervisor. The report contains only compiled data so it is impossible to know the exact source of any comments or the results. The goal of this process is to generate a comprehensive report that will assist both the individual and their manager/supervisor to better understand how the employee is doing within their current role, what the job requires of them, and where improvement is needed. All responses are confidential and feedback obtained from the questionnaires or surveys are only presented to the individual and their manager/supervisor for discussion and follow-up to determine action plans for training and/or development.

The process of the 360° is viewed by many companies as fair and complete, which has increased its utilization over the years due to full acceptance of this tool by employees and managers alike.

True Colors™

Don Lowry founded True Colors in 1978. Lowry wanted to give the world an avenue to enhance the way we live, work, communicate, and interact with those around us. Since its conception, True Colors is widely used throughout the United States, Canada, Latin America, the United Kingdom, as well as parts of Asia.

True Colors is a blend of education and entertainment. Lowry believed the most effective and appealing way to present this idea was to make it entertaining. When people are relaxed and entertained, they are less restricted in new ideas and in participating. Lowry was successful in developing a fundamental and universal way to provide guidelines that are easily understood and applied in everyday life—at home or at work.

True Colors identifies four different temperament styles, each with its own strengths. Lowry felt that breaking down temperament into these styles would be the easiest and most convenient way of understanding and appreciating human behavior. Each participant in the exercise is given four cards, Blue, Gold, Green, and Orange, each one representing a personality type.

The front of the card is a visual aid—a colorful depiction of humans engaged in activity, and surrounded by various symbols. The cards are entertaining and pleasing to the eye. Participants are given time to review the front of each card, and are then asked to put each card in order based solely on the pictures they see on the front of the card. The picture that seems most like them is rated 4, 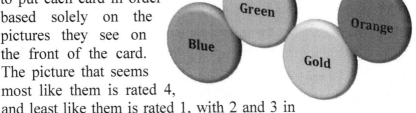 and least like them is rated 1, with 2 and 3 in the middle. Their response is recorded on a score sheet.

Step two consists of participants reading about traits of each type on the back of each color card and again arranging the cards in order of most like to least like themselves, using the same rating process as above and recording their answers on the score sheet.

Step three has participants look at groupings of words. They are asked to score each group of words assigning a 4 for the group of words that seem most like them, 3 for second, 2 for third choice and 1 for least like them.

The fourth and final step is to total each column on the score sheet. The highest score indicates the person's primary, or brightest color and the lowest score represents the color least like them. Most people have a color spectrum, which consists of a dominant colour, influenced by the others.

Here is a brief overview of the four True Colors temperament styles:

Blue

Blue people are imaginative, enthusiastic, and can do almost anything that is of interest to them. They are at ease with colleagues and others enjoy their presence. They are highly creative in dealing with people and are outstanding at inspiring others.

Blues have remarkable latitude in career choices and they succeed in many fields. They prefer a family-oriented and personalized work environment. They dislike jobs that require detail and follow through over a long period of time. They prefer people-oriented jobs that allow creativity and a variety of tasks. They make excellent school counsellors, therapists, and human resource professionals.

Green

Greens are most reluctant to do things in the traditional manner. They are always looking for the next project or new activity. They are entrepreneurs and like to work for themselves. They can succeed in a variety of occupations as long as the job doesn't become too routine. Greens are inquisitive and will ask 'why'. They tend to lose interest when the job is no longer a challenge to them.

Greens contribute immensely to a work environment that allows independence and freedom of expression. They are successful at various occupations such as medical researcher, attorney, artist, or chemist, to name a few.

Gold

Gold people are realistic and curious about new products and ideas. They perform best when following guidelines and regulations. They prefer a work environment where duties and responsibilities are well defined and they can be rewarded for their efforts and loyalty. They are considered to be neat, orderly, and dependable employees.

Occupational choices for a Gold include teacher, occupational therapist, or administrator.

Orange

Orange people are action oriented and are considered to be risk takers who love excitement and trying new things. Having to follow rules and regulations stifles an Orange. They need to be able to contribute in a creative manner using their energy to get the job done.

Orange people make excellent artists, professional coaches, and public speakers.

In examining a person's True Colors, we investigate the various communication styles for each temperament, our personal values, and what others should be aware of when we are each out our comfort zone.

We each have all four of these color groups within us. It is our particular blend that makes us unique. By understanding our colors, and the colors of those around us, we begin to build stronger and more effective teams. Each personality type analyzes, conceptualizes, understands, interacts, and learns differently. We are able to draw on the strengths of those around us in areas we may be lacking. It can help us see the positive qualities of family, friends, and of those we work with.

In 2008 Erica Lowry expanded the concept to True Colors 24, which considers each color in order, in each person's True Colors spectrum. This expanded process can help in understanding of how one's primary strengths and values are "shaded" by their secondary, and tertiary strengths and values.

True Colors is a process of understanding how one person may think or react to a situation differently than you do. This results in breaking down walls and preventing barriers when trying to understand others and most of all, having fun.

Chapter 14.   Job Descriptions: What Exactly is it that You Do?

"Suzanne was dumbfounded when she saw that her job description included picking up her boss's dry cleaning…" And it does still happen!

Definition of job description:

> Written outcome or document of the process of examining a job in an organization and determining the knowledge, skills, and abilities associated with successful performance of the job.

OR

> A collection of information describing the overall responsibilities, specific accountabilities and measurements, as well as competencies and proficiency required to successfully fulfil a particular job.

By itself, the existence of job descriptions throughout the organization is not a Corporate Culture change tool. But it is an essential prerequisite to a healthy and well functioning Corporate Culture.

From an employee / employer relationship perspective, job descriptions can be the greatest asset in which an organization can invest. When job descriptions are created and put in place, they can be and are used for many reasons such as hiring and recruitment, training and development, promotions and succession planning. Job descriptions are also used to establish salary ranges and wages, benchmarking comparisons in the market with competitors and in correcting skill gaps. They are a great communication tool between a manager and employee when determining job performance and evaluation.

No matter what size organization you have or are working for, each position within the company should have a job description associated with it.

A job description provides an understanding of the employee's responsibilities and how their role fits into the overall structure of the organization. It also provides understanding to the adjacent employee's job and function within the organization. To put it another way employees in adjacent or related functions have a clearer idea of their role versus the roles of their colleagues. It can enhance employee engagement and productivity.

Typically, a job description specifies the job duties, along with the skills, knowledge, and abilities required for an employee to be successful in the role. It should not list the credentials or years of experience required, as this can end up placing barriers around the role and can create challenges when promoting from within the organization. Credentials and qualifications are usually determined during the recruitment process and would be listed in a job posting.

Every culture has negative and positive qualities, so assess your current environment. Look at elements in favor of a new employee's success and those that work against the employee. Employees will discover the negative elements on their own (within the first couple of weeks), so show how the positives outweigh the negatives. Identify critical objectives and/or responsibilities of the new employee and focus on the development of those. Identify goals with timetables and assign a mentor as well as arrange for early successes—if possible, something that is related closely to the former job held by the new employee. Provide support but don't over delegate, and don't expect significant results too soon.

Management also needs to overcome any resentment of "bypassed" employees who didn't get the job due to an "outsider" being offered the job over a current employee. Openness in advising the participants will help to defuse any resentment towards the new hire, and counteract possible unjust criticism and refusals to cooperate.

Job Descriptions and Career Planning

Job descriptions identify common job elements (*e.g.* an accountant is required to be accurate when completing trial balances or a payroll clerk must ensure all employee hours are recorded correctly to avoid over or under paying an individual) so that job levels can be structured for career development. When an organization is looking to promote from within, or create a succession plan for a certain role, job descriptions can aid in the evaluation and readiness of an employee stepping into someone else's shoes. They are also a critical tool for determining an employee's performance levels and coordinating the achievement of their career goals.

Job Descriptions and Recruiting

Recruiters generally use job descriptions more than management does. Management often views this tool as being inaccurate and lacking information. This can be true if job descriptions aren't reviewed and updated regularly.

When recruiting and filling vacant positions within an organization, job descriptions are a valuable tool. The requirements of the job as outlined in the job description are used to create a job posting. The actual job description itself is usually given to the candidate when an offer of employment is being made. All employees should be given a copy of their job description in order to prevent an employee later returning to their manager and stating in their review that they weren't aware of a particular responsibility being part of their job. The following story outlines one concern a new recruit had once he started working for a particular organization.

During the hiring process, the Recruiter had shared with all candidates the highlights of the responsibilities that were involved in being successful at the job. This included providing general labor assistance when instructed such as cleaning up debris, sweeping floors, etc. Although the new hire was provided a copy of the job description as part of the company's orientation program, it wasn't until the new hire had been working on the job for several weeks that he approached the Recruiter and expressed his concern that he was finding himself having to complete many general labor type functions during the course of the day. The Recruiter explained to the employee that this was indeed part of the role he had accepted and this was clearly outlined during the interview process and documented on the job description itself. After the employee re-read the job description, he had a better understanding of what was required of him.

The individual was now aware of this responsibility, but the Recruiter revised the orientation process to ensure job descriptions would be reviewed again with all new hires on the first day of employment. All job tasks were to be clearly defined during the review of the job description and new hires were to be told what percentage of time on the job would be spent performing general labor tasks. To prevent this issue from recurring with future new recruits, all employees were asked to sign a copy of the job description stating they have read and understand the responsibilities and that all questions or concerns have been addressed.

Job descriptions allow recruiters and management to match people to the activities. Recruiters will look at all the elements of the position when making decisions such as hiring. Management will use this tool to determine whether someone should be promoted. Elements that should be looked at include whether the employee is required to work with others or individually, or is the job technical in nature? Would the person be dealing with data or performing simple and repetitive tasks? These are all things to consider when filling a vacant role and having that job description in hand will assist in making final choices.

Job Descriptions and Compensation

Organizations also use job descriptions to compare compensation and salary ranges with their competitors. This can assist in gaining equity in compensation and market comparisons—are you paying what the job is worth? This is critical when it comes to employee retention.

The use of job descriptions to determine salary levels can assist management in explaining any decisions to others such as shareholders, government associations, employment lawyers, or unions. It can aid in defending choices that are made when setting salary levels, during recruitment initiatives, or when handling grievances and other legal actions.

Creating a Job Description

Creating job descriptions for all roles within an organization is a worthwhile investment, but many organizations don't use job descriptions—perhaps because they have just never been created and put in place. Job descriptions can be very time consuming to create so people may be reluctant to undertake the process. Writing a job description can take anywhere from one hour to two weeks to finalize.

The benefits of writing job descriptions are not quickly and easily seen, but having this tool in place offers tremendous rewards in the long run. Job descriptions help to manage employees' expectations, and provide an understanding of where and how each position fits into the organizational structure.

Job descriptions must be clear and well written. There are software packages on the market that can aid in the creation of job descriptions but the best way to determine what an employee does is still by interviewing and observing the employee while at work.

The first step in creating a job description is to gather all the required information such as recruiting materials, comments and observations from management and employees, and then determine gaps in training and development and any additional data as required.

The most favorable method of compiling information in order to create a job description is to interview the employee. The employee should be encouraged to keep a diary for up to three weeks, detailing the job responsibilities, specific accountabilities, measures, and competencies they feel are required to be successful in the role. This should provide a clear and concise picture of the role. It is also a good idea to interview the employee when reviewing the diary notes and probe to get further information or to clarify points made. As a follow up to this stage, also interview the employee's manager to clarify any inconsistencies that might arise. Keep in mind that perceptions of responsibilities may differ between employee and manager. At times, the employee may assume responsibilities and authorities that are often not theirs.

The more accurate and specific a job description, the more likely employees will be to perform at their best.

Another method often used to gather information on an employee's position is to have the employee complete a questionnaire, which may contain questions such as:
1. What is the basic purpose of the job? Why does it exist?
2. What are the key responsibilities you perform and how much time is spent on these tasks daily/weekly/monthly? (Primary responsibilities typically consist of four to eight core tasks.)
3. What are the secondary responsibilities and time spent performing these tasks?
4. What type of equipment, technology, or materials is required to perform on the job?
5. How frequently is the equipment, technology, or material used on the job?

252

6. What does the work environment consist of? (Outside, indoors, noisy, etc.)
7. What physical demands are put on you to perform the task? (Heavy lifting, repetitive hand motions, etc.)
8. Who assigns the task and in what way? (Verbally, written, etc.)
9. Who reviews the tasks once performed and how frequently?
10. Do you supervise others and if so how many people? What are their job titles?
11. Are you responsible for making key decisions? What decisions would be referred to your manager?
12. Are any records kept and if so what, and how are they recorded?
13. If you were promoted, what skills, knowledge, and abilities would your replacement require?
14. In order for someone to take over your position due to a promotion or transfer, how long would you estimate it would take someone to become fully trained to do this job?

There may be other appropriate questions, depending on the particular job.

When writing out the actual job description, keep sentences and/or bullets brief and clear, putting emphasis on active verbs as outlined in the chart below. Keep in mind the essential skills that the person must have *vs.* the ideal skills or "nice to have" skills.

Each responsibility should start with an action verb to describe the activity. Commonly used verbs include:

Advise	Clarify	Direct
Analyze	Conduct	Estimate
Appraise	Control	Evaluate
Approve	Coordinate	Expedite
Assign	Counsel	Formulate
Authorize	Demonstrate	Input
Check	Develop	Inspect

Instruct	Organize	Review
Interpret	Perform	Schedule
Investigate	Plan	Supervise
Maintain	Present	Train
Manage	Recommend	Verify
Operate	Resolve	

Job duties are usually listed in order of importance and sometimes have a weight or percentage associated with each task. For example, "conducts job interviews with potential candidates— 30%". Avoid using "trendy" terminology that can become outdated. For example, the term "on-boarding" has been used in some organizations as a replacement for "orientation". If necessary, provide an example of the responsibility to avoid misinterpretations.

Job descriptions must also be consistent in format right across the organization. Therefore, it is best to create a standard template that can be used by the HR team or department heads.

Template headings may include:

- Job Title and reporting structure.
- Job purpose—why does it exist?
- Bullet points of primary responsibilities—usually four to eight tasks—and percentage of time spent performing tasks.
- Secondary responsibilities and percentage of time spent performing task.
- Supervisory responsible and number of people and titles— if applicable.
- Financial responsibilities—if applicable.
- Organizational unit—how it connects with other departments.
- Physical demands of the job.
- Working conditions and environment.
- Knowledge and skill requirements.

Job descriptions need to be more than just the paper they are written on or a document that is kept in a file or binder in the HR office that is given out to new recruits. Employees must know what is expected of them in order to perform to their fullest potential.

As a management tool, job descriptions should be actively used and updated regularly to remain current with trends, equipment and technology changes, and the needs of the company. The average age of a job description is two years. Unfortunately some organizations don't update them as often, and many could be as old as eight years. Job descriptions should be updated at least once a year, and up to four times a year. This adds structure to the position. Any revisions should be discussed between the manager and the employee and agreed upon in writing.

A good time to review the job description is during an employee's performance review. This will ensure that goals and performance are aligned with the role based on the outline provided. If after reviewing the performance the job description is out of alignment, revise it.

A job description that is clearly written gives purpose and direction to the employee. It enables the employee to be more successful within their role, thereby making the company more successful with higher productivity and positive results in performance. A poorly written job description can result in a lack of communications, decrease in motivation to succeed, and confusion as to what is expected of the employee.

Again, job descriptions are not a Corporate Culture change tool but their existence is a critical "housekeeping" item within the organization for the many reasons outlined above. So if you still aren't convinced that you need to implement job descriptions in your organization or that perhaps the ones that exist need to be reviewed, ask yourself the following questions:

1. Do you have/use job descriptions in your organization?

2. When was the last time these were reviewed and revised?

3. What are you looking to use job descriptions for?

4. Do you feel this will bring value and measurable results to your organization and employees?

5. Who used job descriptions in your organization today and for what purpose?

6. Are responsibilities listed in a clear and concise manner?

7. Do job descriptions give guidance to employees to reach goals and fill skill gaps?

8. Are job descriptions used to evaluate performance and encourage employees to evaluate themselves?

9. How often are the job descriptions updated?

10. Does the job description send a clear message?

11. Do job descriptions communicate the direction of the organization and purpose of the job?

12. If you are not using job descriptions for any reason listed in this chapter then what are you using them for?

Overall, job descriptions are a valuable tool used to communicate job responsibilities to applicants and existing employees and also to provide management a basis for job performance reviews.

PART IV: STRATEGIES FOR EXCELLENCE

This section of the book puts strategies and tactics and the implications of these activities into context in organizations and adds further perspective on what to do and how to shape the Corporate Culture. It talks about management, communications, and teams—the essential lubricants of a successful organization.

Chapter 15. Morale Aspects

Let's first look at ourselves as individuals and how those of us who are in leadership positions may want to think about their contribution.

How a leadership can influence culture

Whether a leader comes up through the organization or is brought in from the outside to change the organization, there are ways that leadership can have an impact on culture. Remember – the Culture is always there; it is what it is unless you consciously try to change it.

1. Walk the Walk, Talk the Talk: We've all heard the expression "walk the walk, talk the talk", but do leaders truly act on this? Essentially by saying this, leaders and managers are performing, communicating, and acting in a manner that exhibits the behaviors required and expected to be mirrored by their employees. Actions need to match the words that are being spoken or else employees will lose respect for their leaders/managers. Clear communication is the key, whether verbal, in written format, or even body language and how that is interpreted by others.

2. Employee Engagement and Recognition: Every day employees come into work, whether it's a 9 to 5 job, afternoon, or night shift. Regardless of job title, position, or the type of work performed, leaders and managers need to be active in developing strategies and techniques to ensure

employees are engaged in their daily activities. We can't expect an individual to be a star performer or receive high ratings in their annual review assessment without knowing what truly makes that employee get up and function every day and try their hardest (or not, in some individuals' cases), It's up to the leaders of an organization to communicate with their employees, find out how their workload is, what training they may require or resources that are lacking. Pay special attention to points of frustration to better understand the challenges employees face. Engaging employees in their work and within the work environment can be viewed as different things to different leaders. Whether this is saying hello to everyone upon arrival, bringing in coffee and muffins once in a while, organizing lunch and learn activities on various topics of interest (*i.e.* RRSP or other retirement plan contributions, financial planning). It doesn't always have to be related to work, but taking into consideration the demographics of the workforce and what may be of interest. Recognition doesn't always have to be monetary. Don't forget that simply saying "thank you" in recognition for an employee's contributions can mean so much and you only have to give so little.

3. Enthusiasm: No matter what the industry or type of role a leader or their workforce is responsible for, exhibiting passion and a level of excitement for the type of work performed, the company, and its staff can have an impact on how engaged employees are, and how they may emulate the behaviors and actions of their leaders. As not everyone has the same approach to business, or even the same personalities as each other, it's still important to ensure a level of enthusiasm is presented to the workforce. A leader who comes into the office grumpy and not smiling every day isn't exactly reflecting the type of behaviors he/she may expect from their employees. Smile, say hello, and be jovial when arriving at work, and soon enough, employees will begin to follow their leader's examples. Granted, maybe the drive to work was challenging or there was an issue at home before arriving, but that has to be put aside and leaders must

258

face the day with a positive approach to instill enthusiasm into the workforce. We tell our employees to leave their personal problems at the door and the same goes for leaders.

4. Connecting with employees: there has to be modest amount of social interaction outside the work requirements without being too intrusive. Enquiring about an employee's weekend or vacation is suitable, yet prying into deeper personal or financial matters would not be deemed appropriate. Consider what milestones an employee may have coming up like an anniversary or birth of a child. These may be common or public knowledge to some extent within the workplace so not taboo to ask about.

TEAMWORK

"PARTICIPATIVE MANAGEMENT"
OR
"HANDS-ON LEADERSHIP"

Chapter 16. Did You Get my Message? People and The Rituals of Communication

"I can't believe what happened to me as I was driving to the office/work this morning! Let me tell you what this * ✳#^ ⁄ *#✳! idiot did..."

Whenever idle conversation turns to traffic, cars, or rush hour congestion in many of the greater metropolises, the topic often includes drivers and driving. As they exchange their war stories, embattled commuters often complain about the poor standard of driving these days, and wonder why these idiots behind the wheel have licenses. If you ask anyone in such conversations to rate other drivers on the road, many will likely agree that 75% to 80% of them are poor drivers and that a large proportion of them should be banned from driving. Of course, no one in the conversation is ever in the 75% to 80% group. All will admit to an occasional indiscretion, but none will voluntarily put themselves in the majority group. So if up to 80% of the drivers are bad, how is it that every one that I talk to in this water cooler conversation is part of the 20% and no one makes up the vast majority (the 80%) of the driving population?

It's the same with communication. Almost everyone thinks they are good at it, they know how to do it, they know that they do it well nearly all of the time, and they are convinced that what they communicate is always clear and complete—no misunderstanding. But as for the rest of the people in the world, why can't they be clearer about what they're trying to say?

Consider the message you are trying to convey and what would be the best choice of vehicle to communicate the message. Perhaps just sharing information in email will suffice, or if you need to "engage" employees, a face-to-face is preferred. Front-line managers are the most effective choice for communicating with employees and most employees prefer to receive communication this way. Remember the message must be clear and concise. A human resources manager once said that if you're firing someone, you must make it clear that they are being fired. There's no point in beating around the bush to try to soften the blow. It's the same with all other messages. You must make clear what you want or what information you're passing on.

It is exactly the complexity of communication that makes it such a compelling and critical subject. Put into the context of Corporate Culture, communication is as much the lifeblood of the Culture and the management process as is cash to the financial well-being of the corporation. Indeed, one could make a strong argument that without communication, there is no organization. So, if we accept that communication is the essential "blood in the veins" of the human side of the organization, we can move on to explore the many elements and aspects of communication and its impact on the company.

To communicate effectively, and faultlessly is almost impossible. I would even go one step further—it is impossible to communicate perfectly. One of the ultimate challenges for the human species has to be perfect communication.

My Funk & Wagnall's Standard Desk Dictionary defines communication as "A technique for expressing ideas effectively as in speech. A process by which meanings are conveyed through a common system of symbols."

The essence of communication, then, is the conveyance of meaning. A dictionary catalogues the words and gives the commonly accepted meaning. This is a simple, almost clinical process. The printed word has meaning and the use of the word in a sentence creates communication. The choice of the word, the position of the word in the sentence and, when spoken, the tone of voice, an emphasis here and an inflection there, all have an impact on what is intended to be delivered and what is received.

One of today's communication challenges is that word meaning is often diluted or distorted by common use (or misuse) of a word. Take an example like the word "got". For no real reason, the commonly used word in North America is "gotten", a word that does not exist in standard British English (although it once did and has now been re-introduced). It means the same thing but its existence adds nothing to the ability of individuals to communicate. Another example is the word "preventative", a word that may have been around for centuries but became more widely used during the Second World War by the U.S. army in their quest to provide reliability for their wartime machinery. I have yet to see any rationale that makes the word superior to its root "preventive", which is used five times more frequently than preventative. Lexicographers estimate that there are over one million "official" words in the English language. That's just great when even the better educated of us use no more than 70,000 to 80,000 of that total. As words creep into the language with intent on creating clarity, the effect is sometimes the opposite. And in today's environment of instant communications, the short forms and acronyms flourish.

If communication is an "exchange of meaning", the incorrect use of words and language does nothing to help the communication process. Today our larger mix of cultures and origins of peoples creates additional pitfalls, particularly where the language in question is not the native tongue of one or more of the participants in a dialogue. This is often where the spoken word fails and the written word can be superior. Since sight is the predominant receptive mechanism in the human body, it is clear that speech is off to a poor start. In delivering the spoken word, the communicator must constantly be aware of how the communication is being received. In the spoken word a degree of redundancy is often appropriate. The old adage of saying it three times has a lot of merit: first you tell them what you are going to tell them, then you tell them, and then you tell them what you told them. Body language reinforces the spoken word through emphasis and gesture, the visual part of the communication. This face-to-face aspect is important not only for the listener, but also gives active feed back to the communicator.

Because of the complexity of the subject, I am breaking the communication "vehicles" into groups, which we can then put into the context of Corporate Culture. In general, the groupings relate to the medium or vehicle for communication.

The groups comprise:
- Written or documented word (or pictorial equivalent)
- "Disconnected" voice
- Voice with the physical presence, the emotive communication tools
- Some corporate context aspects.

Documented word as communication vehicle

The documented word includes letters, reports, presentations, notes, memos, email, and faxes. It has often been said that the pen is mightier than the sword. It's true that one person with a conventional weapon bent on some form of destruction can get a lot of attention (particularly in today's media-frenzied and over-dramatized world of reportage). But the message is not enduring unless totally extreme (such as the events of 9/11/01). The destructive communication is noted and heeded, but out of necessity and not out of receptive acceptance. This is where the pen (or the keyboard) can score. A persuasive writer, committed to a viewpoint has the power to reach and change more people than one whose power consists of a destructive threat. The related aspect of the written word is that in the process of being received, the element of sight is involved and thereby the reader is more fully engaged and less distracted.

The only difference between the various types of documented word noted above is the formality of their preparation and the nature of the prospective audience. One way or another these all have a life beyond their original intent. In other words, after they have served their intended purpose of providing a communication vehicle, they then are capable of being placed into "history". That is they can be filed or archived in a number of ways, including being copied several times over (as many have learned to their dismay when correspondence that was thought to be private suddenly becomes available all over the internet). The point is that these communications are critical in that they reach out to specifically inform a very select audience about a very specific issue.

264

Letters, reports, and presentations should be very rigorously crafted, bearing in mind the reason for the existence of the document. Any of these documents should be addressed and worded so that the person to whom the document is addressed has a very clear understanding of the communication intent. It should be in language that is at the right level for the receiving audience—not so junior as to be an insult and not so extreme, convoluted, or technical as to be above the heads of the audience. (See "fog index" in the next chapter). The document must be crafted to meet the addressee's needs. At the same time it must also address the needs of any other audience that is an intended recipient, as well as fit in with the bigger communication expectations of the corporation(s) in which it is being distributed. This type of formal communication must always meet the acid test of "does it say what it must, does it say it clearly, early, concisely, correctly, and simply, is it complete, and are all the right people and only the right people included in the distribution?"

Faxes, notes, memos, emails and multiple fragmented text messaging make up the next level of documented communication. How these less formal communication vehicles are used says a lot about the organization and the Corporate Culture. Check the examples below: "Email overload", "The email blunders", and "Let me see what you wrote".

Faxes are less formal than letters and reports yet somewhat more formal than memos and emails. A slightly less convenient form of technology than email, faxes have limited uses compared to just a couple of decades ago. They are considered as legally enforceable documents under the right conditions and circumstances.

Notes are the least formal of all the written communications, but because they are written they have an equally important contribution to make to Corporate Culture. They are usually meant only for the writer or for the writer plus one other. **Text messages** (*i.e.* cell phone to cell phone and other communication tools) could also fall into this category. These communication tools are viewed as being on the very bottom of the

265

communication heap as being close to inadequate. Looking at the very limited messaging capability and the acronyms used, the communication that results is only as good as how well the people know each other. Even then, we have seen countless examples of where even people who know each other extremely well still misunderstand what was communicated.

Memos, Tweets, and Facebook status updates are also very informal (too informal to be of serious value), and are usually meant for a limited number of people under controlled circumstances. It is unwise to use these as business communication tools. Though there is now a clear movement within several companies to have internal versions of these as part of the communication system. Facebook is actively promoting this option. It is also interesting to observe that in spite of their inadequacies, the tools are getting broader and broader use. I feel that when people start to experience problems with "getting the message out" in this manner it can come back to bite them because they were not paying attention to the detail of what was being said. As a result they are then managing a consumer backlash and will be pedalling backwards furiously.

Email is one of the most abused and overworked of the written communication tools. Who hasn't complained about the onslaught of messages? Like our majority of good drivers, almost everyone is a good email communicator—it's the rest of those guys that are bad. Unfortunately, too much email should never have been email in the first place—it should have been a phone call that perhaps finished up as a voice-mail because the person was not there. Even formal emails  are often delivered to far too many recipients, are too cryptic, and often do not address the fundamental needs of the recipient. Many people would help themselves, their audience, and their company by treating email as formally as a letter. Email is not a voice mail substitute or alternative. It is an informal letter-

266

writing tool that due to its mailing convenience often goes to a wide audience and often misses some of the necessary recipients. Too many people do not think about the fundamental needs of the organization when they get onto the email system. One significant result is that email creates a work overload for the addressees.

Email overload

One of my clients in a large international development and manufacturing organization routinely received about 150 emails every day. Most were for information only, and half of those could be disregarded without being read. Yet each one had to be looked at and a personal filter had to be applied.

- Who is it from?
- Is it directed to me?
- Am I the only one copied or who else has been copied?
- Is it local or international?
- Is it from inside or outside of the company?
- Is it directly or indirectly applicable to me?

If on average it took her 30 seconds to review one email message, just to discard it, then the reviewing process alone would take over an hour.

If people took the time to be as considerate in their email distribution as they would with a letter, then most garbage email would not exist (save for the spammers, who inhabit an entirely different universe). Today, it takes too long to process, copy, and distribute a hard-copy letter. You can hit an email distribution recipient list in a split second. You can hit your entire email sub-group distribution list just as quickly. Then, of course, to reply you hit "reply all" and you have covered your rear end and everyone else has just received another email that most of them did not need.

The email blunder

A recent example I came across in a client situation helps to illustrate the point that emails are a less than adequate communication forum. An individual I know had written a short directive email to some of his own subordinates regarding a recent change in part of the control and monitoring activity in the client company. As a courtesy, this was copied to some of the client staff who were given the note to advise them that some directives had been given to this individual's working group.

One of the senior recipients on the Cc group completely misread the email and assumed it was directed at them (the copy recipients versus the work group). The "wrong responder" went on to accuse the writer of deliberately downplaying an important company policy and deliberately trying to undermine the activity of the "wrong responder" in their quest to implement this policy. The "wrong responder" chose to hit the "caps lock" on the key board for several parts of the memo response and proved further that not only did they not understand the email but they did not even read it let alone figure out what it communicated to whom, and then chose to SHOUT (capital letters and bold text in emails are considered to be "shouting") at the sender (most unprofessional).

Then to compound the felony, the "wrong responder" hit "reply all" and added a copy to their own boss as well as some other senior people not directly involved and thereby erasing any doubt about the "wrong responder's" intelligence and political ability and sensitivity—a classic example of email error by not reading something correctly and understanding what you have read.

A survey conducted in Canada a little while ago on a number of Toronto executives asked how much of their email is useful. The executives reported that 45% of it was junk. They were of the opinion that emails require too little effort to create and even less effort to send to anyone with an email address. Viewed by many as another work-related stress, email is convenient but can also be invasive.

To cope with the deluge of incoming messages, filter out the garbage and unsolicited material as quickly as possible. Focus on the need to know and respond to the important. Learn to use Spam filters to direct junk to the Trash, and set up folders and sub-folders for individual projects for the rest your messages. A worthy goal would be to keep your "In" box emptied each day (although I don't actually know anyone who does this).

Keep in mind these email guidelines:

Do:

- Remember that anything you write could one day wind up as a newspaper headline—as has been seen in a number of criminal trials.
- Use descriptive subject lines that clearly advise recipient of nature of message.
- State the purpose of the message in the first sentence.
- Structure and edit emails using short paragraphs and bullet points to make it easy to read.
- Make it unambiguous.
- Keep emails brief.
- Consider to whom you are sending before hitting the send button.
- Save the non-business messages for non-business hours and non-business email addresses.

Don't:

- Send email without subject line; it sends a signal to recipients of laziness.
- Use acronyms that are not common domain.
- Labor over composing emails as you would a letter.
- Respond to email by copying other parties who you think should be casually informed.
- Send potentially contentious email without sleeping on it.
- Use smiley faces, emoticons, multiple exclamation marks, or all capital letters in business correspondence.
- Forward every joke or humorous message you receive. I'm not against a little humor to brighten up your day, but if it doesn't make you fall down on the floor laughing, it's probably a waste of your time and your recipient's time.

In the area of written communication the norms of what is expected and accepted in the organization set a tone that is reflective of the Corporate Culture.

Let me see what you wrote

A number of years ago I joined a company where every single letter written in the company by anyone, to anyone, anywhere, internally, or externally, had to be viewed by the CEO before it could be sent. This was not a small company, yet the CEO had this obsessive control streak coupled with a huge insecurity complex. To the outside world his characteristics were not that blatant and obvious. To the inside world his approach set an indelible stamp on the organization. You can imagine how things evolved. A large number of important and formal things were arranged and executed without a lot of documented formality since most people did not want the ongoing, sometimes confrontational, discussions surrounding the issuing of a letter.

When I joined the company, they were in a location to which my family and I did not wish to relocate. I joined on a very specific understanding that they were going to relocate to exactly where my family and I were currently living (by coincidence). So, if I wanted to move to the new location it would only be for six to twelve months. We looked at the prospect of moving, but due to the educational differences it made no sense for our children, who in effect would lose a year of schooling. It was only after I joined as one of the executives that I learned that this prospective relocation had been in the planning stage for nine years and was clearly not an active project on any executive's desk.

A relocation of a corporate HQ is not a light decision. It is a change that requires a lot of discussion, planning, and deliberation. This is a process that would normally take a series of reports, reviews, and documentation. Due to the intrusive nature of the letter review policy, one of the other executives and I decided to start the process and take ownership of the relocation. This was all very much above board. Discussions were held at the weekly executive meeting, agreement and consensus was obtained, and the process moved on. All this happened with just a few lines each week in the Executive Committee minutes that were noted, typed, and distributed by the President's assistant— an interesting example of how an intrusive aspect of a Corporate Culture idiosyncrasy could be bypassed without any negative repercussions.

About fifteen months after I joined the company we were relocated and my commute changed from a weekly one-hour flight to a daily thirty-five-minute drive. All but one of the executives relocated, along with many of the key staff. The process was smooth and seamless. Interestingly, the only executive that did not relocate was the one who stood shoulder to shoulder with me and was the other significant instigator in the move. To this day, he and I remain very good friends.

The "disconnected" voice as communication vehicle

By disconnected I mean person-to-person communication in the absence of the human body; in other words, we're talking about phone calls and the ever-present voice mail.

Phone calls are a critical tool since they do allow for some form of human interaction. Much more can be expressed in a phone call to any individual than can be expressed in email or other digital means. If the exact same words were addressed to the same person, once by phone and once by email, the phone call is the stronger and more complete communication to that person. Why? Voice has intonation, pitch, cadence, and punctuation that are beyond commas and periods on the written page. The recipient gets more from the exact same words in a phone call than from the text of an email message. Furthermore, the receiving individual can interject and seek clarification or add his or her own commentary to the process. The result is that the conversation is more complete. The one advantage of email is that there is a record of what was discussed, so that there can be no misunderstanding of what was agreed to. For important calls, it may be useful to send an email summarizing the key points of the phone call.

Voice mail on the other hand is not as good as talking one-on-one over the phone, but because it still contains intonation, pitch, cadence, and punctuation, it is still better than email. Those factors alone make it superior to the written word. But do remember to enunciate clearly when leaving a voice message, particularly when giving your name and phone number.

Human senses as communication vehicles

The third group of communication vehicles, and the most important, includes all the human senses—voice, touch, smell, hearing, and seeing. This is the very essence of communication. The combination of all the senses allows for the addition of "body language" into the human communication equation.

Animals, both domestic and wild, use their senses to communicate, often in highly intricate fashion (*e.g.* a distress cry to the herd from one member, species who sniff one another, birds who put on a show for the opposite sex, and cats or dogs who will flop on their backs to tell us they want to be scratched or petted). For human beings, the use of our senses is the highest level of communication because it allows the most input and output of signals without any mechanical or technological interference (yes I know the other species can't write and can't communicate over the phone). Use of our senses rounds us out as a species and as international cultural entities. Each human culture around the globe has different styles of human communication. Each coming together by two or more people starts a ritual, which is part of the communication process.

All over the world the **first part of the ritual is initiated with seeing.** The first look is often from an approach distance that may be as close as my walking out a door as you are about to enter, to the more distant opportunity where you and I are approaching each other and converging on a meeting place. Sight is a critical precursor to the next steps in the communication ritual. The vision starts to precondition each person about the other. Dress style (suit and tie, jacket and jeans, turban, hijab, bareheaded, sari, or dhoti), demeanor, stance, facial expression (smiles are valued universally), accessories and decorations (briefcase, backpack, jewellery, facial hair, tattoos, piercings, makeup), and how the body is positioned and carried, all start to affect the communication process.

In much of the western world the next step is some form of physical contact, most usually a handshake—maybe a fist pump or high five. Touching and handshakes are the elements that link together the human communication process. This too is a complex and ritualistic step in the communication process. The grasp, the pressure (or gentleness), the duration, the hand motion, and any related body motion all convey a wealth of information about the relationship between the parties when observed. (Why do politicians make such a photo opportunity out of the high profile greeting between world leaders?) Equally, the motions convey a lot between the two greeting parties. The handshake also contributes to the pre-conditioning of the next steps in the communication ritual. In many Asian cultures the bow replaces the handshake, and this too has nuanced shades of meaning. The lowness of the bow can indicate differences in social standing or degrees of respect.

Eye contact is the next element in this communication process. This is beyond the initial sight component of the meeting. It too has critical elements to it, like the intensity of the look, the duration, and where the look is centred or not centred. If you've ever been introduced to someone who did not remove his or her sunglasses in western cultures, you'll know the uncomfortable feeling of missing a vital part of the encounter.

Smell is often overlooked as a critical factor in communication. The presence, or absence, of smell as part of the introductory process can be an unacknowledged entity in the room. If, as you approach an individual in order to have a conversation, there is a lack of smell or a noticeably pleasant (or unpleasant) smell about the individual, this too will begin to have an impact on the communication process that is about to ensue. For some people who have allergies to perfumes, your morning splash of cologne may be a deal-breaker before you say hello. The whiff of garlic on the breath may be enough to create a lasting negative impression.

All of this and we still have not yet uttered a single word. All of the above takes place in a very short space of time, a matter of seconds. The elements all blend into one continuous process that immediately moves into the actual exchange of words. **The next aspect of this increasingly complicated process is the very purpose of the "coming together between the parties", the act of hearing and listening,** arguably half of the whole interactive communication process (speaking being the other half). Some form of salutation or greeting may be the first utterance.

Now the real communication process of talking and listening begins. In most cultures, the verbal exchange and the listening part moves relatively quickly back and forth between the parties. **Voice intonation** has an impact here. The tone, the choice of words, and the manner of delivery all have an impact on what is said and, more importantly, on how it is received.

Language of birth has an impact on how well communication flows between two or more people. For people of the same general origin (or long enough exposure to the language subtleties and nuances) the flow of language is taken at face value. When there are obvious differences, such as the rate of speech or strong accents, the flow takes on another element. Here the listening skills usually move to a higher level and there will likely be more exchange of questions to enhance clarification and understanding.

Body Language is taken for granted as a part of the communication process. This is actually one of the communication aspects that we do share with other species on the globe. All species use some form of body language in their communication process. Indeed, many species can, to a degree, communicate with humans (or with others of their own species) through the body language process (just ask any dog- or cat-owner).

In each culture, body language has a dictionary of its own. The intended party in a particular state of mind or mental preparedness receives the message conveyed verbally. That state of mind is usually preconditioned by the relationship between the parties. Communication is also portrayed by what others see—the non-verbal behavior. Does your face give you away? If it doesn't, it is likely that your body language will (unless you are a first class actor). Body language and facial expressions give perception to employees, co-workers, and management of how your day is going, good mood, bad mood, happy, stressed out, pre-occupied, or bored. Often people aren't aware of the negative message they are projecting. Facial expressions are universal: a smile means happiness, eyes and mouth wide open indicate surprise, wrinkling of the nose shows disgust, and a frown signifies sadness.

As a manager or head of a department, be aware that the look on your face can set the tone for all your staff. If people are constantly asking, "what's wrong?" then you may want to re-assess facial expressions. But do not be fooled into thinking that just by "pasting" a smile on your face that your body language has not uncovered your secret displeasure. A smile on the face goes with a "happy gait" and with open and positive body gestures. (See Chapter 17, Body Language for more on this.)

The "down-trodden" looks

I once had the experience of working with a manager who was highly accommodating and very paternal in his way of managing. It worked well for him when things were going well with the business. If the numbers were up and we were making a profit, he was happy and therefore the people around him absorbed that and felt jovial as well. It was highly motivating. But when we had a rough quarter and head office was coming down on my manager for the lack of money and numbers, he got frustrated and it showed. No matter how hard he tried not to show it, we knew just by the look on my manager's face when he walked in the door in the morning what kind of day it was going to be. It got to the point where the receptionist would approach co-workers and me and let us know if it was going to a good day or a bad day. We could all see it and we certainly all felt it.

Things had become so rough at one point, with the talk around the office consistently about the look of our manager and the tone it set, I decided to take the approach of speaking with him to try and help him see what effect it was having and what I could do to help him. I never saw what was coming. Walking into his office, I closed the door, and broached the conversation. Blasted! He was highly irritated by my concern and his response to me was "Can I help it that I was born with a down-trodden mouth!" I have never forgotten those words, and they stuck with me throughout the remainder of my time with that company. The problem had nothing to do with a "down-trodden" mouth but with how he presented himself to his staff on a daily basis.

On a one-on-one basis a subordinate will likely listen attentively to his or her boss (assuming no undue baggage exists between them). The attention will be clear and alert. The eyes will focus on the boss. The face will be serious, perhaps even studious. The eyebrows may be slightly furrowed as if quizzing the message. The body will be in a relaxed state of readiness. (Scrub this entire scenario if the subordinate knows they are to be hauled over the carpet for some indiscretion.) The subordinate is conveying through body language that they are in an active listening mode, a point that will be very apparent to the boss. This is one of the unique features of the human communication process—the constant feedback and reinforcement of the acceptability and comprehension of the message being delivered.

This reinforcement also occurs in a group situation such as a seminar. First thing in the morning the participants are tuned in, attentive, taking notes. The speakers' eyes scan the group, sitting ready to go, pens poised, looking at the speaker and waiting for the words to flow. The individual's body is relaxed but alert, mostly upright, head up, feet on the floor or perhaps the legs crossed under the table (closed-leg cross for Europeans and open-crossed for the Americans), relaxed but attentive. Imagine the same scene at the end of a long day after a good lunch and much listening and note taking. Many of those same people will be in a more laid back posture, legs outstretched maybe crossed at the

276

ankles, slouching somewhat, shoulder blades over the edge of the chair back, head forward, not quite erect, chin half-way down to the chest, mouth more soft set, arms crossed on the chest. This is the image of the listener who has gone beyond his or her attention span. The speaker's message is lapsing into redundancy. It is no longer being received with the attentiveness that was present at the start of the day. (A good speaker will not only pick up on those clues but will have pre-empted the problem with something stimulating in the program.)

All these subtle elements form an intrinsic part of the communication process. If you ever travel outside your own community, you will soon find that each society in different parts of the world (or even different parts of your region) has slight variations on what is acceptable and what is taboo. In different parts of the world many extremes of the looking or touching process can be considered rude or complimentary. Our purpose here is not to explore all of these but to acknowledge them and put them together as part of the Corporate Culture package.

Dialogue as communication vehicle

The final pieces linking together the elements of the communication process are the very ones with which we started, the **face-to-face meeting** and **dialogue** that ensues. **One-on-one** and **small group discussions** tend to follow and link together the ritualistic items already discussed. **Meetings** on the other hand contain all the elements of the rituals but usually in a more formal setting. Nothing much changes except that we now deal with hierarchy or some form of "pecking order". Here the communication can take on a more sequential form, with the more junior members doing more listening. Indeed, the whole tone of the meeting is set by the relative seniority of the members present since that has a big impact on how things flow.

Earlier I noted an example of a situation where an email message was totally misinterpreted. The receiver sent out an ill-considered response illustrating beyond all doubt that they were "not very bright" and certainly chose to shoot from the hip (but forgot to

277

level the holster first) and finished up with a painful infliction of a wound in the foot. Let's spend a moment reviewing how modern technology in the communications field is actually undermining the art of dialogue.

Help! I'm speechless—my Blackberry is fried

A short time ago an extended communications system failure upset the downtown core of Toronto, a world business centre. The systems that serviced all digital communications crashed and were out of action for the better part of a day. The next day the reports in the paper were very telling. Several extensive comments were noted from frustrated users in the affected business area about how totally out of touch they suddenly were with their colleagues who worked in the same building and on the same floor as they did. The power was not off, lights worked, the heat was on, elevators still linked from floor to floor—but these people were "unable to communicate" with each other because their cell phones, text messaging, Blue tooth-equipped personal organizers, and Blackberry devices could not communicate.

The reports went on at length describing how people had to get out of their offices, walk down the hall, and physically meet with a colleague—"Something they had not done in years". I was surprised—no—even shocked that these intelligent and articulate people would admit that they were at a loss due to this simple failure. I find it difficult to imagine the challenge they faced as they walked twenty-five steps to an adjacent office. How would the dialogue even begin? "Hi, I'm Fred. I work in the office across the hall. Are you the guy that I send my advanced currency hedging trade requests to? Oh yes? Then we need to talk."

Communication when done in an open manner and in person has a tremendous amount of value. This type of contact covers the whole spectrum of communication and is a fundamental to open, honest, and meaningful dialogue. When completed, a memo (assuming the communication to have been important enough to document) will confirm all the key points that may have been

278

agreed upon or need follow up, and another valuable stone has been placed into the bridge of life called networking.

Taken to the next level **communication sessions and presentations** have their own formality where the presenters or speakers have to actively break down the barrier that exists by virtue of the speaker having a commanding place in the communication hierarchy of the event, *i.e.* they are "upfront and centre" and your job is to listen. In the next chapter we will touch on some of the mechanisms that contribute to building or breaking the barriers.

The immediacy of the spoken word is undeniable when delivered properly and received properly. What is equally clear is its impermanence. The mind passes on to other priorities as the senses take in new messages that vie for the person's attention.

Courtesy and chivalry, deference and hierarchy also all have their place as part of the communication rituals. Courtesy and chivalry in their old-fashioned definitions were associated with communication between the sexes, although courtesy is universal in how it is threaded into the equation. Deference and hierarchy are more clearly related to the stature of the participants and to the tone, intent, and purpose of the communication process.

To many people rank, seniority, or stature of an individual in society or business is a challenge when it comes to having to communicate with these "higher beings". The need to go and talk to the President of the Company when you are the Second Chief Clerk Twice-Removed can be very intimidating. Without some practice (or courage) this is a prospect that has you quaking in your boots all the way to the President's office (unless you are a natural born extrovert). It's made no easier by the fact that to access the office you need to get past the "Executive Assistant" who in turn can sometimes be almost as intimidating as the "Big Man (or Woman)" themselves.

I am scared stiff of being in the spotlight
I am indebted to my stepfather for this anecdote and for how much it has helped me over the years. I remember when I first got into industry. I was working on a Co-op basis getting my degree in engineering (six months at the Technical University and six months back in the Company) over a five-year period. The company I worked for was a specialized electrical engineering company and I was one of only two mechanical engineers (my boss was the "official engineer", and I was the "apprentice" since I was not yet fully qualified). Being a small department (of two) we were often asked to handle all sorts of unusual requirements, which would normally have been outside the scope of all the electrical and production staff. On those occasions when my boss was away I was sometimes required to present the mechanical side of a series of customer deliverables since I was the only other one who was available to do that. These presentations had to be made to "the big boss". The big boss was actually three people—two brothers and a cousin, hard-nosed but well-meaning businessmen. The two brothers were Executive Vice Presidents and the cousin was the President. The three of them owned the private business.

The first couple of times that I was required to make a presentation regarding a technical issue I was so nervous that I would dwell in it for all the time prior to the meeting (if I was lucky that would only have been hours, but sometimes it was a day or more). It is not even that these presentations were formal—they just required dialogue, stating the facts, answering some questions, and then dealing with the resulting directive/decision. But I was as nervous as a schoolboy.

One day I had the smarts to ask my stepfather "how do you deal with this fear?" His answer surprised me and has stuck with me to this day. "When you come into contact with people who are apparently higher, more senior, and apparently more important than you, just take a moment to imagine them in the shower. There they are just like you, naked as the day they were born—with more or less the same body appendages (use your imagination boys and girls). Sometimes they will have a little pot belly, sometimes a big pot belly. But when stripped of their clothing and those items of costume and jewellery, they become just like you— another human being with all their frailties and vulnerabilities, just the same as you." That helped me no end. From that day on I never felt inferior or beneath anyone or was ever intimidated again by my own perception of anyone else's importance. I carry that with me to this day and as a result I often feel that my world is my oyster.

The next chapter takes all of the above elements of communication and wraps them into a Corporate Culture context.

Chapter 17. Tobacco and Whisky? Communication Tools and Their Impact on Corporate Culture

> My own experience has been that the tools I need for my trade are paper, tobacco, food, and a little whisky.
> -William Faulkner (1897–1962), U.S. novelist[26]

Faulkner, master of the stream of consciousness technique in his highly acclaimed novels, lived for much of his life as a virtual recluse in his pre-Civil War mansion, "Rowanoak," in Oxford, Mississippi. Like the hermit we imagined in Chapter 1, Faulkner may have had little use for the communication tools of Corporate Culture. Yet despite his Nobel Prize in Literature, he is viewed by some as being difficult, if not impossible, to read.

So lest we be unduly influenced by Faulkner's literary success, we will attempt to bring clarity to all our communications, and in this chapter put the elements of communication into the context of Corporate Culture. We will see how the communication process and the rituals it brings actually help to shape and define the culture of the business environment.

It's important to note that all aspects of communication in themselves do not create the Corporate Culture. They are very important indicators of the culture and how it works. We need to distinguish this a little more clearly. In total and as a process that engulfs the organization, the communication process helps to shape and define the Corporate Culture. The individual elements do not in themselves create the culture, but like pieces in a jigsaw puzzle, the accumulation of all the pieces creates a picture that reflects the culture. They also provide a large number of clues about what the leadership holds as important and hence their influence on the Corporate Culture.

Let's have a look at what I will call "a negative example" of how pieces of a communication style, when added to a well-established culture, can fail miserably.

282

The klutz of a change agent

I was recently involved with an organization that had a very clearly defined Corporate Culture, not by design but just by evolution. While the culture was not perfect and did not drive the business objectives as aggressively and as vigorously as may be the case in many North American businesses, the culture worked and the people identified with it, and for the most part were satisfied to continue enjoying all that it offered. (It was somewhat paternalistic, which the majority actually enjoyed due to the extremely generous benefits and social support it provided.)

One of the senior V.P.'s decided that part of his area needed to be re-vitalized. This individual chose to recruit and bring on board a bit of a "heavyweight", someone who would push the troops in the affected area and not readily take no for an answer. This new person (whom we'll call Pat) came on board and within the first week or so was showing the pushy style of leadership. Unfortunately for Pat, the position, while senior enough to call the shots in one small area was not senior enough to have that same influence across the company. Toes were trodden on, camps were created, and people started and continued to talk about this new person and the changes being thrust upon them. Most were not happy. Many strengthened their own camps and made sure that their preferred colleagues and compatriots were also in the same camp as they were. The result was not a surprise to anyone except perhaps the hapless Pat—who was quietly removed from the organization in a relatively short space of time.

As we have seen in the previous chapter, elements of the communication process that affect Corporate Culture include:
- **The written word**
- **The spoken word**
- **Face-to-face communication including:**
  - **Touch**
  - **Sight**
  - **Smell**

- **Hearing**
- **Speaking**.

We will see later how disproportionately the senior management influences the Corporate Culture. In the previous chapter, a mistrusting and insecure senior manager set the tone of the culture. This was borne out by the fact that he had to know every detail of what all the key people in the company were doing. As a result, most of the senior management almost abdicated from their daily responsibility, since they knew they would be questioned, critiqued, and second-guessed on any decision of consequence. No one wanted to make any decisions. They felt that questions might as well go straight to the top where they would end up anyway.

Communication audits
A quick way to assess how a particular Corporate Culture works is to judge the balance between the written communication, (including the balance between formal and informal communication), the telephone communication, and the face-to-face meetings. Any excess or extreme of any one of the vehicles can often be a direct reflection of the senior management group preferences. The most telltale sign is the delicate balance between the number of formal meetings and the amount of "management by walking around". An excess of meetings prevents the optimum balance of informal interaction. Too much informal interaction leaves an unstructured organization that, due to its informality, often is indecisive and exhibits signs of a lack of leadership.

One way of assessing the organization is through a communication audit. An audit of this type does not need to be complex or handled by an accountant. The process is simple. Gather data such as the following from a representative group over a month:

- The number of reports
- The number of memos

- The number of regular meetings
- The number of informal meetings
- The functioning of the grape vine
- An assessment of how suggestions and complaints are handled.

This audit provides a datum reference point. A quick check on these items every six months gives a trend of the balance between these communication vehicles. An excess of any one or a disproportional shift in any one item is an indicator of a change that exists for a reason.

The fog index

The written communication itself is also an indicator of the Corporate Culture. Lengthy complex documents and letters are not a good sign. **An old technique called "the fog index" provides a way of assessing the complexity of documents.** This simple tool gives a school grade index number to the content and complexity of written documentation of any type. The method is quite simple:

- In approximately one hundred words of continuous prose from any document, count the sentences—including the independent clauses. (Lest you have forgotten your grammar, a clause is a group of words that has a subject and a predicate.)
- Divide that number (*i.e.* how many sentences) into 100 (or the number of words from the passage you have chosen). This gives you the average sentence length.
- Add to the result the number of big words (three or more syllables) excluding proper nouns (*e.g.* Albuquerque), compound words (*e.g.* shantytown), and words in which the third syllable consists of '-es', '-ing' or '-ed' (*e.g.* mentoring).
- Multiply by 0.4.

285

For example (in one hundred words) there may be seven sentences and five big words. So the fog index calculation looks like this:

100 (number of words)
Divided by 7 (number of sentences)
= 14 (the average sentence length)
+ 5 (the number of big words)
= 19
× 0.4
= 7.7 (or approximately 8)

Thus the fog index indicates a paragraph with a difficulty of approximately grade 8 language. Good for a relatively sophisticated operation. (By way of comparison, a randomly selected passage above beginning under the heading "The fog index" and ending at the end of the first bullet point has a fog index of 11, or approximately grade 11 complexity.)

You will notice that many three-syllable words are not difficult. However, the more long words there are in a passage, the more difficult it is for the reader to understand, regardless of the difficulty of the individual words.

Another example more appropriate for less sophisticated operations may be twelve sentences and three big words:

100/12 = 8 + 3 = 11 x 0.4 = 4.4, or the equivalent of grade 4 language.

Don't get trapped into thinking that grade 4 language is below most people. If you want it understood by all people in the organization then remember the KISS principle—"keep it simple, silly".

The written word
This is the first element of the communication vehicles group. The style, formality (or lack of), and the protocols surrounding written

communication give some indication of the Corporate Culture. Remember the CEO who insisted on previewing all written communication? The very presence of such an approach not only put a particular Corporate Culture stamp on the organization, but it also created another element of that company's culture, the avoidance (or minimizing) of formally documented communication.

The spoken word

This is another critical element in the assessment process. We have already noted the importance of the balance between the various communication vehicles. The communications audit mentioned above will give a picture of the balance and the prominence of the verbal communication process. Too little verbal communication shows an insular organization operating in isolated cells of activity. Too much indicates an organization that may lack clear strategic goals and direction.

Size of an operating unit has a big impact on the process, how it functions, and the impact of the balance.

One large multinational company where I worked had a very clear view as to the optimum size of a business unit. Their thinking was that each operating unit in any of their countries of operation should be no more than about three hundred people in size. If it got to more than four hundred it was probably time to see if the unit could be divisionally subdivided. If it was less than two hundred then it was probably a candidate for amalgamation. Each unit should have an autonomous head and sufficient operating infrastructure to be relatively self-sufficient.

Another example at the other end of the scale is a small company that has fewer than twenty employees all in one self-contained office. The primary method of communication is email. Everyone "talks" to everyone else by email yet none of these individuals is more than a four-second walk from each other. The good news is that almost everyone is in the loop since they also tend to copy everyone. The bad news is that there is little personal interaction between the players, just a few formal meetings a week and that is all.

The point again is balance. An excess of any one vehicle is not healthy in terms of a productive and well-connected organization successfully pursuing its goals.

Management by walking around
I am a firm advocate of "management by walking around" and the face-to-face communication process (in balance with the other communication vehicles). Meet Greg, a manager with a well-balanced approach that almost bordered on the extreme of successful styles.

A master of communication

Greg embodied a very specific type of facilitative manager. I had placed him into an operating unit (a factory) that was partway through a critical turn-around. I had brought him in to handle the second phase of a major culture shift we were determined to deliver. The factory was situated in an English-speaking country, but a part of the country where English was not the primary language. Indeed, within the operating unit there were several spoken languages with English being spoken by less than 10% of the employees and probably understood by less than 5%. The parent company was English (of the "stiff upper lip" old school) with lots of paternalistic discipline involved.

Greg was a hard find since I needed a fully bilingual individual who was also bicultural, and a manager who could operate with the iron fist in a perpetual velvet glove. The bicultural requirement needs explanation. To maintain credibility as the factory manager, it was very important that Greg be perceived as typically English by the head office senior management. Even more important was that he be perceived as a native of local origin at the factory, particularly by the factory staff. Greg fitted this requirement perfectly. He spoke both of the official languages perfectly without a trace of an accent that would point to his origins. More importantly, his background was such that he was equally capable of projecting a totally comfortable demeanor in either of the cultures.

Greg was also a master at the subtle art of body language communication. He was one of the best people that I ever knew at integrating all facets of body language into the verbal communication process. Whenever you met Greg, there was always the correct amount of eye contact to start the greeting process. There was always the open and receptive posture and facial expression. The handshake was always warm and open, firm enough to be meaningful, long enough in duration to convey sincerity in the greeting, and almost always balanced with his free arm holding your arm gently—just below the elbow if he knew you, and above the elbow if he knew you well. This gesture adds conviction to the handshake and reinforces friendliness. When coupled with a genuine smile and a welcoming and open tone of voice, the effect was highly positive. He won friends and influenced many people very effectively. He was able to handle the many difficult aspects of the required turn-around and still maintain a high standard of discipline and effectiveness.

In the context of Corporate Culture, Greg was a leader of stature and substance. While the example focuses on the body language subtleties of the communication style that Greg brought to the organization, it also covers a much broader aspect of the leadership contribution to Corporate Culture. Greg was a natural manager, a clear leader with a sufficiently outgoing personality that he became the focal point of that factory. As such, Greg became the icon that set the tone and the standard of the Corporate Culture for that location. His style was distinctive and influential enough that he created a more memorable leadership role, which over time supplanted that of the nearby company headquarters. The presence of the senior management just a fifteen-minute drive away, became secondary in the confines of that location. In the context of Corporate Culture this is not unusual. The top figures in a local operating unit are usually the ones to set the standard. The corporate influence tends to provide uniformity through policy, procedures, budgets, and reporting formality, and thereby exerts its influence. It is, however, the local leadership that shapes the local Corporate Culture.

Face-to-face communication is another critical aspect of total communication. The voice, the use of language, tone, intonation, use of vocabulary, speed of delivery, and punctuation created by both body language gestures as well as the verbal "punctuation" emphasis all combine as a critical part of balanced communication. When done well, the speaker is stimulating to listen to. When done less well, much of the intended communication does not find a receptive ear.

Communication is about influencing behaviors. Face-to-face is still the best way to engage employees and influence them in relation to business strategies. It's about communication styles and credibility. A face-to-face conversation with a direct manager/supervisor is more effective than an employee reading something on the company Intranet or in an email message or hearing it in a voicemail message. A discussion over coffee with employees, video messages from the CEO, or audio conferences are also effective ways in their own right, when used correctly, to communicate with workers.

Engage employees by communicating face-to-face about leadership direction, company information, and the competition or the market place. Building trust between CEOs, staff, and managers is critical to the success of the team.

In a moderate-sized organization where I once worked, our branch manager often flew out west to attend quarterly management meetings with the CEO and other head-office staff members. The intent of the meetings was to look back at where we were as a branch, where we were heading over the next few quarters and obviously where that all fit in with the overall business strategy of the company.

So you'd think our manager would return to us and share with us what had taken place. He might let us know what vision he and head office had for us in terms of growth, or a plan for rectifying any downturns or pitfalls we may have encountered. He could even just tell us we were doing okay and that as long as we worked smart we would pull ahead. Not so. We often didn't get enough feedback, which left us wondering where we fit in the bigger picture within the company. We craved the opportunity to receive word from head office verbally through our own manager. Instead, we would interpret how we were doing by our manager's body language, or we might read about some new venture in an email or company Intranet. Worse yet, we would find things out through the grapevine from other head office staff. It just wasn't an effective way to build a cohesive and motivated team.

Body Language (Non Verbal Communication)

We've all heard the expression "Actions speak louder than words". Have you ever wondered if someone who is talking to you is avoiding a topic, glossing over important details, or otherwise evading the truth? What clues gave them away? Have you ever wondered if others have felt that your own actions are saying more than you could verbally? This is referred to as non-verbal communication or body language.

Non-verbal communication is another way of transferring information from one person to another. Many of us don't realize that we are spending a great deal of time communicating with others just by means of facial expressions, tone of voice, body posture, eye contact, and even motions. During a conversation we are not only communicating verbally, but also expressing ourselves through body language. Sometimes this can give off a mixed message to the receiver and hinder the communication process.

Knowledge and awareness of non-verbal communication is important to leaders and managers for two reasons: first, to function effectively and interact with others successfully as a team, and second, to observe attitudes and feelings of team members. This awareness can work in favor of the leader/manager when looking at the growth of the employee, approval of the work the employee is expected to perform, and recognition for a job well done. All this is assessed through the nonverbal aspects of communication, the posture, the eyes, the position of the arms, facial expressions, and types of movement while speaking and while listening.

In the North American and European culture, it is expected that the non-verbal communication strongly reflects and parallels the words being spoken. It is one of the key mechanisms by which we all judge if the message and the messenger are serious and honest.

If there is an honest understanding of the non-verbal cues given by individuals, the organization has a better chance of being successful. Let's take a look at a few examples of body language.

- Distance. We all have our own "personal space" around us. In some cultures, standing closely to someone is a reflection of status and respect, while in other cultures it may be viewed as uncomfortable and awkward. If you find someone gradually backing away from you while you converse, you might wish to back off a little yourself to give the other person some space. Where we stand in relation to the other person gives different messages. Do we stand beside them to talk, in front of them, or facing them to have our discussion? Even where you choose to sit in a room during a meeting can say volumes about you. These choices reflect the level of comfort, self-confidence, and (sometimes) authority that you have.

- Posture. How we stand or sit in a chair will communicate to others how we feel or potentially what we are thinking at that moment. If we are slouched in our chair, perhaps we are not interested or tuned in to what is going on. If we are sitting or standing straight with our shoulders back, we send a completely different message.

- Contact. Shaking hands and embracing convey different messages. When you shake someone's hand for the first time, do you stand tall and put your hand right out in front of you or do you wait for the other person to initiate contact and take your lead from them? In some cultures, shaking hands is not an appropriate way to greet someone and is viewed negatively. In some cultures, men do not embrace each other, but males and females may do so. In other cultures, business colleagues may not touch, but will instead bow slightly (or deeply) to each other.

- Facial expressions. We can usually tell what someone is feeling just by looking at whether they are smiling, frowning, yawning, or grimacing. A raised eyebrow may mean intrigue or be a questioning look for some. Even a "fake" smile discloses important information. Facial expressions may be similar in most cultures, and are usually monitored closely by the person you are communicating with. Facial expressions tend to communicate emotions and can reveal our emotional state better than any other non-verbal technique.

- Gestures/hand movements. Most people use various hand movements when they are communicating with others. Whether it's a clenched fist or a high-five, we can all relate to and interpret what someone is trying to tell us. In Bulgaria and parts of a few other countries, nodding your head up and down means "no" not "yes", although that nod is usually a simple once-up and once-down movement.

- Eye contact. This one is probably the most significant non-verbal communication tool in most western cultures. Are we looking directly at the person when talking with them or are we distracted and looking over the other person's shoulder? In some cultures, you are expected to look over the person and not directly at them when speaking. In most cases, the manager or leader will typically maintain eye contact longer than their employee when conversing. In Africa, avoiding eye contact is a sign of respect, whereas people in North America may view such behavior as disrespectful, or even label it "shifty". (You may remember the example of speaking to someone with sunglasses on).

- Environment. Even the way you position your desk can communicate non-verbal information to others. Is the desk on an angle? Do you sit with your back to the wall or window? Do you have an informal space within your office where you can sit more comfortably with others to converse or are others expected to sit across from you over the desk? One manager sat in his chair behind his desk and had the only guest chairs positioned at the far end of the room facing his desk. So any guest was left with the uncomfortable choice of sitting ten feet away to try to converse, or standing in front of the desk while the manager sat. Clearly the manager felt some insecurity with his authority. One of the approaches I would advocate in this situation would be to pick up one of the chairs (assuming it to be portable) and bring it to the desk to sit down and begin the conversation. This does two things: first it communicates your self-confidence (but don't overdo it), second, it actually serves to undermine the boss's insecurity even further. Another example that comes to mind is a case where the boss had the two chairs in front of his desk deliberately set so that the front legs were slightly lower than the back legs. The result was that anyone sitting there was always "pitched" slightly forward as if being subtly ejected from the position—a sign to keep the meeting short.

- Tone and pitch. The tone and pitch of your voice will also express to others how you feel. Even the rate at which you are speaking will affect communication. Tone and pitch not only show your feelings, but also convey your message, so these elements will dictate how the message is received. It's no coincidence that James Earl Jones, famous for his deep and authoritative voice, was chosen to be the voice of Darth Vader in the Star Wars films, and later went on to intone "This is CNN" countless times for the television network. The richness of his speaking tone lends an air of confidence, credibility, and power.

- Silence. Silence can be both positive and negative. It can allow others to absorb the information or it may make others feel intimidated or uncomfortable depending on the circumstances. It can be a sign of agreement as well as disagreement. A high school teacher we remember used silence very effectively as a means of controlling the class. If there were whispers or minor disturbances while she was speaking, she stopped talking, folded her arms, and looked out the window until there was dead silence in the room. Of course, one would need to be certain of one's authority before trying this ploy, or it could backfire badly with the group erupting into chatter.

Effective non-verbal communication means knowing your surroundings and the culture you are in, and being a good listener and observer. It's important not to judge non-verbal behaviors by your own cultural standards, especially when visiting abroad. Always read between the lines, and if you aren't sure as to what the message is that you are receiving non-verbally, ask a confidant who is familiar with the local culture.

Training
Training is another communication vehicle that is rarely recognized for its impact on shaping Corporate Culture. Many companies undertake training, both in-house and external, and do not recognize the positive contribution that it makes in framing and reinforcing their Corporate Culture. Most companies view training as an investment in their employees, the skill sets, and growth potential that it delivers. The content of the training is, however, far more than the skill and growth enhancement that it provides. The very process, particularly for in-house training, is a powerful opportunity to constructively enhance and reinforce the fundamental values and expectations of the organization. The content of the material and the delivery convey to every employee attending the course what the company values and what the company expects.

In most companies the senior management endorses the training without actually reviewing the content and taking the opportunity to enhance the Corporate Culture value standards. This is one of those examples where the intent was not to build the Corporate Culture—it just happened to be the perfect outcome.

There has been only one company (a financial services company) that I remember from my personal experience that actually took some time to ensure that the training content reinforced the message that senior management wanted to send. The company wanted to be sure that customer service outcomes were delivered in a clear and concise manner—using particular words and phrases to communicate that they were a genuinely caring company. This company took the time of several senior managers to structure specific parts of the training to ensure that the standard of the outcome of the training met particular criteria. They took the time to review the outcomes by testing and monitoring what the trained employees did, said, and how they each responded to customer questions and complaints. The company was a genuinely caring organization with a strong and positive customer service policy. They even had a public perception that they cared.

While this was a small part of their culture, the training was not intended to help manage or enhance the culture. The primary purpose was to deliver excellence in customer service. So, even in this case the message was not a reinforcement of the culture but an assurance (to the management) that the training was delivering certain clear messages about the importance of the content and management's expectations of the outcome.

Props and visual aids
These provide another powerful way of enhancing the memorable aspects of a message. Why do you suppose everyone knows that a picture is worth a thousand words? Why is a well-prepared visual presentation so much more stimulating than a plain speech? The reason is that visual augmentation stimulates more of the listener's receptive channels, which then become more absorbing and retentive. The speed and frequency with which presenters have embraced the now ubiquitous Power Point or Prezzi presentation programs proves that they recognize the value of enhancing their

296

words with visual aids. With visual aids the message is multiplied without redundancy. The visual receptors greatly enhance the hearing channels, making the result much more memorable. Why is a great movie great? Why is a great play great? Much of that magic comes from being able to engage as many as possible of the human senses in a synergistic and holistic way.

The best presentations are those that do not give the identical information on the screen as the presenter is delivering orally. In fact, there should be very few written words on the screen, and photos, graphics, or other illustrations should enhance what the presenter is saying.

SALES STRATEGY

"SUCCESSFUL SALES COME FROM A SOUND PLAN"

Banish screen clutter in favor of one simple photo or graphic.

The elements of the communication process are only a relatively small part of the overall Corporate Culture picture. The success or failure of a Corporate Culture to engage its employees depends on the senior individuals in the company. The above elements are important as a primary mechanism in conveying the Corporate Culture standards and expectations.

Chapter 18. Industrial Relations and the Impact of Corporate Culture

Industrial Relations is a most critical topic in every organization large or small. There are literally hundreds of books on this subject.

In general the focus of all this literature is to talk about how employee groups are handled within the organization—the structure, the legal, the relationships, the pros and cons of unions, countless examples of "the good, the bad, and the ugly" and the list goes on.

If we take a look from a very high level at Industrial Relations we can break this topic down as follows. In broad terms there are three traditional perspectives on Industrial Relations:
- The unitary perspective.
- The pluralistic perspective.
- The Marxist perspective.

Each of them brings a particular approach to the topic of how management and workers relate to each other in the workplace and on all matters that pertain to the work, employees, and how they are treated.

The unitary perspective sees the work place as an integrated whole where everyone is part of "one big happy family" and where everyone shares common goals and a common purpose. The emphasis is on mutual cooperation. Often this model degenerates into a paternalistic approach to the employees and it becomes a "soft culture" where almost anything is tolerated within reason. Trade unions are not considered necessary since management "takes care of everything". This type of organization is very vulnerable to unionization and there are many examples of these groups becoming unionized since the union offers some of the leadership qualities that the soft and paternalistic culture does not. Employees are therefore often tempted to embrace the union approach since workers in any environment almost always want leadership and the opportunity to respect leadership. In most work environments this form of "Unitary Industrial Relations" tends to be somewhat unique to the organization involved.

The pluralistic perspective tends to be at the other end of a scale where the organization has a number of sub groups—each with its own agenda, loyalties, objectives, and leaders. In this environment the management has to work to be persuaders and co-coordinators. To simplify the management role, trade unions still have their place and serve a useful purpose as the key unification force for the majority of the employees. The trade union is deemed by management and the workers as the legitimate representatives of the employee group. This allows for unification of rules and procedures and puts structure in place for wages, benefits, rights, and grievance handling. Collective bargaining (the Union negotiating with the Management) is the order of the day.

The Marxist perspective (which I would argue is largely outdated in western industrial society) looks at the workers from a capitalistic perspective. Here there is a strong division of interest between "Capital" and "Labor". Here the emphasis is on the disparity that is perceived to be created by the capitalist system and therefore the control it exerts over the workers. Conflict is seen as inevitable and organized labor is the only response.

I do not favor these three categorizations since in today's western industrial society each of them paints an unrealistic picture, as each of them tends to put forward an extreme perspective, with none of them functioning well. While there are no doubt organizations that many employees would see as a "fit" with the above simplifications, I would argue that they are the exceptions and not the rule.

In my experience there are two current forms of employee groups in today's western industrial society. They are either unionized or they are not unionized.

Any smart employer will have a cooperative structure in place that allows the company to operate cooperatively with the employee groups.

In my experience, management gets the union that they deserve. If they are non- unionized (and do not take care of the employee group), management still gets the union that they deserve. If they are non-unionized, then management needs to work diligently and consistently to maintain a non-union environment. The example below gives some indication of what that "diligent and consistent" work entails.

> Over the years I have operated a number of facilities (independent operating units), some of which were unionized and some of which were not. In one case I had several facilities across Canada, several of which were unionized and several were not. In two cases the operating units had a sister facility (making different products) within a block of each other and in each case, one was unionized and one was not. What was interesting was that the non-union groups were happy to stay that way in spite of several repeated attempts by the unions to unionize the neighboring facility. The non-union groups did not want the union. The union group units were happy to keep their union. (By the way, each were under different unions).
>
> The secret of my approach was simple:
>
> In the non-union environment I had the plant management take a consistent approach with the workers and treat them exactly as if they had a union. They had the equivalent of their own contract. All the things that an employee group wanted to know about their work environment, their conditions, their pay scales, overtime, benefits, who can do what, when, and how was all spelled out in a public document. They did not have union representatives but we encouraged them to select "spokespersons" who effectively did what shop stewards did. We allowed them to meet regularly as an employee group, we gave them a form of grievance procedure, and

we gave them structured approach to discipline (if it was required). In other words, everyone knew where they stood and what were the rules and expectations. The point being that the employees had everything that they would have had if they were unionized. For management, this little bit of extra work provided some real benefits. First there was no demarcation of job boundaries—everyone could do what they wanted when they wanted (within reason, subject to skill and within safe practice limitations). There was a tremendous amount of management flexibility available also. When management was training employees or had a particular problem to solve on the lines, they could do so without risk of interference by a shop steward or a disgruntled employee claiming that "management is stealing my work". While not quite the "one big happy family" of the unitary perspective from above it certainly came close to the same outcome, but without the soft paternalistic side of what is described in that approach.

(If you look at the German version of industrial relations legislation, you will see that much of this approach is mandated. Germany has some pretty strong labor relations with some very strong employee participation including Board representation being mandated.)

In both cases the nearby unionized plants also did not have a problem since they could see for themselves that what was done for one group was also done for them. In other words, we did not operate the union environments by hiding behind a collective agreement and a grievance procedure. We treated the workers and the shop stewards as allies and partners in the process of producing the goods that the facilities manufactured. By being proactive with the employees and the shop stewards and the unions, we managed to create and maintain a positive and constructive environment. We would hold regular meetings with the employees and their union stewards. We would regularly meet with the external union officials. When it came to contract time we would try to be preemptive by making sure that the employees and the union knew what was going on in the company. They knew what was coming up next – they knew of our plans and of our financial status so that there were no surprises and hidden skeletons to deal with. Negotiation of the union contract was therefore less of a cat and mouse game and less adversarial than is often the case.

The success of this approach really showed when at one point in time we chose to merge two production units that were near each other into one, with the smaller factory to be housed within the larger factory. Even a radical step such as this did not entice the employees of the smaller unit to engage a union. They were firm and specific in their resolve that they trusted management well enough that they did not require union representation to negotiate closure of the smaller factory. Once the new production area was ready, the transition of the production process took place. Many of the employees moved with the process—after all it was literally just a block down the street. The employees were required to eventually join the union since the larger factory was the unionized location. The employees did not really appreciate this since it gave them no advantage over what they previously had. We were able to negotiate their seniority but the bottom line was that they now had to pay union dues. This was not popular since they had all that the union could offer previously without the union fee attached to the process.

For our purposes I want to categorize this topic into the most obvious high-level aspects that relate the Industrial Relations topic to the Corporate Culture topic. It is back to my point—that management gets the union it deserves. If you choose to ensure that your employees are an intrinsic part of the Corporate Culture, then that is what happens. They become an intrinsic part of the culture. The secret is to make that part of the overall plan, make it public and obvious, and as you "talk the talk" make sure that you consistently "walk the walk".

If the environment is unionized, then make sure that the union is engaged with all the remaining employee groups so that no one is an outcast in the process. If it is a non-union environment, that requires no different treatment.

It is my contention that a non-union work force in a company with a well-adjusted culture will likely stay non-union. For those organizations with a union the same can apply and the on-site labor relations scenario will be significantly better as a result of the ongoing efforts to include the work groups.

I can think of two other examples that make the point of unions and non-union environments within the culture of a corporation.

In one case where the organization was not unionized, their day-to-day relations worked well. Employees could identify with management and the goals of the business since the company was of a size where everyone knew each other. The owner of the company was regularly "on the shop floor" in all areas of the business. Everyone knew who he was and he was not a stranger.

As the company grew, more levels of management were engaged, and as a result the owner, while still widely known and recognized by all, was now more remote.

The added layers of management also bought with it some politics that did not exist previously. In the past, when the company was small, everyone had the feeling that they could approach the owner and ask any question they wanted. They had a sense of belonging. This became more diluted in the larger organization. The new layer of senior management bought their own interpretation of what was to be accomplished. Sometimes this interpretation was laced with their version of the requirements, which progressively gave rise to differences of opinion. Hence politics was born or perhaps, more correctly, mushroomed.

This also gave rise to the employees becoming more interested in hearing what the unions may have to offer and what the benefits of unionization may be. With some hard work on the employee relations front, the company managed to avoid the union. This continued to be hard work since a union with a toe in the door requires more than just proactive labor relations to maintain the status quo.

In another case I can recall the company was firmly unionized in some of its employee areas. This company had a lot of technicians and other junior to middle level employees who were not unionized but had an artisan labor group that was. The overall culture of this company was what I would call "soft and paternalistic" a characteristic that many of the people enjoyed. As I observed the day-to-day operations there was a clear sense that the unionized group was somehow alienated from the organization.

I was not directly engaged in the areas with the union groups though had frequent interaction with several of them on a one on one basis. From my observations I could only surmise that the cause of the apparent alienation was twofold. First, the union clearly formed a strong bond for the employee group involved. One had a sense that they saw themselves as different, even "special" in some way. They were a group that "had some rights, had a contract, had some ability to exert their authority". Equally one had a sense that management had abdicated (well maybe abdication is too strong) from the day-to-day responsibility of communicating with this group. The reason I used that word is that there was no clear management person who was responsible for dealing with the union. The company treated the union employees like all the other employees. They were "part of the group". But I thought something was missing—yes they were "part of the group" but they were unionized. In this case management needed to work to make sure that the group was both part of the group but also treated with a firmer hand in terms of discipline and work habits. The union group was not very productive and gave one the sense that they were hiding behind the strength of their collective power as a form of protection. Several of them took a somewhat lazy approach to the day-to-day tasks. A lot of work was delegated to outside contractors, an approach that cost a lot of money. There were several very good union employees but there were also many that I would categorize as somewhat lazy.

In summary, this gets me back to my basic comment "management gets the union it deserves". Work with the group proactively and they will be an integrated member of the work force. Avoid this approach and you get the outcome you deserve.

Another way to examine the implications of trade unions is to reflect on their role, both explicit and implicit.

The explicit role is the obvious one that a union plays in serving its membership. The union is a force that provides cohesion, support, solidarity, and a "port of safe harbor in a storm". The union is the membership, each of whom has different concerns, needs, and sometimes fears. The union provides structure— everyone involved is under the same collective agreement, everyone knows where they stand and what to expect. The union is the Shop Stewards who are the "on the floor" representatives of the membership. They know the rules and requirements (the contract) very well and they know how to ensure that the provisions in the contract are met for the benefit of the members. The Shop Stewards are also the defenders of the rank and file members. If things go wrong and a disciplinary action materializes, the Shop Steward is there to defend the members involved and ensure that Management does only that which the contract would allow. The Shop Stewards also handle membership complaints by way of a "Grievance Procedure". This is a formally structured process whereby the apparently guilty member gets his day in court and gets either disciplined or given a pardon. The union Shop Stewards have further resources available to them through the Business Agent. The Business Agent is the key external representative and is the person to whom the bigger issues are referred for decision and resolution. The Business Agent is also the key person (often along with some other senior external union people) who sit at the bargaining table to negotiate the renewal or extension of the contract (the legal agreement between the Union and the Company involved). There is no doubt that unions were an absolute essential in the early days of the Industrial Revolution when exploitation of people (anyone and everyone) was the norm. Inferences in Chapter 4.

Unions also provide a number of other supportive features for their members since through their pooled resources they can provide a variety of social, legal, financial, and other services. The larger the union the more capable they are of providing a wide range of supportive benefits for their membership.

The implicit role is often not really thought about since it becomes a given. The implicit role that unions play is in keeping Management straight. After all when it comes to dealing with a large number of individuals (or even specific individuals within the union group) structure and consistency play an important role. If all the employees are treated in a fair and equitable manner and are all treated consistently, there is little need for bickering and discontent. While Management likes to think that it operates from a level playing field and likes to think that it treats all employees equally, personalities creep into the shop floor relationships and one individual (say a supervisor) does not like an employee (a union member) and as a result the supervisor does not treat this individual the same way as he / she may treat another. This is exactly why there are issues on the floor. As a result of the perceived inequity, the employee feels slighted, inferior, even victimized. The other employees will notice this and (depending on the severity of the "discrimination") will often go to assist the targeted employee. It is for this very reason (and many related) that the grievance procedure exists. So, just as the union's presence provides a consistent set of rules and guidelines for the employee, it provides an equal level playing field for the supervision and management.

I can recall an example where the inconsistency of the supervision led to the prospect of unionization of the company's hourly work force. In this case the hourly employees comprised a broadly mixed group of mostly men (and a few women) spanning a wide cultural diversity. A couple of the supervisors were of a specific ethnic background and progressively over a period of a few years had accumulated a number of hourly employees, all of whom were from their own cultural background. As time went on the employees involved were given small favors (to the disadvantage of the remaining hourly employees). This small and subtle series of actions led to dissatisfaction in the ranks of the remaining employees. In a union environment this would have led to a few grievances and the supervisors would have been "forced" to reconsider their actions and ensure that all were being treated equally. In a non-union environment (such as this) there was the inevitable growing dissatisfaction for which there was no ready release. Under these circumstances the more senior management did not get to hear about the concerns except in an indirect way.

Over time the inevitable approach of an external union official started to be greeted with some favor by those employees who felt they were being ignored and underprivileged. This group of employees became a source of fertile ground for a trade union approach. As it happened, some of the senior management were sufficiently astute to keep their fingers on the pulse and their ear to the ground. This intervention proved to be timely enough to allow management to be proactive in dealing with the challenges they were facing, and this allowed them to defend themselves from a unionization approach.

In the context of Corporate Culture union or non-union is relatively less of an issue. The approach has to be that all employees are human beings and need to be treated as an equal part of the employee group. Provide structure and consistency and either of the two types of employee groups will work well with management. But—as always —it is up to management to lead the way. If you "talk the talk" make absolutely sure that you "walk the walk".

Chapter 19. The Pride of Lions and the Herd of Hippos: Teams and Groups

Most conflict style inventories are based on the Managerial Grid Model developed by Robert R. Blake and Jane Mouton (Chapter 5).

The Psychology of Inter-group Relationships

Clayton Paul Alderfer was a forerunner in the area of creating some structure in defining management principles and characteristics. He created a matrix approach of four elements placing "activity" level against a "social" approach to being. His Embedded Intergroup Relations Theory was a forerunner of the Blake Mouton Grid.

Conflict Resolution Grid Analysis and Approach

These tools give insight into how people respond to conflict. The Thomas-Kilmann Conflict Mode Instrument (TKI) asks respondents to choose A or B from each of thirty pairs of statements, and identifies five different styles of conflict:
- Competing (assertive, uncooperative)
- Avoiding (unassertive, uncooperative)
- Accommodating (unassertive, cooperative)
- Collaborating (assertive, cooperative)
- Compromising (intermediate assertiveness and cooperativeness).

Similarly, the Kraybill Conflict Style Inventory identifies five styles of responding to conflict:
- Directing
- Harmonizing
- Avoiding
- Cooperating,
- Compromising.

Its defining feature is its cultural sensitivity.

Both evolved from Alderfer's Theory, and also built on the Blake Mouton Grid approach to defining management characteristics.

I insert these conflict style inventories here as but a small portion of what has been written, said, and practiced in the attempts to move modern management forward. But let's step back and go up one level. These are tools that help to focus on the critical interactions of people in teams and in groups.

So what is a team and what is a group?

Teams or Groups—what's the difference?
The "Pride of Lions versus the Herd of Hippos" describes the difference between teams and groups. A pride of lions conjures up a picture of something organized and purposeful. Each animal has a role. The males patrol the territory against intruders and protect the pride, while the females, being lighter and faster, do most of the hunting for the pride. Females hunt cooperatively, each one having her place and role in the hunt.

A herd of hippos, however, has a flexible group dynamic defined by hierarchy as well as by food and water conditions. A dozen or more individuals will live with a territorial bull, but during droughts many herds may be forced to share small pools of water, disrupting the hierarchical system, and creating constant fighting for dominance. They herd for protection and support—but they do not convey the sense of structure that the pride of lions does.

Teams, like a pride of lions, work together through coordinated efforts and positive synergy—male lions guarding the pride, the female lions on the hunt, all sharing the resulting meal. In management terms a team is viewed as an assemblage with structure, formality, synergy, ownership, and a sense of belonging and motivation.

Groups, like a herd of hippos, consist of two or more people working together towards objectives with shared information—the hippos depending on strength of numbers to sustain and defend

310

themselves. Groups are a more casual and less structured version of a team. Most importantly for our purposes, a team can create a Corporate Culture whereas a group merely accepts what they are and what they have.

We are going to focus more on teams since groups are everywhere—but teams have a more defined place (particularly within an organization).

Types of Teams
Some of the different types of teams include:

- Problem Solving. A problem solving team often consists of five to twelve people, often from the same department (or with related skills sets from an interdepartmental structure), all working towards solving a problem, *e.g.* sorting out why a particular issue keeps reoccurring.

- Self-managed. A self-managed team is typically eight to fifteen people who take on the responsibility of the management role together. They operate with relatively great autonomy and with a broad mandate (also with little more than general guidance). They often have a mandate that covers many facets of a series of problems or challenges.

- Cross-functional. A cross-functional team is usually made up of people of similar hierarchical level but from different departments, divisions, or even from sister companies. These members come together to achieve a common objective or goal, often in a fairly specific area where a common end point is sought from a wide span of contributors.

- Virtual Teams. Any of the above teams can be arranged to be a virtual team. Virtual teams are linked by computer technology or conference calls. Computers and telephones are used to keep the group in touch with each other to accomplish their common goals.

Key roles needed in a team
There are nine key roles of a team and its members. Though a team doesn't require one person to possess each of these skills to be effective, these factors need to be considered when building a team. In other words, a team doesn't need nine members if the various players possess all the elements.

- Creator—the visionary who can put forth ideas and suggestions for discussion purpose or lead the pre-defined mandate.
- Promoter—encourages the ideas of their fellow team members.
- Assessor—offers insights as to why an idea will be effective or not.
- Organizer—the person who holds the ideas and feedback together and keeps structure around team meetings, reference sources, and record keeping.
- Producer—gives direction and follow through.
- Controller—enforces the rules and keeps things on track as it progresses.
- Maintainer—fights the battles and handles the external worries.
- Advisor—searches for more information and resources.
- Linker—keeps it all coordinated and together.

Teams must be given (or need to create) specific measures and goals, have a common focus or purpose, and are able to discuss and agree upon their interpretation of the goals and how to accomplish the task. Successful teams (as judged by the members and those that observe them) increase the motivation of their members to work harder and more cohesively.

Though cohesive teams have greater satisfaction and lower absenteeism, teams may not always operate smoothly. Conflict often arises within teams, but that's not always bad. If there were no conflict, then teams could become stale and less committed to the outcomes. However, too much conflict is detrimental to the team, the members, and ultimately the objective. At the same time all members must be held accountable for the role they play in the team and for reaching the required goals. Members cannot loaf around or rely on others to perform their tasks; each member must pull his or her own weight. In the end, a team's success is measured not only by the performance of the team as a whole but also by the individual performance of each member.

Teams are not always the answer. It's not smart to put a team onto a project that needs to be handled by one experienced individual. Often one person can do the work just as efficiently. When deciding upon a team task or an individual task one needs to ask "Can we save on time, labor, and expenses with a single person solution or are we better off having a broader perspective of multiple players focus on this task?" If the answer is that a team is needed, then it is important to ensure that members of the team share common goals and agree on how to get there.

One final thought on teams—even if they are created to solve the apparently important question that they have under consideration, in some cases the bonus is a broadening and learning experience for some of the team members.

Teamwork
Teamwork can create a positive working environment and decrease anxiety for employees. It can ensure employees are all working towards the same end goal and ultimately result in a better working environment for everyone involved when the company's values and beliefs are exhibited within that team setting.

First, it must be determined if teamwork is the best solution to the problem or if one individual should complete the activity. If the person has the time and experience to complete the task individually, it may be a better choice for saving time and money.

In order for teamwork to be effective, individuals must have shared common goals and a willingness to negotiate changes, approach work/tasks professionally, and be open to the ideas and suggestions of others.

To have a well-rounded team, it's a good idea to get people together from different departments. This provides a wider viewpoint and perspective of the activity and the goal they are working towards achieving. Ensure the team understands what the task is, why it's important to the organization, and that it must be completed and achieved within a specific time period.

Throughout the process positive comments and reinforcement affect the teamwork of the group in a creative and motivational manner. Comments should be sincere and relevant to the task. Constructive criticism is also very important when things appear to be going astray. Addressing human desires such as activity, ownership, empowerment, affiliation, recognition, and achievement can energize a team.

The team members need to listen actively to others and get involved. They should be comfortable in openly sharing their ideas and in making suggestions and at the same time providing solutions or asking for the input of other team members in order to accomplish the activity. The lines of communication need to be open and team members should not be quick to blame others. It's essential to support group member's ideas or at least to consider them before passing judgment and making final decisions. To have a cohesive group, team members should feel confident about the suggestions they have put forward but not boast about the great job they've done if their suggestion is the final choice.

Even though a deadline must be provided in order to move forward with the activity, never rush a team to accomplish a task but make sure the expectations are clear. Rushing them may result in lower productivity and decrease the outcome of product or service you are trying to accomplish. Teams must learn to reach a consensus and support their direct manager or supervisor, avoid political situations, and be pleasant with each other.

314

Team Members need to be competent and have the ability to communicate clearly and most of all have respect for each other and have confidence in their decisions.

Why a team?

The next sections address team building, a process that could have forestalled the sad outcome of this mythical cautionary tale:

> This is a story about four people named Everybody, Somebody, Anybody, and Nobody. There was an important job to be done and Everybody was asked to do it. Everybody was sure Somebody would do it. Anybody could have done it, but Nobody did it. Somebody got angry about that, because it was Everybody's job. Everybody thought Anybody could do it but Nobody realized that Everybody wouldn't do it. It ended up that Everybody blamed Somebody when Nobody did what Anybody could have done.   ~ Author Unknown

Team building can improve on communication skills and help in determining individual and group roles and responsibilities. Team building can assist team members in learning conflict resolution skills, can get to the root cause of poor team performance, and can increase productivity. It can improve the way the team reacts and help the team to develop the ability to solve problems together. Team building can also improve managerial skills and increase support and trust at various levels among employees.

Team building can:
- Increase productivity.
- Ensure properly executed decisions.
- Create interest or involvement of members.
- Clarify activities, roles, responsibilities of members.
- Ensure that meetings are effective with higher attendee ratings.
- Increase the quality of the service/product.

Team building should not be done just for the sake of it, and is ineffective without adequate time and resources. Team building is not to be done if a conflict or problem exists only between two people.

Team Building—prima donnas need not apply
In order to accomplish a task or goal, or to enhance motivation and effectiveness, it may be necessary to reach targets by way of using one or more teams rather than solely relying on one individual to complete a task.

A team is defined as a collection of people with varying experiences coming together for both personal and team-based goals. They are usually brought together in relation to specific activities. Team building is about sharing resources and collaborating on results to produce a finished product.

In putting together members of a team there are various factors to consider. A team should be organized around processes, including functions and skills, and team members must have shared goals and an understanding of what needs to be accomplished. Mainly, teams must agree on the most effective ways to reach their goals.

Team members should be considered based on personalities and preferences. For a team to succeed, technical skills, problem solving ability, and decision-making skills are required. Members also need good listening skills and must be able to give constructive feedback, handle conflicts, and resolve issues. Above all team members must have keen and well-developed interpersonal skills. A balance or blend of these skills is required of a team in order to be effective. Too much of one skill and not the other can result in lower performance of group or skewed results of the project.

To be an effective team, members must be comfortable in their surroundings in order to openly communicate, be able to express and utilize their skills and experience, and shine both individually and within the context of the group—no prima donnas wanted. Give each member a sense of responsibility and ownership of the

316

project or task at hand. Having all members working towards a common goal, sharing opinions, soliciting feedback, and remaining open to the suggestions of others results in not only harmony but in moving towards the end result.

Team size will vary depending on the project or task. A typical team will consist of six, eight, or even twelve members. If a team is too small, it may end up lacking diversity of views; fewer than six can leave a team short of some of the skill sets required to be a fully interactive and engaged team. A team that is too large may result in difficulties in getting things accomplished, in having members take ownership of certain elements or in getting follow-up where required. If a project is so large that a group needs to be more than twelve members, you may want to consider breaking it into smaller sub-units.

In the end, management needs to keep teams aware of their progress and successes and recognize the teams for their accomplishments.

A team that worked
My personal experience of team building has usually been very positive. One team I was involved in was extremely effective at delivering the end results as we had set out to do. We became a team of seven individuals from across branches within Canada. With members located in Edmonton, Calgary, Toronto, and Vancouver, we were a "virtual team".

Our ultimate goal was to create a 360 Degree Evaluation that would be applicable to all administration staff within the organization. The project was being led by Human Resources, which resulted in their having to choose the team members they thought to be most qualified and experienced in working towards this objective. We predominantly consisted of office managers or senior administration staff but we also involved individuals from accounting and corporate services. We had a diverse group of interpersonal skills yet were each considered to be the backbone of a branch or head office's daily operations. (We were the Administration and Human Resource group professionals and our task was to keep the company divisions on track by virtue of how we ran the offices.)

Because we were spread out across the country, all correspondence consisted of email or conference calls. It was challenging coordinating schedules and time zones in order to meet on a regular basis. We made sure we had set agendas, allowed time for questions and answers, and ensured we took minutes of the calls for reference.

During our conference calls, we were able to be respectful of each other, to share opinions as to why something would or wouldn't work, and thus were able to handle rebuttals of those that weren't in agreement with the majority. In dealing with the more difficult individuals of the team, it proved to be beneficial that we weren't all in the same room, and disagreements never truly escalated.

On the other hand, emails at times got a little out of control. There were a number of responses going back and forth between members, which resulted in some members being excluded from these "conversations"—not because anyone wanted to leave them out, but because the correct message wasn't always forwarded to everyone involved. (See Chapter 16 for more about emails getting out of control or missing the point of the communication.)

Nevertheless, the end result was putting in place a tool for 360 Degree Evaluations. We were able to come to a consensus in the long run and implement a time-proven tool for evaluating performance. It was a long process complicated by the distance between team members, but worthwhile, not only for the company's benefit but for our own personal growth as well.

Stages of Team building

Bruce Tuckman proposed his model of group development in 1965. His four stages of Team building are:

- Forming – team members getting to know each other.
- Storming – discovering other team members personalities, thinking and communication styles.
- Norming – appreciating each other's differences.
- Performing – getting the job done and handling conflicts, making decisions.

In 1977 Tuckman, in collaboration with Mary Ann Jensen, proposed an update of the model, which added the step "Adjourning"—also called "Mourning" by some. This occurs when the group dissolves, whether by accident or by design.

The first step in team building is to determine why it's required. What are the concerns or problems? Where is the problem and when does it occur? Where can improvements be made?

When implementing team building, ensure full support of managers and leaders before beginning the process and get employees involved through all levels of participation. This is not a short-term process and must be implemented with both management and employee support.

The process consists of assigning a team leader or facilitator and having members describe the potential problems or concern. They begin working together as a group and rank the concerns in order of importance by breaking into subgroups to develop potential solutions and come up with action plans for those solutions. Once they reconvene as a group, the team should seek management approval before any implementation occurs. Alternative solutions should be generated if required and once a solution is implemented, its effectiveness should be evaluated with regular follow up at specified intervals.

It is recommended that team agendas and goals be set with eight to ten quick accomplishments when a team first comes together and then determine at least five to ten team goals for the next eight to twelve months.

To aid in cohesiveness, there must be clarity on who is responsible for what tasks and avoid overlapping of authority whenever possible. This can assist in avoiding further conflicts. To be effective, team members must have the ability to adapt, cooperate, and change as things progress. A "Team Slayer" is considered to be someone who is unable to deal with change, which results in prejudice against difference. This type of person will have unrealistic expectations, needs to have control of people and not the results, and has an unwillingness to fail. Members must be in agreement to accept goals and understand the purpose of reaching those goals, know what is expected of them and others on the team and know how to get work done together.

When decisions are being made, ensure they are not being forced upon team members and that everyone is involved in the overall process. Be sure to involve the whole team in any decision-making and ensure that these decisions are made at the right level of authority.

Team building doesn't work if an individual or smaller group within the team mainly does work and makes all the final choices. If a member is not participating, be sure to draw them into the discussions and decision-making. Allow employees to have their say and be heard. Some people need to be encouraged more than others to speak out. In order to make conscientious decisions, there must be adequate information available to the team to be effective in their choices. Make decisions with quality, speed, and commitment.

Roadblocks to Team building
There are no guarantees that team building will work and there may be roadblocks along the way. Some of the team building hurdles to watch for are:
- Is there any confusion at any level?

- Are individuals comfortable and able to express themselves openly?
- What happens to the group and processes when things go wrong?
- Who makes the decisions and keeps the cohesiveness?
- How often does the group meet to discuss and review issues/concerns?
- Are individuals getting anything out of the team building?
- Is there improvement in team members' jobs?

Conflict can arise within a team when views, personalities, and thinking styles differ. People who respect each other work together more effectively. Poor performers can demoralize those that are performing, while the high overhead of maintaining non-performers is passed on to customers/clients and other employees, and the cost passed on to shareholders.

Effective Teams

There are 4 C's of effective teams:
- Commitment
- Cooperation
- Communication
- Contribution.

These are cultivated and instilled in team members by providing specific team training using in-house resources or outside professional development. Motivate teams by showing progress and cooperation among members and by exceeding expectations of the project. Problems need to be resolved and members must be open and willing to try new approaches. Cooperation needs to be created and the mission in place must reflect the core purpose of the team, challenge them, and be attainable and congruent with the overall mission of the organization. Team members must have sense of who the customer is. It helps to operate directly from a set of values as laid out by the organization. We've already mentioned the Disney Company, which promotes a family-oriented atmosphere that is entertaining and safe for all ages.

Employees (or cast members as they are affectionately referred to) working at Disney understand these values and perform accordingly in this setting. Goals must be set and measurable and action plans that are developed should outline strategy, accountabilities, tasks/results expected, and deadlines.

Feedback, not only from management but by peers as well, needs to be provided in order to improve on performance of the team. Good feedback focuses on all performance levels and provides instruction. When giving feedback, describe what was done and the result of the action taken, and share what to do next time in order to get full satisfaction from the improvement required. Give "just in time" feedback. Treat conflict for what it is and don't ignore it.

Commitment

Cooperation

Communication

Contribution

Meeting follow-ups are crucial in order to see what has been accomplished since the last meeting. Review notes and make new actions plans. Determine who is doing what and what resources are required. Also, give reward and recognition for a job well done. This assists in appraising self-professional development.

When a task or activity has been accomplished, everyone should celebrate the efforts put forth by everyone. The benefits of doing so include better communication amongst members and the creation of camaraderie for continued success next time. Achievements should be celebrated regularly and consistently.

Successful teams are built on trust and openness. Team members learn their own strengths and weaknesses as well as those of the others around them. Team building improves working relations, improves resource productivity, and achieves organizational goals.

322

Conducting Successful Team Building

In determining who should be a participant in any team building exercise, consider all variables such as deciding which departments require the team building, gender and age of the participants to ensure a good blend, and what size group will it be—small, large, one-on-one?

Ensure start and finish times of the session allow participants time to arrive and depart on schedule. When looking for a location to hold team building, consider again the size of the group and whether or not breakout rooms or space will be required for in-group exercises. Make sure the introduction and instructions are clear and that the targets and outcomes of the session are defined. Consider what materials will be required to conduct a successful session such as flip chart and pens, notepads, handouts, PowerPoint presentation, and access to computers with or without internet.

In order to conduct an outstanding Team building session or meeting, use a variety of presentation styles to match the different learning styles of the participants. Some individuals will find it more engaging to review handouts and take notes while others learn best from exercises and open dialogue. Using open-ended questions to engage participants will also add to the learning. Ask questions such as "How will you apply this learning once back at your job?" or "What has been your experience in the past?"

We all know from our own personal experiences in attending workshops and meetings that most people are willing and open to participating and sharing their viewpoints and ideas while others are quieter. Be sure to involve the whole group and if necessary, approach those individuals who have been less active in participating during a break or lunch session and get their feedback.

Resistance in team building cannot be avoided. There are going to be those individuals who don't feel they need to be part of the group or that they know all the material already from previous experiences. Be prepared to handle those individuals who are more challenging and could be disruptive to the rest of the groups learning. Establishing positive attitudes in regards to the end result is critical in handling resistance from team members. It's best to seek the viewpoints and opinions of all members, but especially from those who are dead set against the whole idea. Encourage resisters to see the value in their knowledge and experiences and in what they can offer to the rest of the team. This encouragement can help in developing the commitment to common goals of collaboration. Developing trust between members and ensuring the sharing of information will aid in accomplishing the end results desired.

Team Leaders/Management should ensure time frames are established and offer assistance in re-negotiating these timelines if necessary. Remember that the concerns may still exist even after someone who is reluctant finally agrees to the process; therefore work continuously to overcome barriers and share in the responsibility.

Follow the group's lead and the direction that the conversation goes, but remain on track. If necessary, make a note of the topic being discussed if it goes astray and let the group know it can be re-addressed at the end of the session if time permits.

As the conductor of team building, be sure not to pass judgement on any feedback or comments made during the session. The idea is to create a safe learning environment where all participants feel free of any reprisal. This can be done by validating a person's thoughts and input.

Lastly, engage the group, regardless of its size, with exercises and games dependent on the purpose of the team building— leadership, communication, planning, time management, cooperation or dealing with challenges and barriers.

Chapter 20. Organizations

Culture Commentary on some Contemporary Companies
In this section I review several well-known companies based on how they are reported in the common business press and related media. My comments and observations are made about how I perceive these companies and their leadership and is not intended to reflect anything more than my perceptions, be they right or wrong.

Each has exhibited some form of "excellence" and I choose to comment on them in the context of the impact that the leadership of that time had on the company involved. In most cases they were more of the catalyst for a coherent Corporate Culture than perhaps any other element within the company.

So, while the prior sections and chapters have covered Corporate Culture in terms of how to define it and deliver it through various tools and techniques, this chapter suggests the obvious—that a charismatic leader can be all that is required to deliver a successful Corporate Culture.

This chapter also confirms the author's belief that Corporate Culture is real, it can be shaped and molded, it is transient (more driven by time, circumstance, and leadership), and it delivers excellent results when properly harnessed.

Excellence Organizations
Let me start with a personal anecdote.

> I am reminded of an example of one of those companies that at that time had what I would define as "an excellence culture". A few decades ago I was the Technical Director of a large multi-million dollar food and commodity processing business—a division of a much larger consumer group, in turn part of an international group of companies. As our existence was heavily dependent on raw commodities (bulk

raw food ingredients delivered from various local and tropical sources to our factory), we had large volumes to process and high technical standards to meet. To allow for this specialized area to retain its focus on the business we had recently been split off into a stand-alone division and a self-contained profit and loss centre. We became a supplier to what was previously "the other half of our business" where the finished consumer products were formulated and packaged for sale. It was as much by luck as judgment for our President (now the overall President of the two divisions) that the team he selected to run this (our) division was one where the chemistry and mutual respect and confidence was very high. The business was not small ($100 to $150 million and well over 100 employees) but it was also not too large. Everyone knew everyone else and mostly on a first name basis.

I had already developed a very hands-on style of management. My approach was to be out on the floor at least once (if not more often) every day so I could see first-hand what was happening. I was already very confident in my staff and had already developed a management style that was open, communicative, and straightforward. I had a reputation for saying it "the way it is", making decisions, and getting on with the needs of the business. I was in no way a micro-manager. I did see most of what went on most of the time. I left the staff to make the decisions, and was available to help, suggest alternative direction if required, make the decision if needed. But primarily it was their decision. The operators had a lot of trust in me and in my management team because they knew we would stay true to our word. This - in a union environment where the main union could be quite hostile - was no mean achievement.

I mentioned that our President had established the team as much by luck as by judgment. The luck portion was really because he had available some key executives with the right experience and the right credentials to make for good leadership. He himself was "in the same mould" an open, honest, and straightforward communicator. He created the teams to lead his Divisions and managed those through his hand picked Executive Group. What made our division excellent was more the chemistry of the individuals involved. Our divisional executive group was quite an eclectic bunch with various international backgrounds and covering several generations. Yet we "clicked"—not in a cliquish way but in a professional and communicative way. We were an open group. There was no obvious politics. We each had a job to do and we each had a great deal of respect for the other. Our focus was on business success. For us that was handling large quantities of bulk materials in a timely and productive manner to provide high quality finished ingredients for our sister division and for the extensive trans-national bulk business that was also part of our portfolio.

At this stage of my career I did not know I was going to write a book on the subject of Corporate Culture—but I had a clear sense of what was required to get people to respond and cooperate. What made this situation excellent was that our division President and our Director of Sales and Marketing and I had a very unique rapport. It was as if we had known each other for many years. It was as if we were long time friends. This was a chemistry that bonded us in a unique way, which led to an openness and trust that was also unique. We knew that there would be no politics from each of our actions. We knew we could make the right decisions for the right reasons and not fear recrimination. Even in the event of some unforeseen crisis, we knew that we could rely on each other to carry the load forward. The benefit of this "open culture" was that everyone knew there was no need to hide things. No other agenda. No surprises. The things that needed to be done were done. Even serious business issues were handled in an open and mutually supportive manner. This, for me at the time, was my first experience of the "excellence" culture in action.

How did this end? Well—all good things come to an end. About three years later the Corporation decided to re-integrate the two Divisions back into a functional structure. I am pleased to say I got a promotion from this experience—though that did not work out quite as planned and expected. More of that elsewhere.

Company examples I will touch on include; GE with its then head Jack Welsh, CN and subsequently Bombardier with Paul Tellier at the helm, Walmart is a candidate in many ways as is Disney World. It should be noted that the review is not intended to be an in-depth study or rationale about these organizations, but rather an opinion about their culture and specifically the leadership contribution that was created by some of the seemingly "larger than life" characters who headed up these companies at their time. In some cases, such as Walmart, the company itself has become the culture. You don't shape that culture—it's there by default. The company is the culture for better or for worse. Obviously all this is viewed from an outsider's perspective through the "tinted glasses" that I choose to wear.

Jack Welsh during his time at General Electric was by all accounts a formidable leader. He came across as very driven and created a clear "stamp" of a cultural style of leadership. The sense one got is that he was a very good person to work for (or with). But only if you were a culture match. I get the impression that he was good at picking the culture matches in his key people. I think that he could be / would be very abrasive and difficult to work for if you were not a "fit". One gets the impression that he may have been a revered leader but also created a harsh reality for many people affected by his style and his decisions. His approach at ruthlessly pruning out the bottom 10% of under-performing units (or people) and rewarding well the top 20% certainly, by all accounts, got both attention and got some spectacular results.

General Electric in my opinion was clearly a Corporate Culture that was driven by the style and nature of one individual who was right for the time.

Paul Tellier had reached some heights within the Canadian civil service as Clerk of the Privy Council and Secretary to the Cabinet during the Mulroney days. As things changed in Government (as they always do), Mulroney appointed him as head of the Crown Corporation CN Rail. He had the mandate and successfully privatized the railway in 1995. That was followed with some US acquisitions that were intended to give CN a continental base

328

instead of a Canadian base. The strategy was successful helped greatly by the advent of the North American Free Trade Agreement (NAFTA), which was one of the hallmarks of the Mulroney era. With the acquisitions, Tellier took on Hunter Harrison as VP (he later took over as President, post-Tellier). One key element of the success was that CN became a "scheduled" freight railway. This service predictability along with streamlining made CN a formidable service provider. Here is an example of the corporate leader using the right tools to focus the business and thereby create a successful Corporate Culture.

Clearly this was a set of circumstances where the right things happened at the right time, which made CN a Corporate Culture success story.

Paul Tellier then went to Bombardier as President and CEO. He left well before his intended three-year contract expired. I am not clear why. First he was a Quebecker and (I assume could speak fluent French—a relative pre-requisite for Quebec). On the surface, reports suggest that he was trying to execute the right things in terms of efficiency, focus, and downsizing. My speculation is that he may have been a "cultural misfit" in spite of his heritage and background. The fact that a family member succeeded him adds to my speculation.

Here we have the same individual under different circumstances not apparently delivering the same sort of success at Bombardier that he enjoyed at CN. My speculation—family companies are different. The opportunity to become the leadership culture catalyst is much more of a stretch.

Let me speculate on Walmart for a few minutes. It has grown into the largest retailer (by revenue) of all time, and is the world's biggest private employer. Its revenues and profits outstrip almost everything else and anyone else. For Walmart lovers they are clearly a valuable entity and for all others, a force to be reckoned with and to be respected. For their critics, they offer fertile ground in many areas. It is clear that they are almost a culture unto themselves. It is also interesting that while most of their expansion ventures are successful, not all are: namely they failed to breach the German market. Part of the reason cited was that they were not a cultural fit with the German people. I personally find it interesting that the US has for many years complained about North American "out-sourcing" yet walk around a Walmart store and my limited sampling suggests that over 80% of what they sell is sourced overseas with the largest portion coming from China and India. My experience with them as a prospective supplier was limited to one venture when I was the President of a Nutraceutical company wanting to get onto the Walmart shelves with a line of unique nutritional products. I did not go far down that road since I do not deal well with companies whose supplier philosophy is "it's my way or the highway". No thanks—life is too short to endure the frustration of making them even richer. But then, as a species we love to take pot shots at the biggest and the toughest out there, don't we? As implied above, they offer fertile ground in numerous areas to their critics.

Walmart is a company that has an enduring culture, but not for conventional reasons. My speculation is that the culture here is one created and driven by socio-economic circumstances of their wealthy founders and especially of their much-less-wealthy customers.

From my limited knowledge and observations about the Disney Company, I think we have something that is actually deeper and more enduring than the leadership. It is clear that it started with Walt Disney—but did it? I think it started with Mickey Mouse. The Disney Empire became and continues to be all about kids' fun characters. As a matter of fact, from the Corporate Culture perspective, Disney seems to work extremely hard at making sure that the essence of the culture is continuously being built, reinforced, re-built and reinforced further. My observations suggest that they have done exceedingly well at maintaining this culture success. I can relate two anecdotes regarding this point. One was during a business trip in Florida. One of our speakers was the then-VP of Disney marketing. He was a very entertaining speaker who spoke at length about the focus of the business and
330

the focus of all employees involved. The whole company seems well focused on ensuring that all of the employees exude "Disney" everywhere and all the time.

My second personal observation happened when I visited one of the Disney theme parks with my grandson and some of the family. I noted that the "Disney" characteristic of communicating the core values of what Disney is all about is absolutely everywhere. It is strong, consistent, and absolute. On one occasion in the park I asked a janitor the direction to the washroom. The gentleman was animated, enthusiastic, almost bouncing up and down with joy. It was to me the strongest sign of a deeply entrenched Corporate Culture that I have seen anywhere.

To my mind, Disney is a Corporate Culture where the Principals know what they have, how to protect it, and how to keep building on it. This Corporate Culture is in my opinion rare since it transcends the style of the leadership and is maintained by the leadership, which recognises how critical this element is to their success.

The bottom line is this: Corporate Culture exists everywhere. In most cases it just "is what it is". In some cases it is really well managed (a rare exception). In many more cases it is there by circumstance (or luck). **In ALL cases it is manageable.**

In every case Corporate Culture exists by virtue of the values, attitudes, expectations, and beliefs that the senior people bring to the table—particularly the head of the organization. In some cases these four characteristics are strongly embedded in the organization itself and thus the organization has an enduring Corporate Culture. But don't be fooled into thinking that this is cast in concrete. **It can easily evaporate and be lost due to inadequate leadership.**

Do you want a winning Corporate Culture? - You have just read the book on how to get there—if you are ready for the hard and delicate work.

Sincerely—Good Luck.

Geoff Sheffrin

The following cartoon is my late Stepfather's view of the quest for perfection.

It is not given to all men to find that which they seek. (Milton)

Appendix A: What do you Value Exercise

What Do You Value?[27]

Following are 24 items. Rate how important each one is to you on a scale of 0 (not important) to 100 (very important). Write the number 0 -100 on the line to the left of each item. The absolute degree of accuracy in the scale numbers is not critical. If 0 to 10 is easier – use that. If you want to use the 0 to 100 scale but in 5 unit increments (0 – 5 – 10 – 15 – etc.) – then use that. The outcome is not that critical that you need to discriminate between a rating of say – 55, 56, and 57.

Not Important Somewhat Important Very Important

0   10   20   30   40   50   60   70   80   90   100

Score	What Do You Value
	1. An enjoyable, satisfying job.
	2. A high-paying job.
	3. A good marriage.
	4. Meeting new people; social events.
	5. Involvement in community activities.
	6. My religion.
	7. Exercising, playing sports.
	8. Intellectual development.
	9. A career with challenging opportunities.
	10. Nice cars, clothes, home, and possessions.
	11. Spending time with family.
	12. Having several close friends.
	13.Volunteer work for charitable or not-for-profit organizations.
	14. Meditation, quiet time to think, pray, and reflect.
	15. A healthy, balanced diet.
	16. Educational reading, television, self-improvement programs, and courses.
	17. A good work environment.

18. Travel – vacations.	
19. Spending time with friends.	
20. Enjoying the company of others.	
21. Supporting less fortunate people.	
22. Reading and contemplation.	
23. Setting fitness goals.	
24. Setting and achieving self-development goals.	

Scoring – What Do You Value?

Transfer the numbers for each of the 24 items to the appropriate column; then add up the three numbers in each column.

	Professional	Financial	Family	Social
	1. ____	2. ____	3. ____	4. ____
	9. ____	10. ____	11.	12.
	17. ____	18. ____	19.	20.
Totals				

	Community	Spiritual	Physical	Intellectual
	5. ____	6. ____	7. ____	8. ____
	13. ____	14.	15.	16. ____
	21. ____	22.	23.	24. ____
Totals				

The higher the total in any value dimension, the higher the importance you place on that value set. The closer the numbers are in all eight dimensions, the more well-rounded you are.

Appendix B: Attitude Survey for Individuals

There are numerous versions and variants of Attitude Surveys. Below are some suggestions about what can be included in a simple Attitude Survey. Respondents are encouraged to create statements that reflect items of potential importance within the organization. The questions need to be tailored to the needs and intended outcome that management has in mind for the survey.

By going to the attitude section in Appendix C (the Word Survey), further statements can be customized to suit the need of the intended survey.

Answer each statement using the following rating.

1 = Strongly Agree	4 = Disagree
2 = Agree	5 = Strongly Disagree
3 = Undecided	

Statements relating to individuals attitudes within the organization could include the following:

This is a good place to work	
Compensation and pay scales are very fair	
People are treated with respect and fairness	
I like my job	
I am motivated by what I do	
I would recommend this company to others	
I know what is expected of me	
I think my boss is fair and reasonable	
I feel I have promotion opportunities	
I like the people I work with	
I can handle my work load	
People are treated with respect and fairness	

Ideally, the above statements are customized to obtain the information management desires within a particular organization. The overall score is achieved by adding up all values from the ratings and summarized by groups, departments, divisions, or the organization as a whole. From there, it is up to management to decide how to execute a plan to improve employee attitudes and develop the areas that are weak.

Appendix C: Word Survey

During the interview process the senior managers of the organization choose from the lists the words that best describe their company. See Chapter 3 for a more detailed description of the word survey process. The following tables show key words that emerge from analysis tasks.

The binary decision matrix in Appendix D can be used to select and refine the attributes within the Corporate Culture being evaluated.

Values

Materialism	Mementos	Superior	Excellence
Influential	To The Point	Subservience	Merit
Notable	Despised	Proactive	Value
Concern	Significance	Philanthropy	Worth
Emphasis	Eventful	Utility	Champion
Greatness	Grave	Profitable	Salt of the
Superiority	Seriousness	Gainful	Earth
Joke	Instant	Effective	Innocence
Urgency	Vital	Practical	Indifference
Principle	Absorbent	Adaptable	Favorable
Essence	Leading	Remunerate	Superior
Kernel	Capital	Profit	Excellent
Salient	Vitality	Benefit	Big-wig

Attitudes

Flattery	Euphemistic	Stewardship	Temperament
Phase	Smug	Husbandry	Condescending
Posture	Conceited	Conduct	Complimentary
Terms	Sentimental	Manner	Polite
Status	Conduct	Practical	Civil
Predicament	Tactics	Executive	Courteous
Crisis	Policy	Civility	Obliging
Circumstance	Strategy	Theatrical	Conciliatory
Provisional	House	Insincere	Gentle
Pedantic	Keeping	Affable	
	Pretentious		

Expectations

Foresight	Anticipate	Reasonable	Pressure
Contemplation	Credibility	Apparent	Take for
Horizon	Plausible	Probability	Granted

Beliefs

Trust	Rooted	Opinion	Credibility
Confidence	Steadfast	Doctorate	Persuasions
Reliance	Dispassionate	Faith	Theological
Principle			

Communication

Information	Network	Scandal	Meetings
Reports	Commercials	Narrator	Letters
Story	Magazines	Grape Vine	Email
Advisors	Corporate Video	Informers	Internet
Bulletins	Image	Memos	Intranet
Telephone	Rumors		

Accountability

Duty	Allegiance	Discharge	Assign
Moral	Conscience	Responsibility	Obligatory
Obligation	Amenableness	Oblige	Answerable
Liability	Fulfilment		
Imperative			

Authority/Responsibility

Influence	Autocracy	Compromise	Autonomy
Power	Democracy	Answerable	Politics
Prestige	Socialism	Ethical	Usurper
Right	Collectivism	Voluntary	Authorize
Jurisdiction	Persuasion	Optional	Expert
Despotism	Moral Risk	Autocratic	Wield
Empire	Freedom	Choice	Head Office
Rule	Discretion	Independence	Ivory Tower
Supremacy	Choice	Originate	Command
Seniority	Purpose	Incumbent	Govern
Patriarchy	Spontaneity	Tied	Sanction
Dictation	Opposition	Conscientiousness	Charter
Control	Inclination	Mob Law	Accountability
Dynasty	Will Power	Bureaucracy	Decoracy
Protectorate	Administration	Feudality	Decorum
		Predetermination	

Appendix D: Binary Decision Matrix

Binary decision matrices were first developed in the telecommunications industry over 50 years ago. They were developed to help rank multiple items in specific order of importance.

The matrix can have as many lines as you have items to compare and evaluate. The more lines you have the better the tool works – since if you had twenty items instead of the seven shown here – the value of the tool becomes more apparent. What is important is that you have exactly the same number of columns as you have lines.

To use the matrix put in the headings that are specific to the issue being evaluated. Then you evaluate which of two characteristics is more important than the other. You do this one with each next item. The zeros are shown since when comparing like with like – there is no preference. You then work down each column making the choice and putting a number 1 in the box that is the more important and a 0 if the box is less important (hence the term "binary"). For example, look at the work column. Is work is more important than money? If yes, then put a 1 against work. Is work is more important than marriage? If no, then put a 0 in the box. If work is more important than family, 1 = yes, 0 = no, and so on until the work column is complete. Then go down the money column but ask the question the other way round. Is money more important than work (it may be depending on where the money comes from)? Is money more important than marriage? 1 = yes, 0 = no. And so on down every column until every box has a number 1 or 0 in it. Then, when all columns are complete, add each up. The column with the highest number is the most important, the next lower numbers are each less important.

Within the context of the book – you can use any of the attributes that are tabulated in Appendix C to be able to determine which of the many characteristics listed in each attribute is important. Within the context of evaluating Attitudes, Expectation, Values, and Beliefs, the key items can each be ranked by the use of this tool.

	Work	Money	Marriage	Family	Social	Health	Fitness
Work	**0**	0	1	1	1	1	1
Money	1	**0**	1	1	1	1	1
Marriage	0	0	**0**	0	0	1	0
Family	0	0	1	**0**	0	1	1
Social	0	0	1	1	**0**	1	1
Health	0	0	0	1	0	**0**	0
Fitness	0	0	0	0	1	0	**0**
Totals	1	0	4	4	3	5	4

Appendix E: Acronyms used in this book

BRC	British Retail Consortium
CEO	Chief Executive Officer
CIM	Computer Integrated Manufacturing
ERP	Enterprise Resource Planning (tools)
GFSI	Global Food Safety Initiative
HACCP	Hazard Analysis Critical Control Points
HR	Human resources
ISO	International Organization for Standardization
JIT	Just In Time
KISS	Key Ingredient Simplification and Standardization
MRP / ERP	Manufacturing Resource(s) Planning/Enterprise Resource Planning
OR	Operations Redesign
PCSS	Packaging Component Standardization and Simplification
PDCA	Plan, Do, Check, Act
RIF	Random Iterative Formulations
RO	Range Optimization and Reduction
ROI	Return on Investment
SAP	Systems, Applications, and Products
S.W.O.T.	Strengths, weaknesses, opportunities, threats
TPM	Total Preventive Maintenance (or Total Predictive Maintenance)
TQM	Total Quality Management
WIP	Work in Progress

Endnotes

Chapter 1
[1] Smith, Bernard T. (2001). *Power Planning for Business*. Butler, PA: B. T. Smith and Associates.

Chapter 2
[2] Adapted from G. Hofstede, "Cultural Constraint in Management Theories," Academy of Management Executive, February 1993, p.91; G. Hofstede, "The Cultural Relativity of Organizational Practices and Theories". Journal of International Business Studies, 14, 1983, pp. 75-89. Mexico's scores were abstracted from G.K. Stephen and C.R. Greer, "Doing Business in Mexico: Understanding Cultural Differences," Organizational Dynamics, Special Report, 1998, pp. 43-59.

[3] Smith, Lawrence, MD. "Medical professionalism and the generation gap". The American Journal of Medicine, Volume 118, Issue 4, Pages 439-442

Data from: Zemke R, et al. *Generations at Work*. New York, NY: American Management Association, 2000.

[4] Adapted from Adams, Michael. (1997) *Sex in the Snow: Canadian Social Values at the End of the Millennium*. Toronto: Doubleday.

[5] From the Disney web site. http://corporate.disney.go.com/careers/culture.html Accessed May 21, 2015.

[6] Festinger, Leon (1957). *A Theory of Cognitive Dissonance*. Palo Alto, CA: Stanford University Press.

Chapter 4
[7] Maslow, A. H. (1943). *A Theory of Human Motivation.* Psychological Review, 50, 370-396

[8] From the Disney web site. http://corporate.disney.go.com/careers/culture.html Accessed October 25, 2007.

[9] McGregor, D. (1957). *Proceedings of the Fifth Anniversary Convocation of the School of Industrial Management, The Human Side of Enterprise.* Massachusetts Institute of Technology (April 9, 1957).

[10] Argyris, Chris. (1993). *Knowledge for Action: A Guide to Overcoming Barriers to Organizational Change.* San Francisco: Jossey-Bass Inc.

[11] McClelland, David C. (1987). *Human Motivation.* Cambridge: Cambridge University Press.

[12] Likert, Rensis. (1961). *New patterns of management.* New York: McGraw-Hill Book Company, Inc.
Likert, R. (1967). *The Human Organization: Its Management and Value.* New York: McGraw-Hill.

[13] Herzberg, F., Mausner, B., & Snyderman, B. B. (1959). *The Motivation to Work* (2nd Ed.). New York: Wiley & Sons, Inc.
Herzberg, F. (1972). *Work and the Nature of Man.* New York: New American Library.

[14] Drucker, Peter F. (1969). *The Age of Discontinuity: Guidelines to our Changing Society.* London: William Heinemann Ltd.

[15] *Peter Drucker's Life and Legacy* from The Drucker Institute web site. http://www.druckerinstitute.com/peter-druckers-life-and-legacy/ Accessed April 24, 2015.

[16] This section of bullet points is licensed under the GNU Free Documentation License. It uses material from the Wikipedia article "Peter Drucker", http://en.wikipedia.org/wiki/Peter_Drucker accessed April 15, 2015.

[17] Drucker, Peter F. "How People Make Decisions", *Harvard Business Review*, July 1, 1985.

[18] Brennan, Tim. Employer's Advantage" Profiles International, Inc. newsletter. January 4, 2006. Available at http://www.energycentral.com/utilitybusiness/humanresources/articles/1177/Top-Employees-Or-Top-Candidates-Which-do-you-select-/Accessed April 15, 2015.

Chapter 5
[19] Blake, R. & Mouton, J. (1964). *The Managerial Grid: The Key to Leadership Excellence.* Houston: Gulf Publishing Co.

Chapter 6

[20] Tynan, Oliver. *"Change and the nature of work. Some employment and organizational problems of advanced manufacturing technology"*, Robotica 3, September 1985: 173-180. http://dx.doi.org/10.1017/S0263574700009115. Accessed September 30, 2015.

[21] Smith L.G. *"Medical professionalism and the generation gap"*. American Journal of Medicine. 2005; 118(4): 439-442.

[22] Deal, Jennifer J., Retiring *the Generation Gap: How Employees Young and Old Can Find Common Ground*, Jossey-Bass and Center for Creative Leadership. 2007.

[23] Drucker, Peter F. "The Next Workplace Revolution," Report on Business, 6, No. 3 (1989), pp. 75-81.

Chapter 8

[24] Finzel, Hans. (2007). *The Top Ten Mistakes Leaders Make*. Colorado Springs: David C. Cook.

[25] Hammer, Michael and Champy, James (1993). *Reengineering the Corporation: A Manifesto for Business Revolution*. New York: Harper Business.

Chapter 17

[26] Interview in *Writers at Work, First Series*, ed. Malcolm Cowley (1958).

Appendix A

[27] Source: Adapted by Geoff Sheffrin with permission from R.N. Lussier, Self-Assessment Exercise 3-3 "Your Personal Values," in *Human Relations in Organizations: Applications and Skill Building* 9e. McGraw-Hill/Irwin, New York, NY: 2013, pp. 70-71.

ABOUT THE AUTHORS

Geoff Sheffrin, P.Eng. C.Eng., is a Principal of OBK Technology Ltd. and of Sheffrin Enterprises Inc.

Geoff is a licensed and certified Professional Engineer who is eligible to practice his profession in North America and Europe. Geoff is a graduate in Mechanical and Production Engineering with a post-graduate diploma in Human Sciences. Throughout his extensive and diverse career Geoff has been in the unique position of being able to combine the rigid, structured, and disciplined requirements of the Engineering Professional with the softer and more intuitive requirements of the Human Resource Specialist. These two unique attributes have equipped Geoff to compose this structured and unusual approach to a critical aspect of organizations and how they function.

The book is the culmination of several decades of careful observations, insights, and reviews conducted in a large number of different organizations – mostly from the perspective of the senior management roles that Geoff enjoyed throughout his career.

Today Geoff continues his career as a Management Consultant and one of the principals of a "boutique" engineering consulting practice. The consulting practice specializes in process, manufacturing, and strategic development for pharmaceutical, food, and personal care product industries along with the turnkey provision of highly specialized purified water systems throughout the continent.

www.geoffsheffrin.com
www.corporateculturebook.com
www.obkltd.com

Dinah Bailey, CHRL, is the principal of HR ByDESIGN, a human resource management consulting practice.

Dinah began her career in the human resource field almost two decades ago where she specialized in recruitment and customer service. As she progressed in this industry, she expanded her knowledge and expertise to other roles such as Career Consultant, Organizational Development, and Human Resource Advisor.

Dinah's passion is providing complete client-focused human resource solutions, with a commitment of continuously providing top-level customer service to her clients and their employees. Her working experience with smaller sized organizations has granted her the understanding and appreciation of what it takes to efficiently streamline human resources in small to mid-sized organizations.

Dinah is an honors graduate of Sheridan College's Human Resource Management program, a member of the Human Resources Professionals Association (HRPA) since 2003, and is a Certified Human Resource Leader (CHRL). She has also been recognized for her outstanding contributions to workplace excellence through Alberta Venture's E-Awards, Quality of Working Life.

See her web site at hrbydesign.ca.

Made in the USA
San Bernardino, CA
17 January 2018